into

THE DEVIL'S DEN

into

THE DEVIL'S DEN

How an FBI Informant

Got Inside the Aryan Nations

and a Special Agent Got

Him Out Alive

Dave Hall and Tym Burkey

with Katherine M. Ramsland

Ballantine Books New York

Published in the United States by Ballantine Books,
an imprint of The Random House Publishing Group, a division
of Random House, Inc., New York.

BALLANTINE and colophon are registered trademarks
of Random House, Inc.

Library of Congress Cataloging-in-Publication Data
Hall, Dave.
Into the devil's den : how an FBI informant got inside the Aryan Nations and a special
agent got him out alive / Dave Hall and Tym Burkey, with Katherine M. Ramsland.
p.   cm.
Includes index.
ISBN 978-0-345-49694-2 (hardcover: alk. paper)
1. Hall, Dave   2. Church of Jesus Christ Christian, Aryan Nations.
3. White supremacy movements—United States.   4. Hate groups—United States.
5. Terrorism—United States.   6. United States. Federal Bureau of Investigation.
I. Burkey, Tym.   II. Ramsland, Katherine M.   III. Title.
E184.A1H2132   2008
320.5'6—dc22   2007032393

All photographs courtesy of the author.

Printed in the United States of America on acid-free paper

www.ballantinebooks.com

2   4   6   8   9   7   5   3   1

First Edition

Text design by Laurie Jewell

Dave Hall

To my mother Peggy, who has always
been there for me

Tym Burkey

To Anne, my sons, and daughter who have sacrificed
in many ways over the years

ACKNOWLEDGMENTS

Dave Hall

First and foremost I want to thank K. C. McGuire, without whom this book would never have been written. It was K.C.'s idea that I write about my time undercover in the Aryan Nations, and her constant support, encouragement, and relentless determination to see my story in print made this book possible. Thank you, K.C., I could never have done this without you.

Thank you to Bill for his help with the photographs that appear in this book.

And finally, thank you to FBI Special Agent Tym Burkey. I had my doubts about Tym at the start of the investigation, but he never once let me down and he became a close and trusted friend. Thanks for watching my back, Tym.

Tym Burkey

I want to thank K. C. McGuire. Her insight, perseverance, and diligence made this project happen.

I would like to recognize my "Boss" at the time, the special agent in charge, Sheri Farrar (retired); the assistant special agent in charge, the late Henry Ragle; my supervisor and friend Roger Wilson; and all of the men and women of the Cincinnati Division who sacrificed time with their loved ones to work this case.

A special thanks to a friend and mentor, Pam Quinn, at FBI headquarters.

And thank you to the rest of the employees of the FBI, then and now, who work to secure the United States and its people every day.

Lastly, to an American hero, my friend and writing partner, Dave Hall. Thank you for risking it all to make this world a safer place.

Dave Hall and Tym Burkey

We would also like to thank our literary agent Kim Lionetti for taking on this project, our collaborator Katherine Ramsland who came up with the idea to tell this story as a dual memoir, and Senior Editor Mark Tavani at Ballantine Books/Random House for his enthusiastic support of this book.

Dave Hall

When you dance with the Devil, the Devil doesn't change,
the Devil changes you.

—OLD APPALACHIAN SAYING

Tym Burkey

Carry the battle to them. Don't let them bring it to you.
Put them on the defensive and don't ever
apologize for anything.

—HARRY S TRUMAN

CONTENTS

19. Terrible Times   200

20. Conspiracy   210

21. Clandestine Preparations   220

22. Earle Cabell   230

23. The Grand Dragon   244

24. April Fools   253

25. Meltdown   269

26. Aftermath   279

    Glossary   285

    Index   293

into

THE DEVIL'S DEN

CLOSE CALL

When Pastor Ray sat down across the table from me, I assumed he'd start ranting as usual about how much he hated the Jews and the mud races. By now, I pretty much knew that stuff by heart. But this time I was wrong. This time, he removed a .45-caliber automatic pistol from where he'd stuck it in his belt. He looked it over, popped out the clip, and took a bullet from the chamber then placed the gun on the table. I waited for more, but he wasn't talking. His dark eyes were on the bullet.

Attempting to lighten the mood, I asked, "Got yourself a new weapon, Pastor?"

He looked at me. "No," he said calmly. "I've had this for a while now."

He picked up an ammo box and dumped some cartridges onto the table. I wondered what the hell he was up to, but I dared not show he made me nervous. Ever since I'd met the man, one of the most ambitious figures in the Aryan Nations, I'd been on high alert. He was both the smartest man I'd ever encountered and the craziest.

Ray selected a cartridge and looked it over, as if to assess its weight or shine. Then with deliberation, he slipped it into the clip and said, "You know, Brother Dave, we've got to be very careful about informants."

I nodded. "I agree."

He looked down at the gun that lay on the table between us, even as he continued to make comments that I could hardly hear. Blood was pumping in my ears, and though the heat was off, the room was warming up. I tried to shift as if trying to keep warm in the chilly air, but the Ohio winter didn't get to Ray. He seemed not to even notice how cold it was.

Picking up the bullets one by one, he continued to place them back into the clip until they were all nestled together. Clearly, he had something in mind. This was a man who had already tried to kill a cop, shooting him several times over a traffic stop, and I'd heard him repeatedly threaten to kill others.

"Brother Dave," he said, "what do you think we ought to do about informants?"

Okay, I knew something was up, and I knew I might not get out of here alive. I had a sudden instinct to grab my side of the table, lift it, and turn it over on him, to crush him beneath it. But somehow I kept my wits about me. If I were just another member of the Aryan Nations, as I'd been pretending to be for the past two years, I'd be assertive on this topic, ready to act. I had to keep that in mind.

"I don't know," I said with a shrug. "I think you ought to take 'em out and shoot 'em."

Pastor Ray seemed to like that response, because he smiled a little, but I couldn't really tell if he believed my act. I'd been wondering that each day since I'd started this assignment. Sometimes he seemed to trust me; other times I wasn't so sure. I watched as he put the clip into the pistol, making it lethal, and cocked it. Then he laid the pistol back down on the table, putting his finger on the trigger and pointing the eye of the barrel directly at my chest. I tried not to swallow.

He nodded a little, as if affirming something for himself. "What do you think we really should do about informants?"

I didn't know if he wanted an answer or was just trying to scare me, so I acted like I was now ready to get serious. "Well, for one thing," I said, "I think we ought to really make sure that they're informants. If we find out they are, we ought to tell them that they're dismissed from the Aryan Nations, they're never allowed back at the church again, and then point them toward the door and make them leave. And when they turn to walk out, shoot 'em in the back of the head."

I waited.

Ray smiled. Then he slowly lowered the hammer on the pistol. In his typical way, he acted as if everything was normal. Looking straight at me, he asked, "D'you mind giving me a ride over to Kale Kelly's place?"

I followed right along as if this had been an everyday conversation. "Not at all," I responded as my insides slowly unclenched. I wasn't going to die today.

Ray got up, stuck the pistol back under his belt, and said, "Let's go, Brother."

When I stood to follow him, I felt a little dizzy, like all my blood had drained out through my feet. But by the time we got to the car, I had recovered: I was fighting off the urge to snap the good pastor's neck.

It had been such a simple test, seemingly easy to pass, but I knew my life had hung in the balance. I couldn't have known for sure what was the right or wrong thing to say, but apparently I'd satisfied him.

Later that night, when I was by myself, I finally got truly nervous. Pastor Ray Redfeairn was an unpredictable maniac with a hair-trigger temper. He acted first and thought about it later—if at all. He seemed to feel no remorse. He watched me so closely I could just about feel his eyes on me, and I began to wonder, not for the first time, why I was even in this situation.

FIRST ENCOUNTER

Tym Burkey

Dave Hall's involvement with one of the most dangerous men I'd ever investigated was due largely to me.

I've been an FBI special agent since June 1991, but it had taken real effort to actually get in. My path was indirect. I'd received a bachelor's degree in construction engineering from the University of Akron, in 1983 and was working for the city Engineering Department in Wooster, Ohio, where I grew up. I wanted to find a new line of work, but in 1984 I'd married my wife, Anne, so I had little room to experiment. My sister-in-law provided media training at the FBI's academy, and she encouraged me to look into employment there. I took the entrance exam but did not qualify. I would have put it behind me, but after getting an MBA, I decided to try again. It turned out that at that time, the FBI was facing the savings and loan scandals and was eager to sign up people with a business background. This time I passed and they accepted me. Although Anne was expecting our third child, she urged me to go to the training.

After I completed the program at the Academy, I was assigned to the Dayton Resident Agency (DRA), an FBI satellite office out of the Cincinnati Division, which put me in southern Ohio, a hotbed of militant groups. But in the early nineties, I was working on crimes such as bank robberies, truck hijackings, and drugs.

On April 19, 1995, the Murrah Federal Building in Oklahoma City, Oklahoma, was bombed. One hundred sixty-eight men, women, and children were killed and hundreds more were injured in the bombing. An alert highway patrol officer arrested Timothy McVeigh on his way out of town, and thanks to McVeigh's stated agenda we learned that a new type of terrorist had emerged in our homeland and that there were many groups around the country preparing for similar acts.

McVeigh espoused white supremacist rhetoric and supposedly envisioned himself avenging the 1993 standoff between the FBI and the Branch Davidians at Waco, Texas, which resulted in a conflagration at the Branch Davidian compound. Four agents from the Bureau of Alcohol, Tobacco, and Firearms (ATF) died there, as did more than eighty members of David Koresh's community. McVeigh's anger may also have been fueled by a book called *The Turner Diaries*, a piece of apocalyptic hate literature written by William L. Pierce under the pseudonym Andrew MacDonald and published in 1978. Approximately eighty thousand words long, it features a racist white "hero," Earl Turner, who joins an underground movement that in the early 1990s resists the so-called Jewish conspiracy that has taken over the American government and confiscated everyone's guns. The book graphically depicts the subsequent extermination of Jews, blacks, Hispanics, other "mud faces," and white "race traitors." Turner's purpose was to establish an all-white separatist homeland in the Northwest.

The book is so full of hate it was hard for me to stomach it. I read it only on company time, not my time, while I was on a stakeout. I would never have read something like that by choice. A particularly disturbing part for me was the fictional bombing of the J. Edgar

Hoover Building in Washington, D.C., which of course houses FBI headquarters. If I needed convincing that groups that embraced the *Diaries* viewed us as the enemy, this did it for me.

Pierce, the *Diaries* author, founded the National Alliance (NA), a white supremacist organization in Hillsboro, West Virginia, around the same time that Richard Butler formed the Aryan Nations (AN). The main differences between the NA and the AN were the level of violence and the religious angle. The AN openly preached from the Bible and used it to justify violence, whereas the agnostic NA advocated violence as a means to an end.

Timothy McVeigh apparently bought into *The Turner Diaries'* racist paranoia, because one passage describes using a fertilizer bomb consisting of ammonium nitrate and fuel oil to blow up a federal building. McVeigh's destructive act would prove inspiring for other antigovernment groups, and the *Diaries* was often found in the homes or possession of members of these groups.

We knew that the central AN headquarters was a compound in Hayden Lake, Idaho, and we knew that its membership hoped for a militant uprising. There was an AN church in our jurisdiction, so we kept an eye on it, especially after McVeigh's attack. As the AN grew in power, the FBI was shifting its focus to prepare for more acts of domestic terrorism, which filtered down to local units that had direct contact with such groups. It was around this time that I met Dave Hall.

Dave Hall

In July 1996, I'd agreed to help out a friend. Mostly in those days I spent time with my friends, partying or just hanging out. I was on disability from a work-related back injury, so I puttered around and enjoyed myself. I had a trailer and a boat up at a lake north of Dayton, and I went there a lot to go fishing. Occasionally I worked on motorcycles for various friends, and I also saw my mom a lot. Basically it was a relaxed, laid-back life. But that was about to change.

I lived in Ohio but had grown up in Kentucky and still had

family there. A distant relative wanted to meet my uncle Mike* for the purpose of selling him marijuana. They asked me to be the go-between—in other words, go get the marijuana—and I said, "No. I'm not gonna do that." So then the guy in Kentucky asked for only an introduction. "Well, okay," I said, "but I'm not coming to Kentucky. You're gonna have to come up here and I'll meet you at a rest stop in Ohio, on I-75. Then you can follow me up to my uncle's house. I'll introduce you and you guys can take it from there. I don't want no part of it."

So we arranged to do that. But unbeknownst to me, this guy from Kentucky had been busted and was working with the feds. He was laying a trap. We met at that rest area, and the next thing I knew, two agents came knocking at my door.

Tym Burkey

In a drug conspiracy case at the federal level, if you're involved in any way, you're just as culpable as the rest.

The Louisville Division gave us this lead on a drug conspiracy, enclosing an arrest warrant for Dave Hall from the federal court in the Eastern District of Kentucky. I found nothing remarkable about the lead—just another mope involved in a drug deal—but I was annoyed. In Ohio, the U.S. attorney's office in the Southern District would not touch a marijuana case unless the amount trafficked was measured in tons: crack cocaine and cocaine cases had taxed our resources to the maximum. But just across the Ohio River, it was a different story. Marijuana was a cash crop that rivaled corn and tobacco. The U.S. attorney's offices and the federal courts in Kentucky took marijuana very seriously.

I looked over the warrant to get the address. I did my usual checks and acquired a driver's license photograph of Hall, which told me he was one big guy: six foot four and 350 pounds. At least he had no record of violence. Normally I would have done a drive-by

*Some names have been changed to protect identities.

of his residence to check it out first—especially since I came in at five foot eleven and 175 pounds. But my partner, Jerry Clark, was six foot one and a former special agent for the Drug Enforcement Agency (DEA), so I decided to grab him and go arrest Mr. Hall.

Jerry drove, and I guided him to a house in the Drexel area on the west side of Dayton, where the violent Outlaws motorcycle gang had a clubhouse. In fact, we were going right around the corner from it.

I briefly reconsidered this arrest, wondering if Hall might be part of this gang. The truth is I was busy and wanted to get it over with. We pulled up to a modest two-bedroom bungalow with white siding and walked to the front door. Standing to either side of it—so as to avoid being shot—we knocked.

Inside, a dog barked, and I could tell it was big. I glanced at Jerry to make sure he was ready. Then the door opened, and the man who answered filled almost the entire entrance, blocking a large black dog that sounded ready to tear into us. From the photo, I recognized him as Dave Hall, but he was much larger than I'd expected. He wore a sleeveless shirt that exposed tattooed arms the size of ham hocks, and sported a light brown goatee to go with his short curly brown hair, which added a sinister air to an already menacing appearance. He was clearly what people in Kentucky call a good ol' boy. I mumbled under my breath, "I didn't bring enough people."

I decided that using the "I'm with the FBI and you're under arrest" introduction would have been like shooting a bear and only making it mad. I introduced myself and Jerry, and as politely as I could I told Hall the purpose of our visit. I said he would have to accompany us to the Dayton Federal Building. To my relief, he responded well, asking only if he could first put his dog away and lock the house. We agreed but told him we would have to accompany him. He ushered us inside. At his command, the dog stepped back, but I could see the animal was bristling and still wanted a piece of us. I kept my hand near my pistol.

As I stepped in, I suddenly wondered if Hall would change his mind. If he'd wanted, he could have teamed up with the dog to overpower us. But he made no such move. Instead, just as he'd asked, he put the dog away, locked the house, and walked calmly to the car with us. Standard FBI protocol is to transport a subject with his hands cuffed behind him, but Dave was too big for that, so we handcuffed him in front.

At the FBI office we fingerprinted, interviewed, and photographed him. I called the U.S. attorney's office, the U.S. Marshals Service, and the court to let them know we had an arrest from another district. I tried to talk with Hall, but he declined to discuss the incident. That was fine with me because I didn't care about his problem. Far as I could tell, he was just another doper who'd screwed up, no different from the scores I'd dealt with before.

For his initial appearance in federal court, he went before Judge Walter H. Rice, a well-respected man. Judge Rice asked the standard questions and told Hall the charges. Then he asked me, "How did he act when you arrested him?"

"He was a perfect gentleman," I replied.

Judge Rice placed Hall on his own recognizance and instructed him to appear in Pikeville, Kentucky, for arraignment. That meant that the Dayton court would record little about this appearance. Later on, that would become significant.

The marshals took him for processing, and I was done. Or so I thought.

One day in October, Hall called me at the Dayton office and said he'd pleaded guilty. Judge Joseph Hood, of the Kentucky federal court, apparently had felt generous, delaying sentencing for six months to allow Hall to "help himself out," meaning to provide information to me. In other words, he was back in my hands. Although I was skeptical that he actually would be useful, I could always use another source. We FBI agents make our living on sources. Despite what's often depicted on TV or in the movies, the FBI simply could not do its job without sources. For that matter, neither could any other law enforcement agency. We're good at investigating large, multistate criminal organizations, but we're not geared to street crime. At any rate, now there was work to do.

Opening up a source involved paperwork and approvals from my supervisor and the front office in Cincinnati. Because I was working criminal offenses at the time, I opened Hall up as a criminal informant. Any accomplishment he produced would be attributed to my Criminal Squad at Dayton. Since I knew that Hall had lived around the Outlaws motorcycle club in Dayton, though he'd never officially joined, I figured he was on friendly terms with them and could provide information about their underground activities. Instead, he told me about the marijuana dealers in and around Dayton. I took the information, but I couldn't have cared less. I passed it off to local law enforcement and thought, *So much for an informant.*

Over the next month or so, Hall sent more such tidbits my way, and I finally had to tell him that the Southern District of Ohio was not all that interested in marijuana cases. I sensed he might be concerned that if I didn't view him as helpful, he'd end up being sentenced, so I decided to work this concern to my advantage. One day I said, "If you really want to help yourself, tell me about the Outlaws."

He seemed reluctant to discuss this topic, so I prodded. Finally he said, "They're for real."

I knew what that meant: they had a history of killing snitches.

"Would you rather go to prison?" I asked.

Hall was silent, and I understood him perfectly. I explained to him how the FBI operates sources. I always avoid terms such as *informant* or *snitch* because they have negative connotations. "It's entirely voluntary for you to cooperate," I reminded him—though he obviously had some extra incentive. "The FBI will protect you, if you agree to do it, and we'll pay your expenses." Safety and money are always prime motivators, and I figured he'd take the bait. He said he'd consider it.

But then his case took a backseat as my own interests shifted. In early 1997, an internal communication circulated in the Cincinnati

Division. The recently passed Nunn-Lugar Act had provided the funding for more resources for investigating domestic terrorism. Cincinnati, a smaller division, was allotted one special agent for the new Domestic Terrorism (DT) program. After six years on major crimes and a lot of missed family events, I was burning out, and I saw this new program as an opportunity. I raised my hand, and they picked me. I was lucky, and I knew it, but it was going to be a while before the unit was organized, so I stayed a little longer in criminal investigation.

Around the same time, the Phoenix Division alerted Jerry and me to a fugitive lead on a white-collar criminal living with his girlfriend in Cleveland. He'd assaulted one agent by running over his foot, breaking it. The information indicated that he would be with his girlfriend that day when she picked up her daughter at a McDonald's in Xenia, Ohio, twenty miles east of Dayton. We were on our way.

Xenia had only one McDonald's, but it was near the high school and very busy. We didn't know what the daughter looked like, or the car the fugitive would be in. All we had was a photo of him.

Jerry and I set up in separate cars and waited. Around midafternoon, as school let out, one of the agents inside the McDonald's radioed us about a brown-haired female who had walked in and picked up a young girl before exiting. Another agent outside noted that she'd gotten into a red Dodge K-car, with a white male at the wheel. Their car pulled out and headed east. It took us several seconds to get out of the crowded lot, but Jerry and I finally got behind the red vehicle. Then an overly zealous local detective blew by us all in his Crown Victoria, alerting the target to the presence of law enforcement. Recognizing his mistake, the detective attempted to turn around and block the vehicle, but the fugitive had already made the surveillance and the chase was on.

We were soon outside Xenia, flying at eighty to ninety miles an hour down rural roads. I radioed the office about it and activated my siren. I then placed a blue bubblegum light on the roof of my car, but it promptly blew off. Having been in two other chases, I knew this one would be dangerous and unpredictable. And as I drove at this breakneck speed, I kept thinking, *Here I am about to be killed chasing this idiot and I will never get the chance to work DT.* And that really pissed me off.

We sped down a steep grade and I saw an equally steep uphill grade ahead of us. I was driving an Oldsmobile with an eight-cylinder engine, so I'd make it, but I believed the K-car would not. As I hit the bottom of the hill, I floored my gas pedal, using Jerry's car as cover while I built up speed. Ahead of us, the K-car lost momentum and I shot past. Before the fugitive could react, I cut over and hit my brakes hard. I released them and hit hard again. With Jerry right behind him, we had the fugitive boxed in. Now we controlled his movements and were able to bring him to a stop.

But I feared he might have a gun, and with the passengers in his car I couldn't return fire. We caught a break when he decided to make a run for it, heading for a nearby copse of trees. Jerry and I followed, but as we gained ground, the suspect suddenly slowed and spun around. Jerry reached for his gun, but I was closer, so I dove right at him and made a tackle that would have thrilled my high school football coach. Still, he wasn't done. He began to fight, and I reached for my belt and grabbed the Cap-Stun pepper spray, emptying it into his face. Finally, howling with pain, he gave up. I cuffed him, and as a local officer led him away, the suspect said to me, "I had that coming."

And so my six years of chasing down criminals drew to an end. I was thoroughly ready to begin my DT assignment. Transferred to Squad 4, the Counterintelligence and International Terrorism Squad, I worked with two agents already dedicated to Squad 4 who were primarily involved with counterintelligence cases at Wright-Patterson Air Force Base in Dayton. Supervisory Special Agent (SSA) Roger D. Wilson was my superior, possibly the best supervisor I've ever had. He was straightforward, even-tempered, and decisive. Also on the squad were Dave Falk and Phil Sandide. Phil was winding down his career, but Dave was in his early fifties, not yet ready to retire. During the 1970s, he'd been in the Los Angeles Division working on the Extremist Squad. He'd investigated the Symbionese Liberation Army (SLA) case involving Patty Hearst and had been securing the perimeter in Compton when the SLA shootout and subsequent fire erupted. He was now on the Aryan Nations investigation, but since his plate was more than full, he was happy to include me.

Since its inception in the early 1970s, the AN has produced or influenced many of history's most notorious events, and the AN of the late nineties had a robust national membership. In fact, the FBI viewed this group as the strongest, most active, and most dangerous DT organization in the United States, and we were concerned with its expansion from the western regions of the country into the Midwest. Since its inception, the AN had used the rhetoric of a dogmatic fundamentalist religion with its own peculiar twist to encourage armed resistance to whatever did not fit the agenda of the supposedly superior and racially pure white American male. The AN hoped to overthrow the U.S. government so they could create a separate nation for whites.

The Ohio chapter of the AN was headed by Harold "Ray" Redfeairn, a notoriously violent man with a lengthy criminal record, including an alleged threat against the life of his own mother. She'd withdrawn the charges, but the incident made it clear to us how ruthless he was. In 1979, he'd attacked a police officer with vicious intent during a traffic stop, shooting the man several times—just for good measure, I suppose—and the officer had saved himself by knocking Redfeairn's gun away before he fired a fatal shot. However, to escape the charges Redfeairn had used an insanity plea, based on a former diagnosis of paranoid schizophrenia, and ended up in a psychiatric hospital for four years. In 1985, he pled guilty to attempted aggravated murder for the shooting and to charges of aggravated robbery for an earlier incident. So he did go to prison, but in 1991 he was released again. It was likely that he'd accumulated even more rage against the government from this experience, and perhaps more effective ways to evade law enforcement.

It was the prevailing opinion of law enforcement that Redfeairn had learned the white supremacist rhetoric in prison. For many incarcerated individuals, joining a white or black prison gang is a survival technique, as the gang provides protection. Once released, they return to their old belief systems. But some disenfranchised white males, such as Redfeairn, continue to espouse these prison-based codes. It becomes a framework for their identity, something worth their energy. They find targets at which to aim their anger—Jews, blacks, other minorities—but they take no responsibility. We've found that most white supremacists have criminal records.

Over the past five years since he'd become a free man, Redfeairn had been in Ohio acquiring power, connections, and resources. He'd also been inflaming others with his hate. A former Klansman, he involved himself only with groups that accepted the use of violence when the need arose. More ominous, this mentally unbalanced man was also the probable successor to the leader of the entire AN organization. An ordained minister in the Church of Jesus Christ Christian, Redfeairn's weekly church services attracted members of such white supremacist groups as the Ku Klux Klan (KKK), the Northern Hammerskins, the National Alliance, and the neo-Nazi National Socialists. The chapter also had ties to the Michigan Militia, the largest antigovernment militia in the United States—and one of the best armed. Ray Redfeairn, paranoid and shrewd, was a man to watch, and we soon had an official reason to do so.

One day, a source reported that Redfeairn and his second in command, Morris Lynn Gulett (who also had a criminal record), were planning to rob a credit union. We followed the source as he accompanied these two around the Dayton area, recording their conversations. They drove by several financial institutions, discussing the layout of the buildings, but never elected to hit any. I suspect that Redfeairn didn't fully trust our source. He was uncanny that way. But even if he took no action, the fact that he was seeking money to fund the Aryan Nations inspired us to make an application to the U.S. attorney, through the FBI headquarters, to initiate an intelligence investigation.

Already, thirty to forty like-minded white supremacists attended "church" every Sunday. People came from Ohio, Indiana, Michigan, Kentucky, Illinois, and Pennsylvania to listen to Redfeairn's racist rhetoric, and we were concerned that he could inspire violence on the scale of the Oklahoma City bombing.

It was around this point that I realized how valuable Dave Hall could be for us.

A Dayton police lieutenant with whom I'd worked a few drug cases called me and said, "Hey, you're working the Aryan Nations now, aren't you?"

"Yeah," I responded, although I hadn't yet crossed fully into DT.

"Well, let me give you a little news. I was in Ikes the other night and Redfeairn was sittin' in there, drinking."

Redfeairn. In an Outlaws bar. In East Dayton. I was uncertain what that meant or how to find out, but then a light went on: I already had a potential informant in place. With his tattoos and good ol' boy demeanor, Hall could easily pass as a member of the AN. In fact, a guy like Hall probably could climb easily through the ranks.

Hall had proven reluctant to pass on information about the Outlaws, but this was something else. Since he was disabled, he had time on his hands. Bad for him, good for us. We could offer him this deal: if he participated as an informant, he could reduce his sentence. I did some checking, then discussed it with Dave Falk in DT. He cleared it, and I prepared to approach Hall. Much as he said he wanted to help, I wasn't sure he'd be keen about this. But I thought maybe I could persuade him.

3

THE INVITATION

Tym Burkey

I saw this as a win-win situation for the FBI, for Hall, and for me. If I sent Hall to Ikes, I was confident that one of two things would occur: he would hook up with the Outlaws or he would hook up with Redfeairn. I personally hoped for the latter.

Redfeairn was fully aware of our past attempts at surveillance. He was cagey and shrewd, and reportedly could spot an informant with uncanny accuracy. That ruled out using an agent, who, try as he might to disguise it, would likely have a certain look. We also couldn't use a disgruntled member, since Redfeairn would probably know about him. We needed someone who could blend in easily and gain Redfeairn's trust.

So I called Hall and asked him to meet me at a specific place on the west side of Dayton. He seemed puzzled but was willing to oblige. When I arrived, he was already there with his big black dog. The dog was barking and growling. I didn't tell Hall this, but if his animal had come at me, I would have shot it.

I pulled up alongside Hall's car and we both rolled down our windows, letting in the winter air. Hall greeted me politely, but I could tell he was uneasy.

"What can I do for you, Agent Burkey?" he asked.

I pulled out a photo of Redfeairn and showed it to him, asking if he'd ever seen the man. He took it, gave it a careful examination, and said that he hadn't.

"His name's Ray Redfeairn," I said. "He's a convicted felon who's served time for the attempted aggravated murder of a Dayton police officer. He's passing himself off now as a minister."

Hall shrugged. "How can I help?"

I came right to the point. "We know that you and Redfeairn have mutual friends in the Outlaws, and we're hoping that through those friends you might be able to get close to him." I couldn't tell what he was thinking, and I knew that providing too much information could be risky.

"Why is the FBI so interested in him?"

"He's the head of the Ohio chapter of the Aryan Nations," I explained. "It's a white supremacist group that's been involved in several acts of domestic terrorism. Since the Oklahoma City bombing, the FBI has stepped up its investigation of these groups. We don't want another incident like that one."

Still, Hall looked puzzled. "What exactly do you want from me?" He fingered the photo. "I don't see how I can help."

"The FBI's goal is to get someone on the inside of Redfeairn's group. But the problem is that Redfeairn is very intelligent and equally paranoid. He can smell an undercover agent a mile away. That's where you come in."

"Me?" Hall laughed, and then our purpose seemed to dawn on him. "I guess you don't have many three-hundred-fifty-pound, tattooed FBI agents, do you?"

I smiled. I knew he was looking me over and evaluating my all-American crew cut. "No," I said, "we don't. I've talked with my boss, and we both think that you'd have a better chance of infiltrating this group than any FBI agent. But I'm not going to lie to you. These guys are not choirboys. It could be dangerous. But it will only be a short-term assignment. Assisting us will also help out with your legal problems. You think about it and give me a call."

He seemed to be pondering the possibility. "Can I keep the picture of Redfeairn?" he asked.

"Sure." I sensed from the question that he had at least one foot in already. He shoved the photo into the pocket of his T-shirt, nodded toward me, and said, "I'll be in touch."

"I'll look forward to it."

We rolled up our windows, gave each other a final look, and drove off. I knew this meeting had been somewhat risky. Hall did have friends among the Outlaws, and if he decided against this proposal and told them about it, our chances of getting to Redfeairn would be minimal, if not dashed altogether. But there was something about this guy. I believed he'd come around. Anyway, it would only last a few months. Just to be sure, I figured out a way to put surveillance on Hall, at least initially, until he proved himself.

Dave Hall

As I headed to my house I thought about what had just transpired. The exchange had surprised me, but the prospect of becoming a spy for the FBI was intriguing. Although I'd never been a member of the Outlaws, I'd been a biker for years. Having run with a pretty rough crowd, I'd seen and done some extremely crazy things. I had no regrets, particularly, but at forty-three years old, I'd started to realize that I hadn't really accomplished anything with my life. My back injury had ended my ability to work at a regular job, as well as most of my craziness. I was definitely in a rut. Just maybe this thing with the FBI would add some excitement to my life.

That night I sat around the house and considered the situation. For every reason I could think of to accept Agent Burkey's offer, I could also come up with a corresponding reason not to. But there was one thing that stood out. I pondered the statement that the Aryan Nations was a dangerous organization. The only thing I knew about such groups was what I'd heard about the KKK over the years. I'd spent most of my childhood with my grandparents in a log cabin in the hills of southeastern Kentucky. There may have been KKK activity in the area, but I never heard about it, and frankly most people were so dirt poor they spent all their energy just surviving.

But as I thought about the deal, I recalled an incident that happened to me when I was four, back in 1957. Another one of my uncles gave me and my sister Linda a dollar to go to the store in Jackson and buy candy. We did that, and when we left the store, a black man approached my sister to ask for money, so she gave him the change we had from the dollar. When we went home, we told my uncle. He didn't like that one bit. He took his shotgun, went into Jackson, and right in front of the store, he shot the man dead. It was Kentucky, so no one gave it a thought. No charges were brought against my uncle, who has since died, for what I knew later was outright murder, and as I grew older and came to understand the nature of this hate crime, it left a lasting impression on me.

In my teens I'd gone back and forth from Kentucky to Dayton, Ohio, where my mom lived with my stepfather and my nine half brothers and sisters. In the late sixties and early seventies, Dayton had pretty much been a segregated town. Blacks lived on the west side of the city, and the schools weren't integrated until the following decade, when the court ordered crosstown busing. But my mom was truly color-blind. She didn't care if a person was white, black, or purple, and she'd raised us to be the same way. In fact, two of my sisters had married black men, and I had several biracial nieces and nephews. I thought about them, and at the end of the day that's what tipped the scales in the FBI's favor.

The next day I called Agent Burkey. "Okay," I said, "I'll find out what I can about this Redfeairn and his group. But I have two conditions." He was listening, so I went on. "Number one, under no circumstances will I give the FBI any information on the Outlaws, and number two, I won't wear a wire."

I'm not sure he liked that last one, but he agreed to my terms. Then I laid out the strategy I would take at the bar. "I don't want to draw attention to myself as suddenly just coming there and staying for hours. I want to do this my way, slow and easy."

"That's fine," Burkey said. "Just let me know when you have something."

With that, it was done. My next move was to set the bait.

Tym Burkey

Ikes, a neighborhood bar that operated on property held in the name of a mother of one of the Outlaws, was far from neighborly. The 1940s structure sat on a street corner, a two-story frame building with white siding. The bottom contained the bar, and an apartment took up the top floor. The back was hidden from view by a wooden fence, but cameras and two-way glass provided security. The Dayton police blotter had recorded numerous violent acts in this place, and the DEA believed narcotics were regularly sold there. In short, Ikes was a good place to avoid.

Hall was pretty much on his own in this bar. The only thing I could do was occasionally drive by. If he turned up missing, I could at least say he had been inside. Also, drive-bys gave me the opportunity to check up on him to make sure he was doing what he said. I carried a pager, and Hall and I set up a code system he could use to let me know if he wanted me to call, was back at home, or was in danger. I knew, but hoped he didn't, that if he was actually ever in danger, there was little I could do to help.

4

BAIT

Dave Hall

I'd been in the bar before and knew I could blend in easily enough, but I didn't want to seem obvious. Fortunately, on my first visit I spotted some old friends, so I sat and talked with them. While I was there, no one who looked like the photograph of Redfeairn came in. But Burkey had told me that Redfeairn usually went to the bar around four-thirty in the afternoon, so I came again a few times, showing up midafternoon and leaving before four o'clock. This way, I could establish a relationship with the various bartenders and patrons. At first, I came about every third day, then every other day. You might think Ikes was empty at this time, but even in the middle of the afternoon it was no place for wimps. Almost every day, some biker broad was running around naked or someone else was getting the hell beat out of 'em. Having friends in the gang and being a big guy spared me from most confrontations, but I had to stay on my toes.

It took over a month, but toward the end of January, I'd become a regular. Then I extended my time, arriving a little later as well as staying later. Burkey called a few times, but I insisted on doing this my way. I knew he was frustrated with the slow pace, but it wasn't him who had to come in here, it was me.

Tym Burkey

Over that first month, I contacted Hall several times, but he had nothing for me. It seemed like he was just putting me off, and I wondered if he was going to be useful to us after all. I wanted him to make contact with Redfeairn so we could get a better sense of his movements before he acted out, but Hall insisted on doing it his own way. I knew he was on disability and was probably spending a lot on beer while he hung out at the bar. I thought I might persuade him by letting him know that the FBI would give him money to compensate him for his expenses only after he gave us something that made clear we were investing in a worthwhile project. But Hall said he wasn't in it for the money, so there wasn't much I could do except wait. Being patient while knowing what this group could be doing, however, proved difficult.

Dave Hall

I finally saw Redfeairn. He was there in the bar when I came in one afternoon, so I sat at the opposite end and asked Tigger, the bartender, for my usual. I took a drink before I risked looking around.

Redfeairn was shorter than I'd expected, about five foot ten, but he was stocky and it was obvious to me that he worked out. He was wearing a short-sleeved shirt with a clerical collar, like a Catholic priest would wear, and his manner was confident. He was talking to an old buddy of mine, J.D., an Outlaw. J.D. was in his late fifties and had been a member of the Outlaws for most of his life. I'd known him for at least twenty years, and he was a good man to have as a friend because his enemies usually didn't last very long. That he knew Redfeairn offered me an unexpected opening.

After a few minutes at the bar, I headed for the bathroom, which took me past the two of them. J.D. saw me and, referring to me by a nickname I'd had for years, said, "What's happenin', Dr. Dave?"

I shrugged. "Nothing much. Just stopped in for a cold drink or two." I gave him a pat on the back, purposely ignoring Redfeairn. I wanted him to see me there a few more times before I reeled him in. Like Agent Burkey said, he was both shrewd and suspicious. I didn't want to lose him before I had him.

I went home that day thinking it had begun: I'd started on this journey. It still made me uneasy, but that's what my dog, Gary, was for. I let him out and watched him run around. His playfulness always made me feel good. Then I called Agent Burkey.

"I spotted your man today," I told him.

"Great!" he replied. "Did you talk to him?" I could feel his anticipation over the phone.

"Naw. I'll give it a couple more times."

He was quiet a moment, but then affirmed, "That's probably wise."

I let him know I'd keep in touch and then hung up. I needed to unwind. I'd barely begun this assignment, but I knew it was serious stuff.

I watched Gary play with a ball I'd tossed out in the yard, remembering how I'd gotten him as a pup about nine years before. I'd stopped by the house of a buddy of mine, Earl the Pearl. His black Lab had gotten the neighbor's pit bull pregnant. She'd had six puppies, but ate four of them that night. Concerned about the other two, he talked me into taking one. This little thing was less than twenty-four hours old. I didn't even know what to call him. When I got home, I called a nearby vet. He told me to feed the pup baby formula with a tiny bit of white Karo syrup mixed into it. He also suggested that I take a small box and a blanket, then put a hot water bottle under the blanket and a wind-up clock in the box. This would mimic the warmth and heartbeat of his mother.

I did what I could and then turned on the TV. An episode of *Taxi* was on, and the Reverend Jim had that horse named Gary in his apartment. So it hit me—Gary was the right name for this dog.

That night and for the next few days, I fed Gary baby food from a surgical glove. I poked a hole in a finger, and when he'd chewed it to where it busted, I'd tie that finger off and move to the next finger. I raised him like that until he got on solid food. And he was a smart dog. I didn't have to train him hardly at all. It's just like he understood what I was saying. He went with me wherever I went, and I'd talk to him like he was a human being. He could play with children at the park, but he was fiercely protective of me. No one got near my car if he was in it and I wasn't.

At the time I got him I was having problems with anxiety and depression, and all of a sudden I had this little life I was responsible for. He saved me. And today, like always, he seemed to know I was out of sorts. He had a sense about him. He came up to play, like he was trying to cheer me up. It helped to know that whatever awaited me down the road, Gary was gonna be there.

Tym Burkey

It was a relief to know that Dave had finally seen Redfeairn. Things had started now, and I hoped it wouldn't be long before we got information. I was certain the Aryan Nations was planning something and that Redfeairn was the key to learning more about it. The criminal agent part of me was confident this would be a quick hit on Redfeairn; we'd get something on him, and the problem would be solved. I did not fully appreciate the value of intelligence and of waiting not for the *right* moment but for the *better* moment. But I was learning quickly.

It was our policy to give as little information as possible to informants, because knowing too much could get them into trouble. It was all right for Hall to see a news broadcast, but we wanted him aware of only basic information about this group, so that he'd come across to Redfeairn as someone who knew very little about the AN.

Dave Hall

It was now early February 1997. Over the next week or so, I spotted Redfeairn at the bar but never had what I considered a good opportunity to approach him. Then one day I walked in and saw J.D. talking with the man. This was it. I ambled over to them and decided to put on an act, like I was upset about something and just needed to talk. That would hide my nervousness, at any rate.

"Those damn niggers!" I yelled. "One of 'em almost ran me off the road. They oughta send every one of those black bastards back to Africa!"

Redfeairn nodded and smiled: he understood my frustration. He extended his hand. "I'm Pastor Ray Redfeairn," he said. "It's nice to meet you."

I shook his hand and let J.D. make the introduction.

"I'm sorry about my language, Pastor," I said.

"That's all right, Brother, I understand. I feel the same way." Redfeairn then handed me a business card. Across the top it said, "Go with the word of God in your mouth and a two-edged sword in your hand." In the center was "Church of Jesus Christ Christian/ Aryan Nations," along with additional biblical verse citations.

"What's the Aryan Nations?" I asked.

"It's a white supremacist organization."

I knew he was watching for my reaction, so I acted ignorant. "Like the Ku Klux Klan?"

"Yes," said Redfeairn, nodding approval. "But we're better organized."

I shrugged as if none of it much mattered to me. "If you guys hate niggers, you're okay with me." I sat down next to them and ordered a drink. Redfeairn picked up where he'd left off with J.D., telling him that Channel 7 had recently interviewed him and that the segment was supposed to air on the eleven o'clock news the next night. I added my comments with a couple of racial jokes. Talking this way was like eating a shit sandwich, and it made me sick to my stomach. I'd never used that kind of language or thought about people that way. I had two black brothers-in-law and several bira-cial nieces and nephews, so listening to this crap without walking away or hitting the people who were saying it felt like a betrayal of those I loved. But Redfeairn seemed to enjoy the jokes. He extended an invitation for me to attend his church on Sunday.

"Well, now," I said, "I haven't been to church in a while, not since I was a kid."

He winked. "It'll be good for you, then. Maybe better than you realize."

I said I'd consider it. He told me how to get to the building in New Vienna, Ohio, a small town about forty-five miles southeast of Dayton. I took the directions and said, "It was good meeting you, Pastor."

"Call me Ray," said Redfeairn. "And I'll look for you on Sunday."

"Okay, Ray," I replied, and then excused myself and walked to the end of the bar to talk with Tigger. I figured for a first contact, I'd done pretty well and I didn't want to push my luck. I joked around until I saw Redfeairn leave. Then I went home to call Agent Burkey.

Tym Burkey

When I heard about this first contact, I was excited. It seemed to have gone as well as we could have hoped.

"Redfeairn invited me to attend the church services," Hall told me.

"And you'll go?"

"Seems like it might be the best way to win him over. Better there than spending too much time with him at the bar. But I don't want to attend too soon."

I considered this. Despite my interest in exploiting this meeting as soon as possible, I knew his idea was sound. "Maybe you're right," I said. "We don't want to scare him off."

"Do you want to see the business card he gave me, Agent Burkey?"

"I'd like to see it, yes." I thought for a moment. He was proving himself, and he and I would be working quite closely from here on out. "And by the way," I added, "why don't you call me Tym?"

"Okay, Tym," he replied. "When do you want to get together?"

I knew we'd have to be careful. I asked him to call me again in the morning and we'd find a time and place. Then he said he'd overheard Redfeairn say he was going to be on the news. That bothered me. It was the first I'd heard about it, which meant we didn't have a good sense of his movements. I told Hall I'd be watching and thanked him for the information.

This was a very good development in the investigation, and for several reasons. Hall had done his job and met Redfeairn. More than that, Redfeairn had introduced himself to Hall. This is the best way to have a source brought into an organization—to have the leader recruit him. I was sure that, prior to inviting Hall, Redfeairn had checked him out with the Outlaws and possibly had another AN member also run a check. My belief was that Redfeairn's inflated ego kept him from doubting his own judgment. But I knew one thing for sure: Dave was in.

5

IN GOOD STANDING

Dave Hall

After hanging up, I looked again at the card Ray Redfeairn had given me. Across the bottom it said, "White Revolution is the only Solution," although *revolution* was misspelled *revololution*. I was curious about the biblical verses, so I found my grandmother's old Bible and looked up the citations. The first one was Genesis 3:15: "And the Lord God took the man and put him into the Garden of Eden to dress it and to keep it." The next was Psalms 110:1: "The Lord said onto my lord, sit thou at my right hand until I make thine enemies thy footstool." Another was Romans 16:20: "And the God of peace shall bruise Satan under your feet shortly. The grace of our Lord Jesus Christ be with you. Amen."

I had no idea what significance these verses had, if any, but I wrote them down to save Tym the trouble.

At my suggestion, we met the next day behind Roth High School, which was in a predominantly black part of town. He agreed that there probably weren't any white supremacists living in that area. When we were face-to-face, Tym asked me to get the license plate numbers of any cars that Redfeairn might be driving. I said okay and handed him Redfeairn's business card. As he wrote down the information, I said, "I hate to bring this up, but for the last six weeks I've been using my own money to hang out at the bar and I just can't afford it."

Tym knew I was on a limited income. He looked up at me. "I'll see what I can do."

"I'd sure appreciate it."

Tym Burkey

Initially, the FBI had not reimbursed Dave for his expenses. In our view he was working off his problems. Plus, if his efforts ever developed into a case against the Outlaws or Aryan Nations and it went to trial, we wanted to be able to show that his motivation was not profiteering.

But I knew Dave was sincere about needing the money in order to continue. Since he was making progress for us, I decided to contact the assistant United States attorney's (AUSA) office in Frankfort, Kentucky. They had prosecuted the marijuana conspiracy that had netted Dave, and at any time they could recommend him for immediate sentencing. I knew that for his six-month trial period, the U.S. probation office was monitoring him as well. I contacted the FBI case agent in Kentucky and was forwarded to AUSA Mark Wohlander. I explained to him what I was doing, and he was glad to learn that Dave was being productive. Oklahoma City was still on everyone's minds, and nobody wanted a repeat. So Wohlander concurred that I could get Dave some reimbursement money. He put nothing in writing, so as not to compromise our security, an act for which I was grateful.

Dave Hall

Agent Burkey was always polite, but I had no reason to trust him. After that meeting, I went home and noticed that there was a message on my answering machine. It was my girlfriend, Terri, who worked as the branch manager of a local credit union. She was a beautiful woman: five foot eight with long auburn hair and a build that any red-blooded male would appreciate. In her late twenties, she'd never been married. I'd met Terri at a tavern and we'd hit it off, but I was slow to notice how much she adored me. After a month of seeing each other, we were at George's Tavern near Trotwood on a Saturday night and both of us had had a bit too much to drink. Terri asked me when I was going to invite her home.

"You want to come home with me?"

She gave me a passionate kiss and said, "Does that answer your question?"

We were out of there. When we got to my house, I opened the door and Gary immediately jumped up on Terri, licking her face. As she leaned over to rub his ears, she said, "You never told me you had a dog."

"Yep, that's old Gary."

She stood up and looked at me. Then she started to laugh.

"What's so funny?" I asked.

She was laughing so hard she could barely speak, but when she did, she said, "Since I met you, you've told me things like 'Gary and I went hiking today' or 'Gary and I are going up to the lake to do some fishing.' All this time I thought that Gary was a person!" We both laughed, but soon she and Gary were friends, too.

I liked that Terri was easygoing and friendly, but better than that, she also enjoyed many of the same hobbies as me—hiking and fishing, watching old movies, and getting together with friends.

At that point, around the time Tym approached me, I'd been dating Terri about a year. It was our habit to spend every weekend together, and during the week she usually stayed with me two or three nights. On the machine, she'd left a message for me to call if I wanted her to stop by after work. I felt guilty. I knew I was putting our relationship at risk, because over the past few weeks I'd spent more time at the bar and less time with her, and had even stretched the truth by telling her I was doing some work for a friend. I owed her some time, so I called her and we had a nice evening together. But after Terri went to sleep that night, I turned on the news.

The Aryan Nations segment began with Redfeairn standing behind a pulpit, flanked on either side by two serious young men wearing blue military-looking uniforms. Behind them hung a large Confederate battle flag and a Nazi flag bearing a swastika. The reporter said, "This is not your usual church service. This is a service by the Aryan Nations, a self-proclaimed white supremacist organization."

It was clear that they were trying to recruit new members. The reporter then said that the Aryan Nations was most often described as a paramilitary hate group founded in the mid-seventies in Idaho, but it had migrated to Ohio with very definite goals.

Then there was a clip of Redfeairn, who looked angry as he said, "The words *racist* and *white supremacist* are adequate in describing what we are. We make no bones about that. We are a white supremacist organization and we're up front about that. To get through the door of our church you have to be white and you have to be Aryan." A picture of a church flashed on the screen, and there was film footage of Redfeairn standing at a pulpit, shouting, "We don't care about white rights! We want white power!"

As the tape played, the reporter said, "This is the church in New Vienna, Ohio. The Aryans hold services here each week trying to attract those who share their racist and anti-Semitic beliefs. The Aryans say forty to fifty people—'believers'—attend every week. Only whites are allowed in. Others, they say, will be stopped."

The segment then returned to Redfeairn, who said, "We have the means to protect ourselves, and our people are well trained. If anyone comes to hurt someone in our organization or our family, we'll stop them." He added with a smirk, "To get to the heart of the matter, if it takes killing them, I'll kill any enemy of my people."

The reporter returned to the screen, indicating that law enforcement groups were ready for them. He added that the Aryan Nations had obtained permits for a rally in Columbus, Ohio, on February 16 and that there could be rallies in Dayton later in the year. There would be additional information in part two of the story, to be broadcast the following evening.

I turned off the TV and sat back in my chair. Tym wasn't kidding when he told me that these guys weren't choirboys. They sounded like a bunch of psychopaths. I began to wonder what I'd gotten myself into. The Ray Redfeairn I'd just seen on TV was a far cry from the friendly man I'd met at the bar. Now that I'd seen this, he appeared to be a mental case. A dangerous one.

On Saturday morning, I found myself needing some fresh air, so Gary and I headed for a nearby park. I had some serious thinking to do, now that I had doubts about Redfeairn and this Aryan Nations thing. I wondered if I'd taken on more than I could handle. On the news Redfeairn had come across as a dangerous lunatic, and if the rest of the members were like him, I was in for a rough time. Still, there was another side: it was clear to me that these people needed to be stopped. I was just one guy, but Tym seemed to think that whatever information I could bring them would be effective in a larger way. I have to admit that despite my concerns, the challenge excited me, as did the possibility of doing something truly important. So by the end of my walk, I'd decided to keep going. I figured it would only take two or three months to get the FBI what they needed, and surely I could put up with it for that long. I'm glad I didn't know that night what I was in for.

I went to Ikes that afternoon, noticing the number of people already good and drunk. I greeted a few friends as I made my way over to the bar. The jukebox was blaring, smoke filled the air, and voices were raised. In some places, those who knew each other were getting pretty familiar, as in shirts coming off. At any moment, I expected to witness an impromptu wet T-shirt contest, which I wouldn't have much minded, or to see someone hauled out the door over a trivial matter. I ordered a drink and started talking to a young woman sitting next to me. A few minutes later, I saw Redfeairn emerge from the bathroom, followed by J.D. I continued talking with the girl but kept my eye on them. They rubbed their noses and laughed like fools, so I figured they'd just done some lines of coke. I picked up my drink and made my way through the crowd. As I drew closer, J.D. saw me and yelled, "Dr. Dave! Pull up a stool."

I nodded, sat down, and said, "What's happening?" I gestured toward Redfeairn to include him in my greeting. "How ya doin', Ron?"

Redfeairn smiled. "I'm fine, Brother Dave, but the name is Ray, not Ron."

"Sorry, Ray, I'm just really bad with names."

He wasn't wearing his usual clerical collar that night, and I wondered why. We talked for a couple of minutes, and I let Redfeairn know that I'd be busy in the morning but might check out his church the following week.

He smiled. "We'd be glad to have you, Brother."

I mentioned the news program, and that seemed to get up his ire. He told me they'd edited out most of what he'd said, so he wouldn't be doing any more interviews. Then he and J.D. returned to the bathroom, and when they came back, J.D. said he'd left me something on top of the towel dispenser. I went in and found a line of coke, enough to choke a horse. At forty-three, I'd done my share of drugs and hell-raising, but I'd given all of that up. So I just blew the coke off onto the floor and after a couple of minutes I returned to my bar stool, sniffing and rubbing my nose. "Damn, that was enough for an elephant," I whispered. J.D. grinned through his beard.

Soon the first fight of the evening broke out. Things got pretty rough and I prepared to move, but it was over in a couple of minutes, and the contenders bought each other drinks. Once things settled down, the barmaid proudly showed J.D. and me the results of her recent breast enlargement surgery.

We all had several more drinks, and I was hoping that Ray was coked up enough to talk freely, but he soon left. I watched through the window as he got into a gray Omni, and made a mental note of the license plate number.

Tym Burkey

Dave called to let me know about Redfeairn's car. He also informed me that the man used coke. Then he reminded me he was running out of cash for these bar excursions, and I assured him that I was trying to get him some expense money. I could see that he was doing what we'd asked, and it had the potential to pay off in some important information.

"We sure appreciate what you are doing for us," I told him.

"Don't thank me," he said, "thank my liver. It's the one taking the abuse."

I urged Dave to be patient, but I'm sure he wondered if I was really going to come through. Bureaucracy ran slowly, and I couldn't do anything more than repeat that money was coming. The policy of the FBI is to stipulate an amount of money for each case, including informant cases. If someone runs low, the amount could be adjusted, but the request had to have the proper documentation and signatures.

I knew that Dave must be thinking that he had quite an investment in this mission already. It couldn't have helped to wonder if we were going to reimburse him.

Dave Hall

I wasn't happy about my mounting bar bills, but I went back to Ikes the next evening. Only four or five people were drinking. Paula, the barmaid, greeted me as I came in. She brought me my drink, gave me a hug, and said, "It's kind of slow. Why don't we go to the ladies' room for a quickie?"

I laughed, knowing she had a steady old man and just liked to joke around with me, and said, "Now, you know there's nothing quick about me."

After a while, Ray walked in. He came right over to me and said, "How ya doin', Brother Dave?"

"Pretty good, Brother Ray. You?"

"Doin' fine, Brother Dave."

It was the first time I'd been alone with him, and he soon started in. "Even though I hate niggers and the mud races," he said, "the Jews are the main enemy."

"The mud races?" I said. "Who's that?"

"All nonwhites. The niggers, spics, and chinks are considered mud races. But the Jews are the evil children of Satan." He seemed to enjoy explaining these things.

Trying to keep a straight face, I said, "I kind of figured that out about the niggers and all, but I don't know anything about Jews."

"That's because they don't want you to know. They keep you from finding out. Everything you see on TV or read in the newspaper is controlled by those vile Jew bastards, but they're clever enough to keep you from realizing it."

I took a slow sip of my drink and then commented, "That all sounds pretty wild to me, Ray."

He looked me straight in the eye. "That's why you need to come to the church, Brother Dave, to learn the truth."

He went on to describe how he'd spent the previous day in Columbus, Ohio, obtaining the necessary permits to hold an Aryan Nations rally on the steps of the state capitol the following Sunday. He then asked if I'd like to attend the rally, maybe even work as security. I paused for a moment and then said, "I don't know about working security."

"Just come to the rally, then."

I shrugged. "I'll think about it."

I asked Paula to give us a couple more drinks, and then pulled out the business card Ray had given me when we first met. Handing it to him, I pointed out the error at the bottom of the card: "White Revololution is the only Solution."

Ray looked at it for a moment and then shook his head. "I must have passed out a thousand of these cards and you're the first one that caught that. I'm going to see the printer and get my money back."

I thought he should invest it in a remedial spelling course for himself. A little later, I glanced out the window and saw a gold Chevy van pull up. A man got out of the passenger side and the vehicle drove off. He came into the bar, looked around, and then headed toward Ray. Dressed entirely in black, his pants stuffed into clunky combat boots, he looked to be in his late forties, about five foot ten with a stocky build and a shaved head. When Ray saw him he stood up and gave the Nazi salute. "Hail victory, Brother Morris."

The man returned the salute. "Hail victory, Pastor Ray."

It all seemed bizarre to me, but I kept a blank expression on my face. Ray introduced me to Morris Gulett. I shook his hand and said, "It's a pleasure to meet you, Morris," but Gulett didn't say a word. He kept looking around the bar. After a few moments, he and Ray walked to a secluded corner and began talking. I couldn't hear the conversation, but Gulett continued to watch everyone as if he expected someone to suddenly pull out a gun. The left arm of his jacket had the same type of patch that I had seen on Ray's jacket, a crown with a sword stuck through it, which I assumed was the logo of the Aryan Nations.

I saw them look in my direction, and just then the gold Chevy van returned and parked. Two young men, also dressed in black with shaved heads, got out and came into the bar. As they approached us, Ray pulled them aside and the four men stood in the corner talking quietly. I nursed my drink and tried to look like I was minding my own business. A short time later, Ray tapped me on the shoulder and as I turned around he said, "Brother Dave, I'd like to introduce you to Brothers Frank Johnson and Dan Rick." We shook hands, and Ray indicated that I might be at the rally.

Dan, the taller of the two, had tattoos running up his neck. He said, "He's a big guy. We can put him right up front." He asked if I was going to come to the church.

"Yeah," I replied, "I think I'll come down and check it out."

"We'll be glad to have you."

I figured I'd made enough progress for one evening and I didn't want to appear overly interested, so I told Ray that I was going to head out. He asked me to meet him at the bar on Saturday evening to discuss the rally, so I agreed. On the way to the car I made a mental note of the license plate number on the van.

Tym Burkey

Dave called with a license plate number and three more names, and said they seemed to be insiders, confidants of Redfeairn's. "It sounds like you're in, Dave," I told him.

"I guess so."

I was impressed that he'd been invited so soon to a significant event, but also wary. "You know, those rallies can get out of hand sometimes, and since it's Black History Month, the protesters will be even more agitated." I didn't want to scare him, but I thought he ought to realize the stakes.

He seemed annoyed. "Do you want me to go to the rally or not?"

I realized I'd given him some doubts, although I hadn't meant to, so I said, "I'll leave that up to you."

"Well, I'll think about it." He told me that he was going to take off a couple of nights to be with his girlfriend. Then he'd meet Redfeairn on Saturday and let me know what he decided. I urged him to be careful. I never wanted anyone to "help out" who doesn't want to. I tell all sources, right up front, that their cooperation is voluntary; they must be square with me and let me know if they're uncomfortable. I will also tell them they can walk away at any time. But I was also aware that if Dave walked away from this assignment, he'd go to prison.

Dave Hall

I noticed that Terri had been in a strange mood, so I took her to dinner, hoping to get her to talk.

"What's wrong?" I asked.

She paused and took a breath, as if this was going to be difficult for her. Then, resolved, she looked me straight in the eye. "Are you cheating on me?"

I was astounded. I hardly knew what to say. I hurt for her, because she must have been really worried, but I also couldn't tell her the truth. I placed my hand on top of hers and said, "Terri, I swear to God that I have never cheated on you and I never will."

I don't know if she believed me. Tears bubbled into her eyes and streamed down her cheeks. I sat there, not knowing what to say. She took a napkin off the table to wipe the tears away.

"Over the past two months," she pointed out, "you've been spending less and less time with me. What else am I supposed to think?"

"I'm sorry, sweetheart, but I've been doing some work for a friend. I can't tell you what type of work, but I promise it's nothing illegal and I should be done in a few weeks."

She looked up. "If it's not illegal, why can't you tell me?"

I thought for a moment about how to phrase my reply. "All I can do is ask you to trust me, and I promise when the job is over I'll tell you everything."

That won a faint smile. "You must think that I'm awfully silly."

Holding her hands, I said, "On the contrary, I think you're the most intelligent and beautiful woman in the world, and I love you."

She seemed reassured, and the subject of what I was doing didn't come up again the rest of the evening. But I sensed that the storm hadn't really passed.

On Saturday, Terri was at my house, with no sign of leaving, so I told her I had to go out for a few hours, but I'd be back as soon as I could. She forced a smile. I left, hoping this little job I was doing wasn't going to damage what I had with her.

I got to Ikes a little before 5:00 P.M. There were quite a few people already drunk and having a good time. Little Mike—all six foot ten and 450 pounds of him—was tending bar. He brought my drink, and after I took a sip I said, "Jesus, Mike! Put some 7UP in that, you maniac!"

He laughed. "Too strong for you, big fella?"

J.D. showed up just then, so we got to talking, and around six Ray arrived with that strange Morris Gulett in tow. Ray was wearing his clerical collar, and Gulett had on the same black outfit as the first time I'd met him. They joined us, and Ray immediately began talking about the rally. He said that Governor George Voinovich had called him personally to ask him to postpone it until after Black History month was over, but Ray had refused.

"You'll be lucky if some nigger doesn't shoot your ass" was J.D.'s comment.

"Brother, I've already had death threats, and they don't bother me in the least."

"That's because you're crazy."

"Maybe, Brother, maybe."

I watched Gulett out of the corner of my eye. His eyes were darting back and forth over the crowd, and he was constantly turning around to look behind him. Ray told me that for the rally, they were all going to meet at the church in the morning. "But I've been thinking, Brother Dave. If you attend this rally, the feds are going to know who you are before you even get home. So why don't you pass this one up? We try to keep some of our members secret."

I was relieved but just replied, "Okay, if you think it's for the best."

"I'd still like to see you at church, though."

"I kind of liked what you said on TV," I responded, trying hard to sound sincere, "and I'd like to hear more." I reiterated that I'd come in about a week.

Ray smiled. "We need all the good people we can get." He and Gulett decided it was time to go, so Ray pointed a finger at me and said, "I'll see you at church."

After they left, J.D. asked, "Why are you getting mixed up with those nuts?"

"I thought Ray was a friend of yours," I said.

"He is, but he's still a nut."

I laughed, then said, "I guess I just don't have anything else to do right now."

I ordered another drink and was sitting there talking with J.D. when I suddenly remembered Terri. I looked at my watch and saw it was almost 7:00 P.M. Chugging down my drink, I told J.D. that I had to split. When I got back home, Terri's car was still in the driveway, which meant at least she hadn't gotten mad enough to leave. As I walked into the house, I found her asleep on the couch with Gary. I was thinking how cute they both looked when Gary jumped up and started barking. Terri woke and seemed happy to see me. To my relief, she didn't ask any questions.

I knew that my next move would take me a lot closer to Redfeairn and probably further from her. But I'd made a commitment and I intended to see it through.

It was a cold Sunday morning, so Terri and I decided to stay home and watch old Humphrey Bogart movies. A little before noon, she went to take a nap, so I turned on the news. The lead story was about a shootout in Wilmington, Ohio—just a few miles from Redfeairn's church. I wondered if it was connected to the rally.

The state troopers had pulled over two men for expired license plates, and the troopers' dashboard camera had caught the whole thing. One trooper was questioning a man at the rear of a blue Chevy Suburban, and he bolted back to the driver's-side door. The trooper followed him, and as they struggled a second man jumped from the Suburban and opened fire on the trooper's partner. There was an exchange of gunfire, and one man ran off while the other jumped into the Suburban and sped off.

Minutes later, the Wilmington police cornered the fleeing Suburban. The driver jumped out with an AK-47 assault rifle and pumped three rounds into the cruiser's windshield. He then fled on foot. None of the officers was injured, but a stray bullet had struck a passerby in the shoulder. The whole thing looked like a scene out of a bad movie. I turned it off, putting it behind me as a random news story. But it wasn't over.

On Thursday, as Terri read her book next to me, I turned on the news again. This time they had more information. The fugitives were identified as brothers, Chevie and Cheyne Kehoe, and they reportedly had ties to the Aryan Nations. I moved to the edge of my chair and said, "Oh shit!"

Terri looked up from her book. "What?"

"Nothing. Just watching the news."

As I continued watching, the reporter said, "It's believed that the two brothers were in town to meet with Harold 'Ray' Redfeairn, the head of the Ohio chapter of the Aryan Nations."

They showed file footage of Ray standing behind the pulpit, screaming about "white power" for "self-defense." He'd apparently said, "The Kehoes are not members of the Ohio Aryan Nations," but that seemed rather transparent, given Redfeairn's criminal history. I listened as they recounted Redfeairn's list of offenses: drunk driving, armed robbery, and the attempted aggravated murder of a police officer. The reporter added that the Kehoes had so far eluded a nationwide search and were considered armed and dangerous.

I wanted to call Tym, but with Terri sitting there, I couldn't. I needed to know more about this, but I'd have to wait. For years I'd ridden with a pretty rough group of bikers and had found myself in some dangerous situations, but I'd never intentionally walked into trouble. I wondered what I was in for.

Tym Burkey

I heard from Dave just as I was about to call him. He wanted to know more about what he'd seen on the news. I did know a few things about the Kehoe brothers, but I didn't want to say too much. Chevie Kehoe appeared to be the more violent of the pair, but both had been raised in a racist, anti-Semitic home. Chevie grew up to become an aggressive antigovernment radical who hoped to establish a whites-only Aryan homeland. When they discussed the government—their enemy—they used the term ZOG, an acronym for "Zionist Occupied Government"; they literally believed that the Jews controlled the U.S. government and sooner or later ZOG would begin hunting down all Aryans, putting them into concentration camps, and exterminating them—the Holocaust in reverse. Some of these white supremacists believed that in Indiana, on a military bombing range, there was an underground crematorium.

Chevie Kehoe held grudges, especially over the government

standoff in August 1992 with white separatist Randy Weaver's family at their home on Ruby Ridge in Idaho. The incident had inspired widespread outrage among antigovernment groups, and Kehoe was among those who wanted to avenge it.

It was known that he'd associated with Timothy McVeigh before the Oklahoma City bombing and that he'd supplied weapons to the Aryan Republican Army, members of which went on to rob nearly two dozen midwestern banks. Kehoe was also wanted for his association with several murders, including three members of the Mueller family in Arkansas. They were gun dealers, and their supply of guns had been stolen. In addition, Cheyne had implicated Chevie in a bombing. He was a dangerous fugitive.

In the incident that Dave had caught on the news, the police found weapons, thousands of rounds of ammo, and federal law enforcement paraphernalia in the Kehoes' Chevrolet Suburban. The two brothers had escaped in separate directions, and we knew they would find cover in the Aryan community. What they were up to was anyone's guess, but they clearly meant business. Chevie, at least, was not averse to killing people.

"We don't have any hard evidence that the Kehoes were in town to meet with Redfeairn," I told Dave. "Do you plan to go to the church on Sunday?"

"I wouldn't miss it for the world."

"Just keep your ears open, Dave, in case the subject of the Kehoes comes up."

"Well, this being my first trip to the church," he said, "I'm going to be careful, but I'll try and get as much information as I can."

I knew he would. Even as I reiterated that he should be watchful, I did want information about the movements of these fugitives. They were a serious concern to us, and we had no idea as yet what they'd planned. Dave was our eyes and ears. His trip to their church could be instrumental not only in getting him involved with Redfeairn but also in gathering other kinds of important information. I doubted we would locate the Kehoe brothers this way, but we might learn what they'd intended in this area.

6

INTO THE DARK WORLD OF WHITE SUPREMACY

Dave Hall

I arranged to meet Terri for dinner the next night and then prepared to go to Ikes. Gary stood at the front door, his tail wagging,
his eyes saying, *I want to go, too.* He was used to going everywhere
with me, and lately I'd been leaving him at home. Lately, I'd been
neglecting everyone.

"Okay, you can go," I told him, "but you have to stay in the
car."

Tigger was tending bar that evening, and all the regulars were in
their usual seats. For a Friday, it seemed kind of quiet—which was
good, because I didn't want to stay. I joined J.D. at one end of the
bar just as Ray walked in. He gave the Nazi salute and said, "Hail
victory, brothers!"

We exchanged greetings, and I asked, "What's up with that Nazi
salute thing you guys do?"

As usual, he was only too happy to explain. "The open-hand
salute is actually a greeting rooted in ancient Scandinavia and used
mainly by the Vikings. By extending your open hand to an ap-

proaching neighbor, it showed you were holding no weapons and they were welcome."

"I thought that all started with Hitler," I said.

"No, Brother Dave, that's a misconception. Take the swastika, for instance. That's a rune or symbol also used by the Vikings, as well as people in India and China thousands of years ago."

I nodded my head. "Guess a fella could learn something new every day."

He mentioned his church again, and I said I'd come. I toyed with the idea of bringing up the shootout in Wilmington but then just asked about the rally. He said that Mo Gulett had gotten testy with one of the protesters, but offered nothing more. Rather than prolong our meeting, I ended it there, picking up some jerky for Gary, and went home, promising to be in church the next day.

And I did go. In New Vienna, I found the aging building where I was supposed to park and went to the rear to head up a set of rusty metal stairs. I spotted a man walking on top of the roof, wearing a blue uniform and baseball cap. He carried binoculars and wore a sidearm. As I ascended the steps to get to the room where services were held, he glanced at me and pulled out a walkie-talkie, obviously announcing me to someone inside. I acted like I should be there.

At the top of the stairs, I found a door with three small windows covered by a curtain. I knocked and waited. After a few minutes, a man pulled back the curtain and, with a suspicious expression, asked, "How can I help you?"

"My name is Dr. Dave," I said. "Ray Redfeairn invited me."

He told me to wait, and after a few more minutes the door opened. I stepped onto an Israeli flag, apparently used as a doormat, and spotted a large "Whites Only" sign on the wall. Below that was "No profanity. No tobacco or alcohol products allowed." The man who accompanied me was dressed in the same uniform as the guy on the roof, and he wore a 9mm pistol in a side holster. I wasn't afraid of guns, but I wasn't as certain about the paranoid temperaments in the room. Others watched me, clearly wondering who I was.

Approximately twenty-five to thirty people were standing around in a kitchen area talking, and several children were running around. Six uniformed young men with semiautomatic pistols stood near them. This was unlike any church I had ever been to in my life.

I didn't see Ray, but I remembered Frank and Dan from Ikes. Dan recognized me, smiled, and gave me the Nazi salute. "Hail victory, Brother! Glad to see you could make it. Have any trouble finding the place?"

"No, Ray's directions were pretty thorough. Where is he?"

"The pastor is working on his sermon, but he should be out soon. Make yourself at home and have a look around."

There were a lot of pictures on the walls, mostly of Adolf Hitler and other Nazi leaders, along with Jesus Christ and several crosses. The ceiling must have been eighteen feet high, and there were several large, mostly red flags hanging in a row from it—some Confederate, some Nazi, and the rest I couldn't identify.

Suddenly Ray appeared. He saluted me with "Hail victory, Brother Dave." He gave me a big hug, which I hadn't expected, and I suspected he was checking for a wire. Then he introduced me to others. He told me to address him as Pastor Ray while at the church, and added, "Most of the brothers and sisters are parishioners of the Church of Jesus Christ Christian. The ones in uniform are members of the church, too, but they're also members of the Aryan Nations, our militant arm."

We soon took seats for the start of the service, while Ray discreetly disappeared. Dan walked to the pulpit, where three of the red flags hung—to good effect—and said, "I'd like to welcome you to the Church of Jesus Christ Christian, Aryan Nations. If you will all stand, we'll begin with a prayer."

As we rose, all the men held up their right arms in the Nazi salute. I wasn't sure what to do, so I just watched. Dan began to pray to "Yahweh," ending with "Hail victory!" Everyone around me shouted "Hail victory!" and then sat down. I sat as well, on a hard metal folding chair.

Ray emerged from a door at the rear of the room and made his way to the pulpit. He stood beneath one of the flags as Dan and Frank went rigid next to him, their eyes locked in a solid gaze across the room that said they were ready to defend their leader with their lives. Ray launched right into his sermon with passion, at times yelling, at others speaking in a hypnotic tone.

"As you know," Ray said, "we're in the middle of so-called nigger history month. What a joke." He then raised his voice in anger. "For thousands of years, we, the Aryans, the true Israelites and chosen people of our God, Yahweh, have built empires and civilizations. We have created great artwork and music. We have discovered electricity and the secrets of nuclear power. We developed industry and invented the automobile and the airplane. But is there an Aryan history month? No. Yet these niggers have the audacity to proclaim February as nigger history month. The only history these picaninnies have is the history that we, the Aryans, gave them. They didn't even have a written language until that nigger lover Abraham Lincoln freed them from so-called slavery. That's when a few weak-minded white people taught them to read and write. So what great accomplishment has the nigger made since their history began? The only one I can think of is when that nigger George Washington Carver jumped up and down on a peanut and called it peanut butter."

I dared not flinch.

Ray paused for a moment, as if to let his cleverness sink in, and then went on. "As most of you know, we held an Aryan Nations recruitment rally in Columbus last Sunday." This made me listen more closely, but he only reiterated how he'd told the governor that he wouldn't postpone it. The congregation applauded, and Ray reveled in it. Then he punched the pulpit and held up his fist. He yelled something about Jews. "They're using the media to promote race mongrelizing!" Ray shouted. "These sons of Satan control our economy through that serpent Alan Greenspan."

I got it: this was a real theater for him. He was in his element. But what I didn't get was why these people were so mesmerized. To me, he just seemed crazy. But then, I guess, that's how Hitler was, and he'd managed to get control of a nation and then some. I understood now why Tym was concerned. This maniac could actually incite people into some pretty serious violence.

Ray finally wore down. "At the end of a thousand years," he said in a theatrical voice, "Yahshua will return and lead us to our victory, and the streets will run bridle deep with the blood of our enemies. We praise Yahshua and in his name we say, hail victory!"

The congregation jumped to its feet, the men giving the Nazi salute and everyone shouting "Hail victory!" over and over. Ray smiled. The whole scene looked just like a documentary I'd once seen on Hitler, except that crowd had yelled, *"Sieg heil!"*

After people resumed their seats, Ray said, "Just one more thing before I call services to an end. No doubt most of you have heard about the two gentlemen who were attacked by state troopers a week ago not more than twelve miles from where I'm preaching to you today. The media and the feds have been trying to tie those two individuals to the church and to me. I'm telling you the same thing I told the media. Those two men are not, and have never been, members of the Ohio Aryan Nations." That seemed to skirt the actual issue, but he said no more and invited us to join him for food and fellowship. I wondered if there was something he wasn't revealing. Their not being members of the Ohio AN did not actually mean that he wasn't associated with them. Pastor Ray was crafty. He knew how to get attention or deflect it, as it suited his purposes.

I went to tell him how much I'd enjoyed the service. He was talking with Dan and Frank, his back to me, and I heard him ask, "What day did we meet those guys?"

Dan said, "I'm not sure. I think it was two or three days before the shootout."

Ray then sensed me and turned.

"I really enjoyed your sermon today, Pastor Ray," I said, disappointed I hadn't heard more.

"Thank you, Brother Dave." He patted me on the back and invited me to eat with them. We entered the kitchen, and a pretty young woman handed us plates piled high with fried chicken and all the trimmings. Ray invited me to sit with him at the table where the uniformed members were sitting. As we ate, I commented on how good the food was.

"You can't beat a good Aryan woman's cooking," said Ray.

The dinner conversation was light, and when we finished, I leaned back in my chair. One of the women took my empty plate and asked, "Do you want another? We've got plenty."

"Thank you," I said. "But if I had to swallow a walnut right now I'd surely explode."

She laughed and cleared the table. Ray said, "Come with me, Brother Dave."

He introduced me to people from Cincinnati, northern Kentucky, and several other states. Aside from their extreme racist views, they reminded me of the friendly down-home folk I had grown up with in southeastern Kentucky. I felt pretty comfortable, despite the conversations about government conspiracies. As I got set to leave, I requested some pamphlets about the church. Ray gave me several and I asked him what the "Hail victory" salute meant.

"Yahweh is the name of our God and Yahshua is the true name of Jesus Christ. Soon Yahshua will return and lead us in battle against Satan's children, the Jews. That's why we say 'Hail victory.' It's our impending victory over the vile, unholy Jews."

I said I understood and then descended the stairs. But in an afterthought, I turned at the bottom, looked up, and said, "Hail victory, Pastor Ray."

"Hail victory, Brother Dave."

I hoped I'd given him the impression that I was tempted to join. I noticed a lot of cars in the parking lot and realized I'd have to devise a way to remember these license plate numbers. I was pretty good with numbers, but I needed to be shrewd as well. I set myself to thinking about this problem, even as I memorized a few, just for a start.

When I got home, I invited Terri over, but she said she had things to do. It was never good to be apart from her, but I was relieved not to have to answer any questions about my morning.

Tym Burkey

When I answered the phone that Sunday afternoon, I was surprised.

"Hail victory, Brother Tym."

It was Dave's voice, and I was sure he was joking, but it concerned me a little. I didn't know him that well yet, and I had to be watchful for signs that he might become sympathetic to our targets.

"I assume you went to New Vienna today," I commented.

"I sure did."

"How was it?"

"I guess it was educational. The reason I called was I have one quick bit of information."

"Fire away." I was hoping he'd have news about the Kehoes, and when he told me what he'd overheard, I believed, as he did, that it was probably about the fugitive brothers. "This is good stuff, Dave." It was just as we had suspected, despite Redfeairn's denials: he knew the Kehoes and had wanted to do business with them.

Dave apologized for calling on a Sunday, but I assured him that whenever he had something of interest to me, he should call. I also told him I had expense money for him, and we arranged to meet the next morning. I sensed that he was relieved. It was the first formal sign he'd had in two months that the government was actually supporting him.

The next morning, I brought along Bob Hlavac, another agent, because it was FBI policy to have two people involved in any exchange of money. Dave had Gary with him again. He seemed cautious about meeting a new agent, but we needed to do it this way in order to pay him. I sensed that he still didn't trust me entirely. Nevertheless, he was going through with the mission, so I figured I'd give him some time. He handed me the pamphlets that Redfeairn had given him, and after he described his experience at church, noting that Gulett had been absent, I asked, "Did Redfeairn carry a weapon?"

"No, but practically everybody else did. At least the ones in uniform." He then told me the names of people he'd met.

"You have a helluva good memory," I commented. I truly was impressed.

"Yeah, it comes in handy. I'm even better with numbers."

"Then I'd like you to get as many license plate numbers as you can from cars belonging to people at the church."

I watched his face. He wasn't fazed. He just said it shouldn't be a problem. I also asked if he could re-create the layout of the church. He said he had some drafting skills, so he'd try.

Then, as Agent Hlavac watched, I handed Dave the money. As I counted it out, I noted Dave's disappointed expression. Clearly, he'd expected more. I gave him a clipboard with a receipt for him to sign. He accepted it and was about to write when I stopped him. "We've given you a code name," I told him. "For your safety. It's Saint. Anytime you sign for money, use that name." He acknowledged that.

I was impressed with his ready acceptance. Most sources scream bloody murder and demand more money, then attempt to extort it by telling you that unless they get paid, they're through helping the FBI. It's a game we play. I asked Dave if he planned to attend next week and he thought he ought to skip a week. I didn't like that.

"I think you ought to go to the church a few times before you miss a Sunday," I said.

Dave shrugged his beefy shoulders. "You're the boss."

Before we parted, Agent Hlavac added that it was a pleasure making his acquaintance and warned Dave to watch his back.

I knew I'd disappointed Dave, and that could start to erode his sense of commitment, so I'd have to see if I could get more money. He was doing a good job, and we needed to be responsible to him. The deeper in he went, the more risk he took on, in more ways than he probably realized. But I couldn't tell him that.

Dave Hall

Later Monday evening, I looked over the pamphlets. The first one was "Ike the Kike." It alleged that even after the Allies declared an end to World War II, General Eisenhower ordered the firebombing of Dresden, an industrial and cultural center in central east Germany. The bombing, it said, resulted in the deaths of 250,000 men, women, and children, including American POWs. The next pamphlet was called "The Holocaust, a.k.a. the Big Lie." I couldn't believe what I was reading. Whoever thought this crap up was sick, and I'd had enough. In fact, I took a few days off to go boating and camping with Gary and Terri, to renew my relationship with both of them. It felt good for us all.

Sunday morning arrived before I was ready to go at it again. Terri was over, asleep in bed. I let Gary in and he raced to the bedroom to wake her. She laughed, and it did me good to hear her sound happy. I said I'd be gone for a few hours, and did she want to go to dinner later?

"That sounds nice," said Terri as she rolled over.

This time, I put on a Harley T-shirt. Having worn dress clothes the first time I went to church, I'd clearly been overdressed. When I arrived at the building in New Vienna, I saw about fifteen young men standing at the foot of the stairs, all with shaved heads. Most of them wore black jackets that said "Northern Hammerskins" on the back in large white letters. As I approached, several of them gave me the Nazi salute and said, "Eighty-eight."

I had no idea what that meant, but I returned their salutes with "Good morning, gentlemen." Climbing the stairs, I ran into Pastor Ray. I saluted him as well and asked what "eighty-eight" meant.

He smiled. "*H* is the eighth letter of the alphabet, and eighty-eight is short for '*Heil Hitler.*' " He also told me that the Northern Hammerskins were a group from Indiana that he'd invited. The crossed hammers on their jackets signified the working class.

Dan Rick walked over with an elderly man and introduced me to Hoge Tabor, a member of the KKK for some fifty years. "If there's anything you need to know," Dan said, "this is the man to ask."

He then called the congregation to order. I made a surreptitious scan of the room and estimated about fifty men, women, and children in attendance, although there was no sign of Morris Gulett. I also scanned the place to get a sense of the dimensions for making a drawing of the layout. We all stood, prayed, and saluted. Then Ray emerged from the rear of the room. He went behind the podium and began with, "Welcome, kindred, to the Church of Jesus Christ Christian, Aryan Nations, and a special welcome to our skinhead brothers and sisters."

I expected the same routine as the week before, but suddenly Ray said, "If all of you will excuse me for a minute . . ." He walked down to a young man sitting in the front row. After whispering something in his ear, he escorted the young man out the door, closing it behind him. I wondered what that was about. After a couple of minutes, they returned and I saw that the boy had no shoes on.

Back at the podium, Ray said, "I apologize for the interruption, but I want everyone to understand that this church is for Aryans only, and while you're here you're expected to conduct yourselves as Aryans. This includes your manner of dress; for example, we don't allow nigger clothing like Air Jordan basketball shoes. Or those baggy pants niggers wear. I also noticed that one of you had a yin-yang charm on your necklace. That's a Chinese symbol and has no place in an Aryan church." With a self-righteous flourish, Ray demanded, "Does anyone have any questions?"

No one spoke.

Apparently satisfied, Ray continued. "I have an article from one of the Columbus, Ohio, newspapers. In this article the head of the Anti-Defamation League makes comments about our rally. This line pretty much sums it up: 'These people are nothing but dangerous hatemongers.' " He paused, smiled, and then said, "I agree. We are dangerous. Dangerous to the Jews, niggers, and anyone else who poses a threat to the white race. What I find especially disturbing is the niggers." He ranted again about Black History Month, and added, "The Anti-Defamation League is manned by the children of Satan, and we have ways of dealing with these vile creatures!"

Applause broke out around the room. These people really liked this stuff. A few of them shouted, "Hail victory!" I also heard some skinheads shout "Rahowa," which I later learned meant "racial holy war."

The sermon continued for over an hour, with more screaming and more warnings about threats to the white race. Again, I stayed afterward to eat and listen for information. I did overhear several people speculating on the whereabouts of the Kehoe brothers.

Then Ray commented, with a hint of restrained agitation, "I heard that Morris Dees is suing another KKK group into bankruptcy."

Dan Rick erupted. "Somebody needs to kill that bastard!"

I asked who Dees was.

"He's an enemy of our people," Dan replied.

Ray elaborated with, "Dees is a so-called civil rights lawyer who works out of a place called the Southern Poverty Law Center in Montgomery, Alabama. It's a Jewish organization that sues white supremacist groups on behalf of niggers who feel their civil rights have been violated, and Dees is the worst of the bunch. He isn't even Jewish, which makes him a proselyte of the Jews and twice the child of Satan."

I felt somebody pressing against my back and, being somewhat paranoid around this group, I quickly turned. A young lady was leaning over to take my empty plate. She replaced it with a full one. "Thank you, ma'am," I said, "but do I look like I'm starving to death?"

She smiled and said, "We don't want any food to go to waste." She gave me a wink and walked away.

I turned to see the guys looking at me with smiles on their faces.

"I think someone likes you," said Ray. "You need a good woman to have some Aryan babies with."

I wasn't prepared for a conversation this personal, so I just grinned to deflect them and started eating food I didn't even want. To my relief, they left me alone and continued to talk about their business.

I was invited to a KKK party celebrating Hitler's birthday, to take place in April, complete with a cross-lighting ceremony. Ray then introduced me to Jeff Courtney, head of the National Socialist Party of Northern Kentucky. He was in his early twenties, with a medium build and the requisite shaved head. After a firm handshake, he handed me a business card for the American National Socialist

Movement, which had a post office box in Bellevue, Kentucky. I also met his cousin George Courtney, the leader of the Northern Hammerskins, a group out of southeastern Indiana and Cincinnati, Ohio. The bearded, six-foot, twentyish man was heavily tattooed with racist symbols, and he squeezed my hand with a viselike grip.

When we went outside, I noticed something about the black combat boots that most of the young militants wore: they all had red bootlaces. Jeff explained red laces symbolized blood that was being spilled and was yet to be spilled in the race war.

Startled, I changed the subject. "So are you guys coming to church next Sunday?"

"Personally," said Jeff, "I'm not all that religious, but it's always nice to be around people who feel the same way I do."

"I know what you mean," I replied.

Finally, I headed for my car. Along the way I made mental notes of license plate numbers on the cars the skinheads were driving. About halfway home, I pulled into a gas station and wrote down the numbers. I realized again that I'd need a better way to record these things. If someone followed me and wanted to see what I was writing, I'd be a goner. For next time, I was determined to have a solution.

I went out to dinner with Terri that night, expecting her to come home with me, but she declined. I was relieved to be alone, especially after I saw an item on the evening news that caught my attention.

"A white supremacist was arrested today," said the anchor, "after a high-speed car chase that began in Dayton and ended in a crash in nearby Beavercreek."

They showed a film of the crash scene—a van lying on its side in the middle of a busy intersection. I sat up. I knew that gold Chevy van.

"The driver of the van has been identified as forty-one-year-old Morris Gulett, a member of the white supremacist group the Aryan Nations."

So I was right. He'd been in an accident. I wondered if Tym was watching.

"Gulett had left this Dayton-area park and was driving the wrong way on a one-way street." As they showed film footage of the park, I recognized it—a place notorious for homosexual activity and illegal drug use. The reporter explained that when a Dayton police officer tried to pull Gulett over, he allegedly rammed the cruiser and then led the police on a high-speed chase through several jurisdictions before finally crashing. He was taken into custody without incident. Gulett reportedly said that he fled because he didn't have a driver's license and he "was just in one of those moods." That was rich. I added it to my list for Tym.

Tym Burkey

I received a call at home from Dave Falk asking for assistance with Morris Gulett. The Clinton County sheriff's office had arrested Kale Kelly the night before, near the AN church, for carrying a concealed weapon—a revolver stuffed in a twelve-pack of beer next to him in his vehicle. Falk was heading down to the Clinton County SO to oversee the vehicle inventory of Kelly's car. He then received a call from the Cincinnati office regarding Gulett, who had gotten into a chase with a Dayton police officer and crashed in Beavercreek, in the next county over from Dayton. I lived in Beavercreek, so Falk asked me to go to the crash scene and learn what I could.

I was glad to do this. I knew that Gulett had been Redfeairn's second in charge until right after the Columbus rally. He'd had an argument with a black journalist there, which went against Redfeairn's rally protocol. This had caused a rift between them, so Gulett was no longer attending AN Sunday meetings. I had suspected that there was more to it. After all, Redfeairn used the Bible to show how God condoned violence against the "mud races." With this type of philosophy, what was a little heated discussion at a rally? This traffic incident seemed like an opportune moment to exploit the trouble to see if Gulett was bitter and wanted to talk. Maybe he'd tell us something about the criminal activity of AN members.

That chilly Sunday, it was overcast and raining on and off. From my house, it took only moments to reach the rural intersection where the crash had occurred. I saw Dayton and Beavercreek police cruisers, as well as emergency vehicles, so I moved through them by using my FBI blue light. Then I saw, amid debris, a blue sedan off in the ditch, with heavy damage on the rear passenger side. East of there, an older-model gold van was turned upside down. From past dealings, I knew most of the police at the scene. They all knew of Gulett's AN affiliation and thus guessed why I was there. To them, any friend of the cop shooter Redfeairn was a threat to law enforcement.

The Dayton detectives filled me in. Over the past several Sundays, someone had broken into vehicles belonging to churchgoers to steal property while the owners attended services. The Dayton police had increased patrols around the city's churches in an effort to stem the break-ins. An officer in a marked cruiser observed a gold Chevy van driving near a church and pulled the plate number. He found that the van's plates were expired and the vehicle's owner, Gulett, did not have a driver's license. The officer drove the cruiser back around the block and up a one-way street, where Gulett was driving the wrong way. The officer blocked his path and then stepped out. Gulett gunned the engine, driving right for him. The chase was on, and it ended one county over when Gulett struck the blue sedan and flipped his van. Despite how it looked, no one was injured.

Gulett was taken to the Dayton Police Department's Detective Section, and when the police searched his van they found crack cocaine strewn around the inside. After the detectives finished with him, they let me have my shot, so I went in with Detective Randy Brannon. Gulett, a small-featured, defiant redhead, had facial bruises and a split lip. He was forty-one at the time but looked much older. He made it clear he did not like ZOG talking to him. Any mention of the AN induced even more anger. He denied being a member until it was pointed out that he'd been seen on television next to Redfeairn, wearing an AN uniform. Further, AN cards and patches were in his van. Gulett conceded his membership and his addiction, and said he was at odds with Redfeairn. He expected his membership to be revoked, since Richard Butler, the AN national leader, expressly prohibited drug use.

Still, Gulett refused to discuss the AN and denied knowing either the Kehoe brothers or Kale Kelly. To his knowledge, he said, no one in the Ohio AN had aided the Kehoes after the shootout in Wilmington.

"Mo," I said, quite deliberately, "I think you know more than you're telling us."

I could tell I'd caught him by surprise. "What are you doing?" he asked.

I ignored the question and tried to get more from him, but in the end Gulett failed to provide any useful information and I decided that further questions would just give him information that he could pass along to Redfeairn.

Thus, I already knew about Gulett before Dave called that Monday morning, but he assured me he had more. "If you've got your crayon ready," he said, "I've got some stuff for ya."

"Fire away," I told him. He gave me individual names and the names of groups that had been mentioned or who were in attendance at church, along with news of a significant gathering on Hitler's birthday. He assured me that he hadn't written anything down that might endanger him or us, but after he offered a fourth license plate number, I insisted, "You had to write these down."

"You're right," Dave acknowledged. "I stopped on the side of the road halfway home and jotted them down. I can only hold that many numbers in my head for a short time. But I'm working on a way to do it carefully." Then he caught me by surprise. "You are a white Aryan," Dave said. "Why don't you come down to church next time?"

I didn't know how to respond. "I, uh, um . . . I've got too much yard work to do."

We both laughed, fully aware of what would happen to an FBI agent in that den of snakes.

"Good work, Dave," I told him. "Keep it up."

I was genuinely impressed. It seemed as if Dave was becoming a genuine part of the team. I was curious about the discussion Dave had reported about Morris Dees. He was a unique individual and always in danger. Although he'd been successful in business, he'd grown up in Alabama and had witnessed terrible hate crimes. It bothered him that certain white groups were treating other people so badly, so he did some soul-searching and decided to change his life's focus. Dees sold his company in 1969 and, with attorney Joseph Levin Jr. and activist Julian Bond, founded the nonprofit Southern Poverty Law Center (SPLC) in 1971 to support civil rights.

Dees began filing civil suits, successfully halting the planned construction of an all-white university and integrating the YMCA in Montgomery, Alabama. In the face of numerous death threats, he also sued several hate groups, getting expensive judgments from brutal incidents that crippled their resources. His most recent book, *Gathering Storm,* was about the danger in America from domestic terrorism—especially the militias. No matter what threats he received, he continued the fight.

If the AN had Dees on their minds, they were probably concerned that he might turn his forces against them. I hoped Dave could get us more specific information. To this point, it sounded like a lot of hot air, but it was never safe to assume anything.

Three days later, Bob Hlavac accompanied me to see Mo at the Montgomery County Jail in Dayton. Gulett looked much better this time and not nearly as defiant. He'd probably had his first good food in a long time. I presented an article from the Dayton *Daily News,* dated March 5, in which Redfeairn had publicly distanced himself and the AN from Gulett. I'd hoped to rattle him, but he wasn't surprised. He gave us no new information. I suspected that Redfeairn had something on him, perhaps a crime they'd committed together. I left my card and told him to call anytime.

I might add a fact that always gave me a chuckle: both "Aryan warriors" lived at home with their mothers.

7.

TAKING RISKS

Dave Hall

The weather was beautiful on Saturday, so Terri, Gary, and I spent the day hiking. We got back to the house around 4:00 P.M., just as my mother called. I was glad to hear from her, because I'd been pulling away from the people I loved. I didn't want to; I just didn't know what to tell them, so I saw less and less of my family. Mom and I talked for a while, and after I hung up, I noticed that the house was unusually quiet.

I walked down the hallway and peeked into my bedroom. In the middle of the bed were Gary and Terri, lying like spoons in a drawer, fast asleep. She was as sweet as she could be, but the poor girl snored like a sailor, and I had to swallow a laugh. I would have reason to remember this moment, because soon enough my life would be devoid of such peaceful times.

On Sunday morning, March 9, I went back to church. When I pulled into the parking lot, I noticed the skinheads and National Socialists were back. Most everyone was standing outside, so I figured

I'd take advantage of the situation to get some measurements of the church's interior. Inside, Dan and Frank, armed and garbed for a military standoff, greeted me. But they went outside, leaving me alone, so I casually paced off the length and width of the two main rooms, committing the measurements to memory. I also made a mental note of the smaller rooms, as well as which doors opened in and which opened out.

Just then, Dan stopped me. He was now armed with an SKS assault rifle, and I tried to act natural, but I was nervous that I'd been caught already.

"I'm sorry, Brother Dave," he said, "but I've got orders to search everyone today."

"Do you need that thing?" I asked, gesturing at the weapon. Frank patted me down as Dan explained that they were expecting a special guest today and it was a precaution. He would reveal only that it was someone from the Aryan Nations World Headquarters.

When they finished with me, I went into the kitchen area. As I walked through the doorway a young woman took me by the arm and said, "We haven't been properly introduced. My name is Laura."

"You're the young lady that tries to stuff me full of food every Sunday, aren't ya?" I said. She smiled at this, and I added, "My name is Dave. It's a pleasure to make your acquaintance."

As we talked, I learned that she was from northern Kentucky and was a member of the KKK. She continued to flirt with me, and for a moment I enjoyed it, but I finally came to my senses and excused myself. The Northern Hammerskins had arrived, as had Jeff Courtney with a group of National Socialists. There were several new faces in the crowd as well. Dan and Frank searched each person as they entered. As soon as everyone had found a seat, Dan asked us to rise for the opening prayer. This time I joined the salute, because I had no excuse not to.

Ray came out of his office at the rear of the room, walked to the podium, and began by saying, "As most of you may already know, two of our good brothers have been arrested over the past week. Morris Gulett and Kale Kelly are now prisoners of the Zionist Occupied Government, and I hope you will remember them in your prayers. I have tried to make pastoral visits, but so far ZOG has refused to let me see them.

"Moving along, we have two special guests with us today. Our first is a recognized authority on the Civil War years, and she'd like to say a few words. May I introduce Ms. Jo Kinder."

Pastor Ray stepped aside, and as everyone applauded, a small dark-haired lady stepped up to the microphone at the podium. She was an attractive woman who looked to be in her mid- to late forties, wearing a long old-fashioned print dress.

"Thank you, Pastor Redfeairn," said Ms. Kinder. "I'll try to be brief."

She told us about the trial of Byron de la Beckwith, accused of killing civil rights activist Medgar Evers in 1963. He had been tried and acquitted twice, and on March 17, just days away, the feds were going to put him on trial for a third time; she asked us to pray for him. She handed out her newsletter, *The Copperhead Update*, explaining that during the Civil War, Northern sympathizers of the Confederacy were called "copperheads."

We applauded as Ms. Kinder stepped down. Then Pastor Ray took the podium to introduce the man I was interested in, the Aryan Nations international ambassador, Vince Reed. I knew Tym would want every detail.

Reed had gray hair, a short beard, and a stocky build, and he appeared to be in his early fifties. He paused for a moment as he looked out over the congregation. "As international ambassador," he said in an authoritative manner, "it's my job to coordinate all chapters of the Aryan Nations. If there are any ZOG informants here today, this is your chance to hit the door, because you will be found out."

Again he paused and scanned the crowd. I could only guess that he was looking for some sort of reaction—something that would give an informant away. After a minute he resumed.

"I also meet with other groups around the country like the skin-heads, the Ku Klux Klan, and various militia groups. I've just come from a meeting with the West Virginia Militia."

Reed went on to tell us that he was a Vietnam War veteran and had been a member of the white supremacy movement for twenty years. He'd done time in prison for assault on an ATF agent and had been in Waco, Texas, during the Branch Davidian standoff. He added that he was a personal friend of Randy Weaver, whose wife and son had been killed by ZOG agents during the shootout at Ruby Ridge, Idaho. He seemed to have been in all the hot spots, and he encouraged us to uphold our beliefs with bravery. Eventually, Reed concluded by thanking Redfeairn, and once again there was applause as they exchanged places.

Back at the podium, Pastor Ray explained the concept of the two-seed line in Christian Identity beliefs. It was a long explanation, but it amounted to this: when God created the earth, the beasts of the fields were the mud races. Then God created Adam and Eve, white people made in God's image, and gave them dominion over all but warned them to remain separate from the beasts. Soon Satan came along and corrupted Eve by luring her into having sex with him. She shared the experience with Adam, and that's what got them cast out of Eden, as well as cursing Eve and all women with the pain of childbirth. Eve eventually bore fraternal twins—Abel, the son of Adam, and Cain, the son of Satan. Cain later killed Abel and was cursed to wander aimlessly upon the face of the earth. The descendants of Cain are the Jews. Some years later, Eve would bear Adam another son, whose name was Seth, and his descendants would be the Aryans, "the true Israelites and children of Yahweh."

Pastor Ray screamed some invectives against Jews, using his bulky body for emphasis, and then wrapped things up with a salute. The frenzied crowd was on its feet, shouting over and over, "Hail victory! Hail victory!" I stood, raised my arm, and shouted right along with them. They say that hate starts in the heart and its first weapon is a vicious tongue. I was beginning to believe this old saying carried some weight.

Then we went to eat. After Laura gave me a plate of food, I found a place to sit where I could see through the hallway into the church area. Pastor Ray was now talking privately with Ambassador Reed, but I couldn't hear anything. I wanted to move closer, but the last thing I needed was this experienced ambassador, with an eye for traitors, getting suspicious of me. Frank and Dan sat down at the table with me. Dan looked at my dinner plate and smiled, then asked, "Are you hungry, Brother Dave?"

"It's that Laura woman," I replied. "I think she's trying to fatten me up for the kill."

Dan laughed and said, "She just likes you, that's all."

"If she keeps on liking me, I'm going to have to buy larger pants."

As we ate, I learned that Dan had been a member of a skinhead group in Denver before moving to Ohio with his girlfriend, Tiffany. That's when he joined the Aryan Nations and settled in the small town of Leesburg, Ohio.

Soon Pastor Ray joined us.

"Where's Ambassador Reed?" I asked.

"He had to leave early to make it to a meeting with a militia group." Then, to my surprise, Ray added, "For some reason, I just don't trust this guy." He didn't elaborate. Instead he changed the subject and urged me to consider becoming a uniformed member of the Aryan Nations. Then Dan's girlfriend came over to the table and held up a small doll wearing a convict uniform. The doll had the head of Moe of the Three Stooges. Much to my surprise, everyone at the table started laughing, including Pastor Ray. He shook his head and said, "I don't know what I'm going to do with poor Mo. Every time I think he's going to straighten up and fly right, he does something stupid."

Ray then told everyone to be careful when leaving the church. He urged us to obey all the traffic laws because the cops were looking for any reason to stop and search us, especially in Wilmington. As we walked down the stairs to leave, Ray asked me again to consider joining the Aryan Nations. I told him I wanted to attend church a few more times before making a commitment.

"Take all the time you need, Brother," said Ray as he patted me on the back, but said there would be no services the following Sunday, due to a Klan meeting on Saturday. Ray asked me if I wanted to go to the meeting and I said sure. He told me to meet him at the church on Saturday morning.

As I walked to the parking lot, I noticed two cars with out-of-state plates, so I committed the numbers to memory. I stopped just outside town at a Quickie Mart and wrote them down. During the drive home I had time to think. Most of the people I had met and talked with at the church seemed to be friendly and kind, but their hatred and racist views left a poisonous taste in my mouth. What could make a person hate someone they didn't even know? The color of their skin or the fact that they were Jewish? Deep down inside, I didn't really want to know the answer.

Tym Burkey

I was quite interested to hear about the special guest, Vince Reed, and was disappointed that Dave didn't know which group he'd gone to visit afterward. I was especially intrigued by Redfeairn's impression of the man. I knew that Redfeairn coveted a more powerful position than he currently had and would one day make his move. Maybe he just sensed a threat to his ambition, or maybe he suspected the truth—that Reed was a federal informant. He'd been inside the AN since 1992, renting a house near the Idaho compound. He'd become a trusted insider. But all I said about this to Dave was, "That damn Ray wouldn't trust his own mother."

"He seems to trust me," Dave said. "He even asked me to consider joining the Aryan Nations."

This was good news. "What did you tell him?"

"That I wanted to learn more about their beliefs before I made any commitments. I felt if I jumped right into it, Ray would become suspicious."

"You're probably right. It doesn't take much to put him on guard."

Dave mentioned the KKK meeting and suggested that his invitation was just dumb luck. He then added that he'd drawn the church's interior.

I thanked him and then asked, "What about that girl who's been flirting with you?" There was more than one way into the heart of this organization.

"I'm prepared to make certain sacrifices for my country," Dave joked, "but that's not one of them."

I laughed, glad for the levity between us. Dave was relaxing, I thought, and trusting me. I laughed even harder when he told me about the Moe doll. We ended our call on a high note.

Dave Hall

That Wednesday, March 12, I learned from television that Morris Gulett had been indicted for felonious assault as a result of fleeing from police. What really amused me was that the county judge had appointed Charles Smiley Jr., a prominent black attorney, to defend him. The irony was too rich.

The next day, I had an opportunity at Ikes to ask Ray about the KKK meeting.

"What I want to do," he explained, "is gather as many racist groups as I can together under the umbrella of the Aryan Nations. The problem, especially with the KKK, is that if one person disagrees with the leadership of their Klan group, they can move across the street and start their own group. It's this kind of activity that's weakening us all. If we, the Aryan Nations, can unite these groups and stop all the infighting, we would have a powerful force in our quest for an all-white homeland."

I nodded. "That sounds like a great idea to me," I lied.

"It's going to take a lot of hard work," said Ray, "but I think it's doable and will be worth the effort."

"I believe so, too." After taking a sip of my drink I asked, "How's Brother Morris doing?"

"I've been trying to see him in jail, but they've been refusing him pastoral visits."

Trying to keep a straight face, I said, "I saw on the news that the court appointed that nigger attorney Charles Smiley to be Mo's lawyer. Do you think they did that on purpose?"

Expecting an angry reply, I was surprised as Ray smiled and said, "You know they did. The government is going to take advantage of every chance they can get to make us look bad. That's why I urge everyone to stay out of trouble. In Morris' case, trouble follows him like a stray dog. I've known Mo since high school and I love him like a brother, but he has to get his act together." Ray finished his beer and nodded toward me. "Brother Dave, I've gotta go, but I'll see you Saturday. Hail victory."

"Hail victory."

I don't know if it was my personality or my having friends in the Outlaws, but Ray seemed to like me and was beginning to trust me more and more. He certainly wanted me at the event on Saturday.

By this time, I had come up with a way to memorize things and write them down in the form of a code, so that if anyone ever saw my writing or came across my notebook, I'd have a disguise. The answer was simple: use an alphabet that most people weren't familiar with. I did some research and found the Phoenician alphabet in *Webster's Collegiate Dictionary*. There were twenty-six symbols, mostly just primitive lines and circles, so I memorized it, added some adjustments of my own, and made numbers and letters from the English alphabet correspond to specific Phoenician letters. It wasn't that hard to remember, once I used it often enough.

On Saturday morning, I headed for the church. People were already gathering, some of whom I knew and some I didn't. Most wore uniforms and sidearms. Soon John Graham arrived from Cincinnati. A young man in his early twenties, Graham was a member of the National Alliance, another white supremacist group. I'd learned that Pastor Ray had asked him to join the Aryan Nations, but he was reluctant, citing his loyalty to Dr. William Pierce, founder of the National Alliance and author of *The Turner Diaries* and its sequel, *The Hunter.* These books were practically required reading throughout the entire white supremacy movement, and I knew that I'd have to read them. I heard that during his time in the army, Timothy McVeigh urged his fellow soldiers to read *The Turner Diaries,* and he even slept with this blueprint for a race war under his pillow.

Pastor Ray called all of us together and thanked us for coming. He asked that all firearms be left at the church and urged us to be on our best behavior at the meeting. Surprisingly, he asked me to collect everyone's pistols. I did so, and Pastor Ray locked them in his private office. As we were getting ready to leave, Mitchell Adams, a National Socialist from Cincinnati, arrived with a few of his people.

Soon we had loaded everyone into three cars, including mine, and headed for Grove City, a suburb of Columbus, Ohio, an hour and a half away. The station wagon I drove was full of young neo-Nazi National Socialists. They giggled as they told stories about how they would gather together and assault gays and blacks by beating them with baseball bats and kicking them with their combat boots.

"My buddies and me kicked two niggers unconscious," one of them bragged. "Later that night I noticed something sticking out of the toe of one of my boots, and when I looked closer I could see it was a tooth."

The car nearly burst open from the maniacal laughter. I failed to grasp the humor of the situation, but I tried to laugh along with them. Finally we arrived at the Grove City Public Library. As the young men with their shaved heads, combat boots, and all-black clothing emerged from my car, people in the parking lot began staring. The Klansman who had arranged the meeting spotted us and led us into a library conference room reserved for us.

The Klan had set up several tables displaying their literature and clothing patches, available for purchase. I bought a couple of patches and loaded up on the free literature. Soon the leader of this particular Klan group began to speak. He thanked us for coming and added that he hoped this would be the beginning of a long and productive association between the two groups. Then he introduced Ray.

Pastor Ray did his usual routine—pray and rant—and then explained that both groups had the same basic goals: the eradication of the unholy Jews and the return of the mud races to slavery or their countries of origin. "We must stop all of the fighting and bickering within our respective groups," he insisted. "I used to belong to the KKK, but there were too many chiefs and not enough Indians. It seemed that every time someone disagreed with the man in charge, they would just move across the street and start their own group. I became tired of this and began exploring the concept of Christian Identity. The strong religious beliefs and solidarity of the Church of Jesus Christ Christian/Aryan Nations soon convinced me to take a different path. So I quit the Klan and joined the Aryan Nations.

"The Aryan Nations is a well-structured international organization with a clear chain of command and one leader, Pastor Richard Butler. We're always actively recruiting new members. I'm not necessarily suggesting that you quit whatever group you're affiliated with, but should you do so, we will welcome you. What I would like to see is one unified national Klan group with one elected leader, also one national skinhead group, one National Socialist group, one national militia group, and so on and so forth. Imagine the power we would wield if all white supremacist groups in the United States worked together toward our common goals. We would be unstoppable. I am prepared to offer my services as a mediator to any group that shares this vision of the future."

With that, he presented a strategy. "We need to get our people into positions of political power, everything from city government to county, state, and federal government. This way we could effect change from within the now Zionist Occupied Government."

He then fielded questions, so I sat back. *My God, could this maniac actually pull this off?* People seemed to listen and respond. Again, I was reminded of the clips that I'd seen of Hitler. I wondered if Ray purposely modeled himself in Hitler's image. I wondered how many people he might actually reach and convince.

When the meeting adjourned, Pastor Ray introduced me to two uniformed members of the Ohio Militia.

"I didn't even know Ohio had a militia," I said.

One of them smiled and replied, "Yes, we've got well over a thousand members."

I shook hands with them. "It's a pleasure to make your acquaintance, gentlemen."

Finally, it was time to return, first walking through the embarrassing gauntlet of stares from ordinary citizens and then driving through town as the young neo-Nazis in my car shouted racial slurs at every opportunity. I felt bad for the black people walking down the sidewalks, but there wasn't much I could do about it.

Sleep was elusive for me that night as I reflected on the looks on the faces of the targets of racial slurs shouted from my car. I could only imagine how they must have felt. After a few minutes of tossing and turning I sat up on the edge of my bed, cursing my conscience. I felt truly awful that I had participated in all of this. I went to the kitchen and poured half a pint of vodka into a glass and drank it down. Then I returned to bed to try to sleep.

Tym Burkey

It was now time for me to interview Kale Todd Kelly, recently arrested for carrying a concealed weapon. Since he was a convicted felon, he was not permitted to possess a firearm. He was housed in the Warren County Jail in Lebanon, Ohio, just north of Cincinnati.

He'd done time before. He'd been in the U.S. Army, in Germany, and got nailed for selling hash, so he did time in Leavenworth. He'd floated around until he'd found the Aryan Nations via Redfeairn. After a traffic stop in Wilmington, Ohio, a search of his vehicle had yielded a loaded .38-caliber revolver and a small amount of marijuana. Although he seemed at this point to be just another AN member, Kelly would later become a very significant part of the investigation.

On March 13, Bob Hlavac and I went together to interview him. He was in his mid-thirties, approximately five foot nine, and a muscular 180 pounds. His brown hair was cut close to his head, military style, but I could still see that he was slightly balding. To emphasize his appearance as an Aryan warrior, he sported tattoos, including a swastika on his chest. Despite his intimidating demeanor, his hands were constantly in nervous motion. He carried folded pieces of paper and kept making notes while we talked with him.

We said that the FBI had observed him on the roof of the Church of Jesus Christ Christian, the New Vienna Aryan Nations church, during Sunday services. He'd been armed and wearing an AN uniform, as if he were guarding the service. Further, the sheriff's office had searched his vehicle and found several handwritten pages of what appeared to be military training, set for that month. There were also written references to April 19 and 20, the anniversaries of the Waco conflagration, the Oklahoma City bombing, and Hitler's birthday. These were important dates to any neo-Nazi white supremacist.

Kelly admitted being a member of the AN, but he gave the obligatory "I don't know the Kehoes" and added without our asking that neither did Pastor Redfeairn. He stated that he was unaware of any criminal activity conducted by the Ohio AN membership. Regarding the military training documents, Kelly claimed he was a freelance military trainer and would provide training to any group, including the AN. He denied knowing of any upcoming "events" planned for the nineteenth and twentieth of April. When asked about Timothy McVeigh, Kelly's true side briefly appeared: he said McVeigh should have killed more federal agents and not so many innocent people. But he denied knowing the man.

Proud of his AN membership, he discussed it in detail, giving us more information than he probably realized. He described the organization as multilayered. The first layer was attending Sunday Church of Jesus Christ Christian services. The next required sponsorship. He wouldn't specify the other layers but said that each required different access. Kelly conducted background checks on new members, and said "security clearances" were needed before moving to the next level.

That meant Dave was being checked out.

Quite abruptly, Kelly ended the interview. My impression of him was, *Watch out—this guy is serious.* His military training only heightened my concern, and I sensed he was a lone wolf who could form new cells.

That's where the trouble begins. Lone wolves like to plot violent acts to promote a cause, especially if they think the leadership is remiss. McVeigh, for example, had interacted with only two others. Aryan Nations member Buford Furrow was alone when he fired into a Jewish day-care center, injuring five and killing one. The Kehoes traveled as a pair, and there had been two Midwest bank robbers in the Aryan Republican Army, a white supremacist splinter group. This was what Kelly seemed to me—a lone wolf. I made a mental note to tell Dave, once Kelly came back out, to keep an eye on him. Later, I would be glad I did.

8

MEMBERSHIP DUES

Tym Burkey

After the meeting in Grove City, Dave accepted Redfeairn's invitation to join the Aryan Nations. This proved fruitful because Dave received an application that revealed to us the types of questions Redfeairn and the AN asked. Along with the expected inquiries about racial lineage was a request to list special talents. Dave wrote that he had competed in semipro archery tournaments, had a third-degree black belt in tae kwon do, and once worked as a karate instructor. He wasn't certain about supplying a recent photo, so he called me to find out what he should do. We arranged to meet so I could snap a couple of Polaroids of him.

As usual, Dave was at the parking lot long before I got there. He was out walking Gary when I pulled in. He looked at his watch meaningfully when he said, "Hey, Tym."

"I know, I'm late again."

"That's all right. I'm getting used to it." He showed me his application, and I asked about the black belt in karate. He assured me it was genuine and earned, so I said, "I hope I never piss you off."

"Don't worry," he laughed. "I'm not easily riled."

I positioned him for some photographs and then asked how he was holding up. I knew all too well what could happen to informants when they start to submerge more deeply into the target subculture. I wanted to be sure I kept tabs on his personal perspective.

He was quiet for a moment before he said, "It's difficult not to let these maniacs get under your skin, you know?"

I heard a note of stress in his voice, so I cautioned, "Just remain focused, Dave. You know you're better than they are."

"Yeah, but it's still tough. It's easy to see how Pastor Ray casts his spell, especially on the younger people. He's a dynamic speaker, and with his knowledge of the Bible he somehow makes everything he says make sense."

I looked at him. "Dave, don't let this psycho get into your head."

"I'm not. I'm going to get into his."

I smiled and nodded. I hoped he was right, but I wondered. It was all too easy for informants to become sympathetic toward the group they were infiltrating. Human consciousness is fairly malleable, even if we don't want to accept that. These influences can be more insidious than we realize.

We looked at the photo, and Dave didn't think it resembled him. "That's the idea," I told him. He mentioned the application fee and said that between drinks and gas, he was going broke.

"I'll do my best to get you some more money to cover your expenses," I promised. He told me he'd appreciate that, and said nothing more on the subject. Then he pulled out the blueprint of the church he'd drawn. I was surprised at how professional it looked. "How did you remember all these details and measurements?"

"I just have a very good memory," he said. "In fact, I can remember all the way back to the moment of my birth."

I gave him a skeptical look.

"Yeah, the shock was so bad," he quipped, "I couldn't talk for a year and a half."

I just shook my head and let Dave laugh at his own joke. "We've got to do something about your sense of humor," he said.

"I'll develop one after we take care of Redfeairn and his cronies."

Dave Hall

Terri came over early Saturday morning and we spent the day together. My conscience was eating away at me because I'd lied by telling her I'd taken a part-time job on Sundays repairing motorcycles in Xenia, Ohio. I'd convinced myself I had no choice, but it still bothered me. She seemed to accept it but remained distant. I was relieved when she agreed to stay the night.

On Sunday morning, Terri was sleeping soundly and I left her a note on the kitchen table that I'd be home midafternoon. Gary had been running around the backyard, so after my second cup of coffee I opened the door and, like a bat out of hell, he headed straight for the bedroom. As he landed on the bed, I bit my lower lip, anticipating Terri's scream. But there was only silence. I walked quietly toward the bedroom and looked in. When I saw Terri still asleep with Gary lying quietly beside her, I breathed a sigh of relief. Deciding to leave well enough alone, I headed for New Vienna, knowing Terri would be unhappy when she found me gone again.

Pastor Ray had read through my application, and he mentioned that if he ever needed a bodyguard, he'd know who to ask. He told the others that day that I'd decided to become a member of the Aryan Nations, so I received their enthusiastic congratulations.

"Welcome to the fight, Brother Dave," Ray said.

The church was crowded with more members from the various groups, which suggested that Ray's persuasive tongue had at least drawn their interest in the idea of joining forces. After the service, I looked around the parking lot and saw far too many cars to be able to memorize all the plate numbers, so I concentrated on the out-of-state tags. I memorized several from Kentucky and Indiana, and then made my usual stop at the roadside store a few miles from the church to write down the tag numbers. When I got into Dayton, I went to take my exit off the freeway, but a black driver cut me off.

"You stupid fucking nigger!" I screamed.

I sat back in my seat, stunned at what I'd just done. Having never been one to use racial slurs, I realized that the company I'd been keeping was changing me. I knew right away that I would have to be more careful about its effect.

The following Sunday I invited my mother over to see her "granddog" . . . and to enlist her as an ally.

My mother had grown up in a log cabin in the hills of Kentucky, later moving to Dayton, and raised my nine half brothers and sisters despite a difficult marriage to my stepfather. When he died in the late 1980s, she'd gone back to work as a nurse to support us kids who were still at home. She didn't retire until she was seventy-three, and then only because a shoulder injury finally forced her to. She still had the energy of ten women and was constantly on the go, usually doing something for one of us when she wasn't reading, watching the news, or listening to classical music. She is one of the strongest women I've ever known, and nothing seems to faze her, no matter how much trouble her kids or grandkids get into.

I'd already confided to Mom that I'd been attending a church in southern Ohio. Although she was pleased, I could tell she knew there was something fishy about it. She knew of my legal problems. I sat her down and told her about being a federal informant, explaining how it would reduce my sentence. She got really mad at me for my dealings with Uncle Mike—the incident that got me into this situation—and just as mad at Uncle Mike. She didn't like it, but by the end of the conversation she said she understood, and urged me to be careful. I also told her that it was very important that my brothers, sisters, nieces, and nephews not be seen anywhere near me or my house. I didn't want my new "friends" to realize I had biracial relatives.

"We'll figure something out," she assured me. "I just hope you know what you're getting yourself into."

So did I. That next Sunday was to be my formal induction into the AN. When I got to church, Ray asked all the uniformed members to line up behind him. Six men, all wearing sidearms, responded. I had the impression I was standing in front of a firing squad. Pastor Ray told us all to raise our arms in a Nazi salute, and then said, "Brother Dave Hall, do you swear that you are of Aryan descent?"

"Yes," I replied, "I am of Celtic Aryan blood."

Ray then handed me a card with the Aryan Nations credo on it, and despite my disgust I stated out loud the words written on it. Afterward, I heard three cheers of "Hail victory!" followed by handshakes from everyone. Pastor Ray told me to start arriving at the church one hour before services for the weekly members-only meetings. He also gave me a law enforcement supply catalog from which I could order my uniform pants and shirts. To get the arm patches and collar, Ray said he would call the Aryan Nations National Headquarters. He added that I'd be expected to obtain a firearm to wear while at church. That part alarmed me; it would violate the terms of my pre-sentencing release.

Before closing our meeting, Pastor Ray told Dan and Frank to produce some recruiting flyers for us all to pass out in the Dayton and Cincinnati areas. He assured us that if we happened to be arrested while doing something to further the cause, he would stand behind us 100 percent, but if it was for something stupid, we'd be on our own. In that context, Ray added that he had recently talked with Morris Gulett and told him if he screwed up one more time he would be out of the AN.

The only unusual thing that happened that day was the entrance of two young men, built like weightlifters. Pastor Ray introduced the first one as Jason Swanson, the temporary leader of the Michigan AN chapter. Tattoos covered his arms and, in contrast to the Ohio AN members, he wore his hair down to his waist. (He would soon change this to a military buzz cut after Pastor Ray told him that an Aryan warrior should look "like a man.") Max Burton was his right-hand man, but the purpose of their presence at our church was not explained, so finally I left.

When I arrived home, before I even opened the door, I smelled food cooking. Clearly Mom had been busy. In fact, she'd cleaned the entire house and had a large pot of beef stew on the stove. That was just like her. She couldn't do much about my situation, but she would see to my needs.

"Mom," I said, "you didn't have to do all this cooking and cleaning."

"Well," she replied, "the devil finds work for idle hands."

"I don't think you'll ever have to worry about calling the devil boss."

She laughed and asked how everything had gone at church. I told her it was the usual hate-everybody-that's-not-white crap.

"You know, that's a sickness that's easy to catch," Mom said, "so you be careful."

"Don't worry," I replied, "I know what I'm doing."

She gave me a look. "I hope so."

Tym Burkey

Dave told me about the uniform requirement and I assured him we would cover that expense, but when he added that he was required to have a weapon as part of his uniform, it presented several problems with his pre-sentencing agreement, which we moved quickly to address.

The next evening, on April 12, Redfeairn and AN member Frank Johnson were in Redfeairn's vehicle, with Johnson driving them through rural Warren County, Ohio. A Waynesville police officer saw the vehicle and ran the plate, finding it to be expired. He attempted to stop the car, but Johnson continued on until he found a secluded dirt road. Then he pulled over. Since the officer also worked at the Montgomery County Jail in Dayton, he recognized the name of the registered owner—Redfeairn—so he called for backup. Then he approached the car. Johnson and Redfeairn exited the vehicle and stood beside it but refused to comply with the officer's request to step away from the car. At this point, backup arrived and the officer observed Redfeairn, on the passenger side, toss something into the backseat. Together, the officers handcuffed the two men and searched the vehicle, finding a steak knife. In Redfeairn's pocket was another knife, so he was arrested for carrying a concealed weapon. Johnson had an ASP baton, so both men were taken into custody.

When I heard this, I believed the incident could have ended badly. Had the Waynesville officer not recognized Redfeairn's name and called for assistance, he very well might have been killed. Redfeairn's actions, later described to me, indicated that he'd been attempting to draw the officer from cover in order to attack him. He'd done it before.

I knew that Dave would learn about the arrest incident soon. But as it turned out, he heard about it the very next day.

Dave Hall

When I got to church on Sunday morning, I could tell by the tone of Dan Rick's voice when he greeted me that something was wrong. In the rec area, five other uniformed members sat around a table, as if engaged in a meeting. After I joined them, Dan said, "Brothers, I've got some bad news. Last night Pastor Ray and Brother Frank were arrested in Warren County for carrying concealed weapons. I haven't gotten all the details yet, but I do know that they're in the Wilmington jail, being held on a twenty-five-thousand-dollar bond. We need to collect enough money to at least get the pastor out, so at ten percent that means twenty-five hundred dollars. I've been in touch with everyone whose phone number I have so we can get as much as possible."

I stood up and pulled out my wallet. "I've only got forty-two dollars," I said, "but you can have it."

"Thanks, Brother Dave," Dan replied.

About eight or ten people Dan couldn't reach by phone showed up for services only to learn that Pastor Ray and Frank were in jail. Around 1:00 P.M., Dan told everyone to leave so he could lock up and go collect money pledged by various parishioners.

When I got home, I called Tym right away, and I wasn't surprised that he already knew. He told me that Redfeairn and Johnson had been pulled over for an expired plate.

"What a couple of idiots," I said.

"Yeah, and now I've got to go down to Wilmington tomorrow and interview them."

"You'd better make it early," I told him, "because according to Dan Rick, he'll have enough money to bail Pastor Ray out first thing in the morning."

"Where's he getting all the money?" asked Tym.

"He called around asking for donations from parishioners and everyone at the meeting donated cash. By the way, you owe me forty-two bucks."

"You didn't."

"Sure did. Dan was standing right beside me when I opened my wallet, so I felt if he knew I gave all I had it would help with my standing in the group."

"Thanks, Dave."

"Hey, you gotta walk the walk and talk the talk," I replied.

Tym laughed and said, "Next time, walk away and keep your mouth shut."

I also told Tym about a two-day KKK World Congress in Centralia, Illinois, scheduled for June 20. He thanked me for the information. I later learned that Pastor Ray had attended the Congress and persuaded KKK member Dennis McGiffen to quit the Klan and become the Illinois AN state leader.

Tym Burkey

As we'd hoped, DT approved the request for Dave to carry a weapon. Next, I sent a letter to Assistant United States Attorney Mark Wohlander in Lexington, Kentucky, explaining the situation. AUSA Wohlander went to Judge Joseph M. Hood, a federal judge, and he granted permission. Judge Hood and AUSA Wohlander agreed that the decision should be kept out of written court records for the sake of Dave's security. This decision was extremely important to the investigation, and Judge Hood was taking a great risk by putting trust in a felon, as well as in me to control the situation. I was grateful that these two officials had looked beyond their personal concerns to the importance of what we were doing.

Dave Hall

Around the third week of April, I received a call from my federal probation officer, Tom Atkinson. He wanted me to come to his office in Covington, Kentucky, and asked me to be there the following day, which was unusual, since I'd just seen him three weeks before. He was at least a week ahead of schedule, so I sensed that there was something important that he wanted to say.

When I arrived, Mr. Atkinson asked me to have a seat and then handed me a list of rules that I was supposed to follow while I was waiting for sentencing.

"You already gave me this," I said, reminding him of our first meeting.

"There've been some changes," he said. "Take a close look."

I read through it, seeing the same information I'd seen before, but then I noticed the change: I was now allowed to carry a firearm and to associate with felons. I looked up, unsure what to say.

Atkinson leaned back on his chair and clasped his hands behind his head. "Dave," he said, "I'm retiring next year, and in all my years as a federal probation officer, I've never seen a federal court make an approval like that. What the hell are you up to?"

He was a federal agent and my probation officer, but I wasn't supposed to reveal my status as an informant to anyone. I was in a tight spot, but I knew he wasn't going to let me leave without giving him some sort of explanation. Finally, I decided just to tell him. After swearing him to secrecy, I described my assignment from the FBI. Atkinson listened intently, occasionally shaking his head as if he could hardly believe it. When I finished, he leaned forward.

"All right," he said, "that explains the change. If you need any counseling or advice, don't hesitate to call me. I've had a few white supremacists as probation clients and they can be very dangerous. So be careful."

I assured him I would, and after shaking my hand, he wished me well.

When Sunday rolled around, I wondered what I might find out at the church. Neither Ray nor Tym had contacted me all week, although I knew that Ray was out of jail. In the parking lot, Dan Rick told me that two men I'd recently met had resigned from the Aryan Nations and turned in their uniforms. They were both in their forties, two of the older members of the group. Apparently Andy's wife had insisted he quit and the other man was just afraid of getting arrested.

"Well," I commented, "we don't need members who aren't dedicated."

Soon Hoge Tabor, Kevin Burns, and John Graham arrived. John gave me a copy of *The Turner Diaries,* in case I hadn't read it, so I'd know more about how it had inspired so many anti-government groups. I thanked him.

Pastor Ray, free since Monday, had not yet arrived, so as we waited for him, we were joined by a couple of members of the Ohio Militia, as well as four members of the KKK from Eastern Ohio. It was shortly after noon when Pastor Ray showed up, and he proceeded to offer his side of the story. He'd been charged with a misdemeanor, he said, but the FBI and the Anti-Defamation League (ADL) were pressuring the prosecutor to charge him with a felony. He didn't stay long, as he wanted to visit Frank, still in jail. He assured us his attorney was working on the case. My main concern was that if he went to prison, that would extend my time with this operation that much longer.

Tym Burkey

By this time, I'd made the transition to full-time work with the DT Squad, thanks largely to Dave's contributions and the need to focus on the Ohio AN members. I was happy with the change, but there was a lot to keep track of. Once Dave became established with the AN, I lived this case seven days a week.

DT and the Aryan Nations became my main duty. I'd start off on Mondays debriefing Dave, either in person or over the phone, on events from the previous Sunday. I would call my supervisor, Roger Wilson, and the FBI HQ analyst, Pam Quinn, with any important developments. Then I would type the information to be distributed around the country to the appropriate FBI divisions. This generally took me into Tuesday. On Wednesdays I would cover leads on other investigations or conduct interviews and brief my local law en-forcement partners on the Ohio AN. Thursdays I would meet again with Dave and discuss the upcoming weekend. I would also pay him. Fridays were spent catching up and dealing with any last-minute details for the weekend.

Since Dave usually went to Ikes on Thursday and Friday evenings, I would do drive-bys. Then on the weekends, I'd sit by the pager and wait. As appropriate, I might do an occasional surveil-lance or drive-by of AN members.

Dave traveled frequently, which caused a considerable amount of phone calls and written communication between the Cincinnati Di-vision, FBI HQ, and the division in whose territory Dave was trav-eling. He and I spent many hours strategizing the investigation or preparing for a meeting or a trip. Our time was spent talking about the what-ifs—which was extremely important for Dave's safety—and one of our most frequent discussions involved the possibility he might be confronted as a snitch.

From my days of working criminal cases, primarily drug-related, I knew Dave would be tested as to his veracity, so I went over and over his response—he was to lie, lie, lie, make counter-allegations, and never under any circumstance admit any involve-ment with law enforcement. Such an admission was the quickest way to die.

Around the same time as Redfeairn's arrest, Dennis McGiffen, for-merly a night hawk with the Illinois KKK and now Illinois AN leader, had formed The New Order in southern Illinois. It was named after Robert Mathews' 1980s group, The Order, which committed armored-car robberies as well as the assassination of a Denver, Colorado-based talk show host, Alan Berg—a Jew despised by all white supremacists. The Order met its end with most of its members in jail and Mathews dead after a shootout with federal authorities. Similarly, McGiffen planned robberies to raise money to promote the race war that the AN so desperately wanted. That spring, McGiffen had become a regular at the Ohio AN meetings, and since Redfeairn favored him, it was no surprise that Redfeairn's young protégé, Dan Rick, began to travel with McGiffen.

At first, McGiffen's effort lay in racist rhetoric, but by all appearances he was a lone wolf, forming a cell that consisted of himself, Rick, and two others. Redfeairn, although not directly participating, seemed to be in the shadows, directing at least some of their activity. It was difficult to know precisely what was going on, but over that summer, our concern would grow about McGiffen's intent. We also watched Redfeairn, as his attorney kept delaying legal proceedings against him. Since Redfeairn remained out of prison, Dave was able to continue his work.

9

RECRUITMENT RALLY

Dave Hall

By this time it was obvious that Ray had problems with alcohol and cocaine, but I never said anything about it, except to Tym. I believe that existence of this unspoken secret between us led Ray to trust me more and more.

I had my own problem: I was struggling with my identity. My life was slowly being consumed by the Aryan Nations and Pastor Ray's constant bombardment of white supremacist rhetoric. And it didn't help that every Sunday for church I was now wearing the AN uniform—a light blue shirt, dark blue tie, dark blue pants, and black combat boots. Before leaving, I'd put on the pants and boots, but at Ray's instruction (to avoid being hassled by cops) I held off putting on the shirt, tie, and gun until I arrived at the church building. I could feel my personality changing, even as I constantly tried to remind myself who I really was. At times I felt as if Lucifer was on my left shoulder and the Archangel Michael on my right, with my head in the middle for their battleground. My only saving grace was that in times of doubt I had my mother to turn to.

And times of doubt there certainly were. During a members meeting late in May, Pastor Ray told Frank Johnson to lock the door and admit no one. He said that if any law enforcement showed up, he was not to let them in unless they had a warrant. Leaving Frank at the door, Pastor Ray had me accompany him to the kitchen area. About halfway across the room, I glanced back in time to see Frank remove an SKS assault rifle from its hiding place behind the Confederate flag.

I wondered what the hell was going on, especially when I saw the rest of the members seated at a table. As Pastor Ray called the meeting to order, he said, "I fully expect that law enforcement may try to arrest me today. That's why I'm not wearing my usual clerical clothes. I didn't want to be shown on camera in handcuffs wearing those clothes. In the event of my arrest, Dan Rick will become number one in charge and Kevin Burns will be promoted to number two position as a lieutenant in the Aryan Nations."

Ray then turned to Hoge Tabor and me, and said, "Dave, I expect you and Hoge to help and to provide guidance to Dan and Kevin as needed."

"I would be happy to," I said, "but if you don't mind my asking, what do you think you might be arrested for?"

"They're trying to tie us in to the Kehoe brothers, and there may be indictments coming out charging me with buying weapons from them. The only thing I can figure is that the cops were already watching them or us."

When Ray said this, both Dan and Kevin nodded. Then Kevin said, "We'd only seen them once, and that was two or three days before those state troopers pulled them over and started the shootout."

"The information that I've been getting is coming out of Cincinnati," Ray continued, "and I've been checking on it." As he went on, it seemed to me that much of his so-called information was from a Channel 12 news exposé that had aired the previous week, painting Pastor Ray as a violent and dangerous individual. In fact, he referred to this exposé as he spoke to us. I thought he was just being more paranoid than usual.

"If the police show up," he said, "I want you to keep your weapons holstered and your hands above your heads. We don't want to give them any reason to start shooting."

He then excused himself and went into his private office. We all looked around at each other, not really knowing what to say, so we got up and went to the church area to welcome the arriving parishioners.

After all the drama of that morning, nothing happened. But in the context of press reports about Redfeairn, there was an item about how he'd once shot a cop. Tym had told me this when we first met, but I was curious about Ray's version. When I had an opportunity, I asked him about the incident, and he freely described it.

Having been stopped for a traffic violation, he'd pulled out a gun and shot the police officer five times, and when the man fell to the ground, Ray walked over and said, "I'll bet that hurts. Here, have another one." But the officer had knocked the gun away and, despite being badly wounded, had survived. Ray hadn't been happy about only wounding the man, but with amusement he went on to tell me how he'd sidestepped the system, because he'd studied psychology at Urbana and knew how to appear crazy. So he'd spent four years in a mental hospital and later got a light sentence for pleading guilty. He thought that was pretty clever.

In June, Pastor Ray formally promoted Dan Rick and Kevin Burns to the rank of first lieutenant in the Aryan Nations, presenting them with certificates of merit from the Aryan Nations World Headquarters, signed by Pastor Butler. It was then that we learned that Frank Johnson had been bailed out but that Ray had been charged with a felony in the concealed weapons incident. He reassured us that he would deal with it.

At the end of services I asked Pastor Ray if I could talk with him privately. I wanted to address a situation before anyone got wind of it. One of my sisters lived across the street from J.D., and although she was married to a white man, my two older sisters, who liked to visit her, had married black men. They had biracial children, which they brought with them on their visits. I knew it was just a matter of time before Pastor Ray would learn about this from some source so I'd come up with a plan.

Pastor Ray led me into his personal office and invited me to have a seat in the chair by the desk. I noticed a copy of *Mein Kampf* lying there next to a Bible. As I sat down, Pastor Ray sat on the edge of a bed in the other corner and asked, "What's on your mind, Brother?"

"If I confess something to you," I began, "do you have to keep it in strict confidence like a Catholic priest would?"

"Yes," Ray assured me. "Anything you tell me goes no further than me."

"Okay, then. Since I've been coming to church, I've learned that the Jews are our primary enemies, but I know you also realize my deep-seated hatred of niggers."

"That's okay, Brother, I hate niggers, too."

"But I have special reasons for hating those black bastards," I said. "Remember when I told you I had three half sisters?"

"Yes."

"Well, technically, I have five half sisters, but I've disowned two because they married niggers, and even worse, they both have several mongrelized children with those bastards."

Pastor Ray thought for a moment before he said, "I'm glad you feel that you could confide in me. This information in no way makes me think any less of you, Brother. We simply can't always control the actions of others."

"Thanks, Pastor."

Ray stood up, placed his hand on my shoulder, and said, "This conversation never took place. Now let's go join the others and grab a bite to eat."

I felt disgusted about speaking of my kin this way, but it seemed to increase Redfeairn's trust in me. I had to reassure myself that this was all for a good purpose.

Tym Burkey

For the rest of the summer of 1997, Dave attended church services and gathered intelligence. I was aware that among those attending the services was Larry Wayne Harris, a microbiologist and Aryan Nations member who'd previously been arrested for fraudulently obtaining samples of bubonic plague from an East Coast biotech lab. Dave offered the details of a disturbing conversation with Harris, during which the scientist explained in detail how to use dirt and hamburger to produce botulism neurotoxins, telling him that "the germs on the head of a pin could be used to kill more people than an aircraft carrier."

It seemed to me that these people could be preparing for large-scale, organized violence, which could include biological terrorism. In fact, Dave soon told me about a recruitment rally coming up in September. It was to be a joint effort by the AN and the KKK, to be held in Hamilton, Ohio. Since the Internet was not nearly as popular during the 1990s as it is now, white supremacist groups relied heavily on rallies for recruiting. Yet they were controlled by law enforcement and no weapons were permitted inside a safety perimeter. Each person—even protesters—was searched as he or she entered the perimeter. And white supremacists typically would have a "war wagon" nearby, a vehicle driven by other like-minded individuals that was full of weapons, both handguns and rifles. The theory behind a war wagon was that if trouble broke out, the vehicle could be driven to the rally participants and the weapons quickly distributed. The potential for violence from either side was always high.

Dave Hall

During that summer, I attended church every Sunday, but trying to do my job to the best of my ability finally came crashing against my personal life. One afternoon in August, I entered my house, knowing Terri was there. Gary greeted me at the door, and as I rubbed his head, I called out, "Where's your mommy?"

"I'm in the kitchen," she said.

I went in there, ready to enjoy her company, but she sat at the table with a serious look on her face. I looked on the table. In front of her sat the open shoe box in which I'd been keeping my Aryan Nations literature and membership card. Apparently I'd forgotten to lock the desk drawer.

Holding up the card, Terri said, "You've been going to this Aryan Nations church every Sunday, haven't you?"

I was trapped, so I admitted it.

"David, I can't understand this. I know that you're not a racist. Maybe if you had explained to me why you were getting involved with these people I could have understood, but you've been lying to me all this time and it's unforgivable." She stood up and headed for the front door. There she turned and said, "Good-bye. I hope you have a good life."

As she paused to give Gary a quick hug, I asked, "You're not going to give me a chance to explain?"

Without a word Terri walked out the front door, slamming it behind her. I felt numb, not quite believing what had just happened. I sat down on the recliner, and Gary laid his head on my lap. I rubbed his ears and said, "I really did it this time, didn't I, buddy?"

I tried calling Terri several times that evening, but she had taken her phone off the hook. A couple days later I finally got her, but she reiterated that our relationship was over. I apologized for lying to her. Terri accepted my apology, then hung up. As I sat there I thought, *Maybe it's for the best.* Lying to Terri had been stressful, and I didn't need that with all the rest of the pressure. I could only hope that after the whole mess with the FBI was over, maybe we could get back together. But it still hurt to have things end this way. My one consolation was that at least I wouldn't have to worry about Terri seeing me on TV at the rally.

Pastor Ray told me he'd gotten all the necessary permits to hold the rally in Hamilton, where blacks had rioted after a black man had died under suspicious circumstances in the Butler County jail. Ray apparently chose this spot for its potential to incite another riot, and said he was going to do his best to make that happen. I could only hope that he'd get hit by a truck or something so that I wouldn't have to go. The thought of wearing an Aryan Nations uniform in the middle of a race riot was more than a little unnerving.

I also learned around this time that Ray was looking at as much as eighteen months in jail on the concealed weapons charges. I'd had conversations with Tym about this, and he wanted me to stay in the AN until Ray got out of jail—until we got something on him that would put him away for a much longer sentence. But the prospect of remaining a member of this group for another year or two was disheartening. If Ray did go to jail, I'd have to make some serious decisions. I'd made a promise to Tym that I would stay with the investigation until Redfeairn was in prison. There seemed to be no end in sight, but a promise is a promise.

In any event, I had to focus on the immediate task at hand—the approaching rally.

Tym Burkey

I knew Dave had to attend this rally, but I was concerned. He worried that his family would see him on the six o'clock news and believe he was a member of this hate group. To be sure he felt some measure of protection, I prepared to attend as well, posing as a news photographer. The FBI talked with other law enforcement, so quite a few police officers and sheriff's deputies were to be on hand.

For my part, I arrived early to make sure I had a good position from which to spot Dave, knowing he'd be in his uniform and storm trooper boots. He'd also be wearing sunglasses to disguise himself as much as possible. There were other members of different hate groups mulling about, many in their respective uniforms of black or brown, but I kept looking for Dave. At six foot four and 350 pounds, he would stand out.

I had admonished Dave that if he was arrested, under no circumstances should he reveal his relationship with the FBI. I assured him that because he was assisting us, he was covered and would not be in trouble. I also told him that if he involved himself in any violence other than self-defense, he would be on his own. After all, I reminded him, cameras would be rolling.

Dave Hall

Before going to the rally, I'd mingled at the church with skinheads, members of the National Alliance, neo-Nazis, and National Socialists. Troy Murphy, the imperial wizard of the KKK in Indiana (not the Indiana basketball player), was also on hand. I'd run into Dennis McGiffen, a former Klansman from Illinois who'd joined the AN earlier in the year, and as he'd changed into his uniform, I'd seen that his entire body was covered with racist tattoos, with the one on his back depicting several Klansmen standing around a burning cross. I knew he was among the most serious members and that he was ready for action. Some of the wives and girlfriends were also there, but they wouldn't be attending the rally. Instead they would stay behind to prepare the after-rally dinner. That was their rightful place, according to the AN's beliefs.

About five miles from Hamilton, we met up with the Butler County sheriff's deputies at the Liberty substation. I had never seen so many deputies in one spot. They had us line up and pass single file through a makeshift gate, where they checked everyone with metal detectors. Soon two buses arrived to take us the rest of the way into Hamilton. As I read the lettering on the side, I had to bite my tongue. It said "Butler County School for the Developmentally Handicapped."

On the bus, Ray told us that if we were physically attacked, we should stand our ground and defend ourselves by any means necessary.

As we drove into downtown Hamilton, it looked like an armed camp. The streets were barricaded and there were crowds of people everywhere. Hundreds of law enforcement officers were herding them, and no one seemed to notice us as the buses passed by on the way to the rear of the courthouse.

We entered the rotunda, where Pastor Ray assigned us our places, and as luck would have it, I was to stand at the bottom step in the very first row. Putting on my cheap sunglasses, I stepped out onto the porch, sparking sneers and jeers from a couple hundred protesters. There was also a group of supporters to my right, though they numbered only about five or six people. The whole front of the courthouse had been fenced off, and police officers stood every few feet, some with dogs. I noticed that there were people on the roofs across the street, taking pictures. I would later learn that they were from the FBI, the ATF, and the Ohio Bureau of Criminal Identification. Tym was among them.

About this time, Pastor Ray called everyone back inside. He lined everybody up and carefully choreographed how each person would take his place on the courthouse steps. Since yours truly was of course the largest person there, I got the honor of being first in line. By the time we went back out, the mob of protestors had whipped themselves into a frenzy. As I led the group down the steps, I looked into their angry faces. I thought that we were supposed to be the "hate group," but these people were acting like crazed cannibals foraging for someone to eat. I guess hate goes both ways.

After we were in place, Pastor Ray stepped up to the microphone. As he started to speak, the crowd chanted, "Hey, hey, ho, ho, Aryan Nations gotta go," and made clear their disapproval with the universal hand gesture. Undaunted, Pastor Ray used every racial slur in his vocabulary. He'd told me he was going to do his best to incite a riot, and it looked like he might succeed. I stood fast, expecting the worst.

With every statement Ray made, the crowd grew more enraged. There were a couple of openly gay men from the Gay and Lesbian Alliance who bent over and bared their rear ends. Ray immediately replied with, "God has a cure for homosexuality, and it's called AIDS!" This really got the crowd going. A few of the women bared their breasts and pressed them firmly against the chain link fence that separated them from us. I have no idea what this was supposed to symbolize, but it was the only moment of the rally I really enjoyed.

By this time, more of our supporters had shown up, around thirty in all, and obscenities were flying back and forth through the fence. It seemed that things were on the verge of chaos when Troy Murphy, in KKK robes, hood, and the full regalia of an imperial wizard, took over the microphone. The first words out of his mouth were, "Look out nigger, the Klan's getting bigger!"

Needless to say, the crowd roared. He went on to say, "We haven't got a problem with the niggers in Africa that are jumping up and down and beating on a log—in fact, more power to them. But we do have a problem when niggers want to move in next door to us and marry our sisters. As far as black history goes, you niggers didn't have a history until your own village kings back in Africa sold you into slavery. The biggest mistake made by the white man was allowing you monkeys to learn to read and write! That's where your history began. So how does three hundred years of nigger history compare to three thousand years of white history? And what contributions have niggers made? Your only claim to fame is when that nigger George Carver jumped up and down on a peanut and created peanut butter; I guess that's not bad for nigger progress."

When Murphy finally stepped back from the microphone, the protesters were going crazy, and I fully expected them to start climbing the fence to get at us. By this time, I'd been standing at attention for over an hour and my back was killing me. I was almost hoping that something would happen just so I could move. The large AN arm shield I'd been holding weighed a ton, and I was praying that this circus would soon end. The protesters' voices had become one great roar, and with the public address system blaring in my ears, I thought I'd go deaf.

But then Dennis McGiffen stepped up to the microphone, and it was more "nigger this" and "nigger that." McGiffen railed on and on about blacks being the beasts of the field, and said that they were to be looked upon as a farmer would look upon a horse or a mule. He also attacked the Jews, proclaiming them to be the children of Satan, a scourge on the face of the earth.

Yet even so, the hate that I saw on the faces of the protesters was far worse than anything I had ever seen, even among the rank and file of the AN. It was unnerving that racist speeches from a few individuals could transform a group of somewhat peaceful protesters into bloodthirsty animals. Words had more power than I'd given them credit for.

Then, just as I thought that I would pass out from the pain in my back, the rally came to an end. As we filed back into the rotunda, my ears rang from the noise. Ray told us he was proud of the way we had conducted ourselves, especially the volatile skinheads. As soon as we had secured the PA equipment, the deputies rushed us away. Somewhere along the way a few protesters caught up with us. Most of them just shouted obscenities, but rocks were thrown as well, so the deputies turned on their lights and sirens and drove us nonstop out of town.

Back in New Vienna, we could smell the food the women had prepared, and it was like we were warriors returning from battle. As we ate, we discussed the events of the day. I guess Ray was pleased with me, because he asked if I would be interested in studying to become an ordained minister.

"I haven't really thought about it, Pastor," I said.

"Take some time, Brother Dave, take all the time you need. Just consider it."

I counted this as another step in my acceptance into this organization and decided to make it a goal.

After everyone left, I got into my car, laid my head back on the headrest, shut my eyes, and just sat there. My brain was going a hundred miles an hour, and I needed to calm myself before the long drive home—especially since I was going back to a house without

Terri. After a couple of minutes and a few deep breaths, I headed back to Dayton. As I drove along I couldn't get the roar of the crowd and the cries of *"Sieg Heil"* and "Hail victory" out of my mind. Even turning the radio up didn't help. Finally I stopped at a park along the way and went for a short walk.

Autumn was setting in and the leaves were turning. I came upon a large rock by a small stream and sat down. As I watched the leaves float by, I asked God for the strength to carry on. I wondered how much longer this was going to last. When I had agreed to help Tym in this endeavor I had no idea of the stress that would be involved. But after this rally, I was convinced that these people were capable of just about anything and needed to be stopped, so I had to keep going, but I knew I'd need all the strength I could muster.

10.

WHITE NOISE

Tym Burkey

As Dave dealt with rallies, I kept my eye on Redfeairn's fate. He had been convicted of having a concealed weapon and he awaited sentencing, so late that summer I had tried to make an appointment with the sentencing judge to suggest probation. I was convinced that, given time, Redfeairn would overtly involve himself in McGiffen's plot, whatever it was, and thus get himself a life sentence when they all got arrested. But the bailiff had told me that the judge would not meet with me. The Anti-Defamation League and others were lobbying for a stiff sentence for Redfeairn, and the judge wanted to avoid any influence in his court. I had to chuckle. I'd liked to have seen his reaction to an FBI agent pleading for a light sentence for a white supremacist.

On October 1, Redfeairn received his sentence: six months in jail. He'd gotten off easy, and I could live with that, but I knew that Dave was fretting over the fact that this would extend the time he worked for us. I'm sure he wondered whether it wouldn't have been better just to have gone to jail for a year on the drug conspiracy charge than to remain immersed among these hatemongers. But there was nothing we could do to change the situation now.

Jason Swanson traveled from Michigan to assume temporary leadership of the Ohio chapter, and he made some changes. Effective immediately, he insisted that members now pay $25 a month to defray the church's delinquent accounts. We gave Dave the money, and he accepted the position of Ohio propaganda minister. That meant he had to write flyers. He also helped to prepare for an AN television show that aired on public access channels. I knew that he was reading the Bible, taking a course of indoctrination, and studying Hitler's *Mein Kampf* so he could impress Redfeairn when he got out of prison, and he continued to suffer from the façade. He told me of nightmares and bouts of nausea. He was also losing his footing at times, because "walking the walk and talking the talk" drew him deeply into the attitudes and behaviors of this group. Since he'd become distanced from his family, he had little support, so I kept tabs on him.

With Sunday services suspended due to Redfeairn's incarceration, finances deteriorated for the group, which made us happy. Soon the church's heat and electricity were turned off. But Swanson was not deterred. He suggested that the Ohio chapter sponsor a concert in Detroit. Dave told us that Swanson had financed the Michigan chapter using concerts put on by racist rock bands from the Resistance Records label based in Oak Park, Michigan.

I didn't like this development. Any rock concert can be dangerous, let alone one meant to fuel a hate group. I alerted my superiors and we tried to stop the concert. Failing that, I knew that Dave would have to attend, but I could not be with him, so I arranged for a contact agent in Detroit and gave Dave a code word to use to call the agent in the event he ran into trouble.

Dave Hall

It was October, getting cold, and as I entered the church one morning after Ray went to jail, I wiped my feet on the Israeli flag and noticed the chill inside. Jason and Dan Rick greeted me with a Nazi salute, then Kevin Burns and John Graham arrived, followed by Bob Hill, the Aryan Nations' answer to Hans Christian Andersen. I was curious as to what new adventure Bob would relate this time, as he always seemed full of tall tales, supplied by an obviously overactive imagination. Since he usually annoyed the others, I tried not to stand too close to him. The decision would prove to be a wise one.

Jason had three skinhead rock bands ready to perform: the Involved Patriots, Steel Cap, and the Vineland Warriors. The concert was scheduled for November 29 at VFW Post 9507, located at 630 East Eleven Mile Road in Madison Heights, Michigan. The VFW didn't actually know the nature of what we were planning, and in fact, we were instructed not to wear uniforms. Jason passed out *The Klansman's Handbook* and two small pamphlets, "Auschwitz: The Big Lie" and "Ike the Kike." I felt like taking my gun from its holster and shooting him in both knees.

At this same meeting, I learned that Dan Rick, who once had been a skinhead in Denver, was planning a trip to Colorado, supposedly to meet with other AN members. I believed in my gut that Dan was up to something, but I couldn't figure out what could be so important that he would drive nearly three thousand miles roundtrip. And how did Dennis McGiffen figure into all of this? I knew he and Dan had stayed in contact lately, and I was sure McGiffen had a part in whatever was going on.

I asked Tym if I could take a few days off just to clear my head. He agreed that it was a good idea. I loaded Gary into the car and headed for my place on a lake. My involvement with the Aryan Nations had slowly infected virtually every facet of my life. Not only had it cost me my relationship with Terri, it had also alienated me from others. Being at the lake, alone with Gary and his boundless energy, proved to be good medicine.

Tym Burkey

After Dave took a breather and returned, I learned from him that John Graham had been at the church with a couple of friends from Cincinnati, one of whom was a gun dealer. He'd brought catalogs of various weapons and their prices, and had everything from 12-gauge street sweepers to AK-47 assault rifles. He had even showed Dave how to convert semiautomatic rifles to fully automatic.

Dave had as yet heard nothing about Dan's trip, although the area where he'd gone, the "four corners" that joined Arizona, New Mexico, Colorado, and Utah, also lent its name to the Four Corners Militia. I guessed that an arms deal was in the works.

Dave Hall

Severing ties with my family had been one of the toughest aspects of this whole mess. When one of my biracial nephews asked me why I never took him fishing anymore, it broke my heart. The only thing that I could say was that Uncle Dave was just too busy right now, but soon we'd be going fishing again. This whole thing had snowballed from a simple investigation into a way of life, and I had a terrible feeling that I was in so deep that I could never get out.

In October I was in court again, in front of Judge Hood, to have my case reviewed. He sentenced me to five years of probation and a fine of $50, addiing "upon motion of the government as a result of defendant's substantial assistance, sentence departs from guidelines." At this point, if I wanted to be, I was done. I could have walked away from Tym and the whole investigation, and it was tempting to do so. But I'd promised Tym that I would stay with it. I was in this until Ray was either in jail or run out of town. Difficult as it was to continue, I returned to the services and meetings.

It was early November before I spotted Dan Rick's car back in the church parking lot, which meant he was back from his trip. When I went inside, I saw him talking to Jason. He sported a new shoulder holster and a .45-caliber semiautomatic pistol, which he proudly told me he'd picked it up in Colorado. I knew he'd been financially strapped before he went, and now he suddenly had enough to purchase a nice new weapon, with all the trimmings. He also said he'd been spooked at one roadside stop by a police car, which led me to believe he'd had more than a new pistol in his car.

Later, I overheard conversations that included names such as Dennis McGiffen and Vince Reed, the AN international ambassador. There was a reference to weapons, but I couldn't make out what was said. In fact, over the next three weeks, these guys withdrew from the rest of us, including me, and became more secretive. I made a conscious effort not to change my personality, to just focus on producing flyers, and acted as uninterested as possible in Jason and Dan, at times purposely ignoring them. On the other hand, Bob, the storyteller, pestered them like a child trying to get a baseball player's autograph. By this point, everybody had begun to avoid him. At first, his tall tales had been a source of amusement, but we were all growing tired of hearing them.

I passed what little information I was able to acquire to Tym. I didn't know if any of it was significant, but I wasn't in a position to interpret it.

Tym Burkey

Dave told me he thought Jason and Dan suspected that someone in the group was an informant, and hoped they hadn't targeted him.

"If you're ever confronted," I told him, "deny, deny, deny, and make counterallegations."

He was aware that admitting his status could—probably would—mean a bullet in the head. He reminded me that he carried a gun and if pushed into a corner he wouldn't hesitate to use it.

I let Dave know that we hadn't been able to stop the skinhead concert but that we'd alerted certain groups about the concertgoers, so there would probably be protesters on hand.

To my surprise, Dave said, "I almost look forward to Pastor Ray getting out of prison."

"Why?"

"Because I feel like I'm spinning my wheels and the investigation's getting stagnant."

I suspected it was more than that. It was obvious to me that his own life had gotten out of control and he wanted it to be normal again. "What you've done for us," I assured him, "has been very helpful. In fact, the information you've given us has allowed us to extend the investigation beyond what we'd originally anticipated."

He seemed to feel better when I told him this. And by the following week, he'd supplied several significant items.

Dave Hall

Another Sunday and I was running late, so I threw my uniform and sidearm in the trunk of the car and headed out. When I arrived at the church I saw more vehicles than usual in the parking lot. Inside, I gave the group a Nazi salute, noticing several new faces. As I went over to John Graham, I realized that Jason and Dan were nowhere in sight. John introduced me to five of his friends, all in their early twenties, from the Cincinnati and northern Kentucky area. I learned that all five were members of the National Socialists Resistance, a neo-Nazi organization.

They wanted to know more about our beliefs, and as I explained them Jason and Dan emerged from a small private room adjacent to the worship area. They walked over to the group and listened to the way I used selected biblical passages to emphasize Aryan superiority. As I finished my impromptu sermon, I made it a point to tell them that I was not yet an ordained minister, but everything that they needed to know was in the Bible; all they had to do was to read it for themselves. With that Jason said, "I believe you're going to make a good pastor, Dave."

He called the meeting to order, and Kevin Burns asked if he could address the group. He said he'd attended a meeting at the Jewish Community Center in Dayton and that a number of Jews and blacks, as well as representatives from the Bureau of Criminal Identification and the Montgomery County sheriff's office, were in attendance. Kevin said that among other things, they'd discussed the recent increase in hate literature being passed out in the area. Everyone looked at me and smiled. That was my job. Even Jason gave me a rare nod of approval.

We discussed preparations for the concert, and then Dan Rick told us that the next meeting would be December 21 and at that time they would be fingerprinting all members. We sat there, waiting for him to explain. Bob came right out and asked why.

"Because someone has been leaking information," Jason said. "I think it's someone right here in this room."

My blood ran cold.

"I can't see how fingerprinting can do any good," Bob stated.

Jason and Dan looked at each other as if they had been waiting for a reaction like that. Both looked at Bob, and Jason said, "Everybody gets fingerprinted and that's that."

For the first time, I was actually glad to have Bob around. He'd drawn all the attention with his dumb remarks.

When I reported all of this to Tym on Monday morning, I suggested he consider shaving his head so he could come with me to the concert.

"You know, Dave," he said, "you've been working awfully hard lately and you deserve to have all the fun."

"Thanks a lot, pal."

I spent most of the rest of the week working on my Bible study course. Whenever I got to the point where I thought that I would lose my mind from reading this stuff, I took a break. Walking Gary or playing Frisbee seemed to help me keep at least one foot anchored in reality.

Finally the day of the concert arrived. The night before, I'd had terrible dreams about Hitler, jackbooted skinheads, fiery crosses, and swastikas. In fact, around 3:00 A.M., I'd woken up out of breath and in a sweat. As I sat on the edge of the bed, I realized that going back to sleep was out of the question. My hands were still shaking as

I headed for the kitchen to put on a pot of coffee. I watched old movies and chugged caffeine until daybreak.

It rained for most of the five-hour drive to Detroit. I checked into a motel and then drove around until I found the VFW post. Back at the motel, I lay down for a while and tried to recall what my life had been like before I'd met Tym. I'd barely been aware of the Aryan Nations or the KKK, and I'd had no idea that the Christian Identity movement even existed. Now, nearly a year and a half later, not only was I involved with one of the most violent hate groups in America, I had moved up through the ranks to become a trusted member and had successfully created an impeccable façade of loyalty.

The phone rang, and I nearly jumped out of my skin. I had forgotten that I'd asked for a wake-up call. I went to the bathroom and splashed some cold water on my face.

To my surprise, I actually felt a little excited.

As I drove up Eleven Mile Road to my destination, I could see a multitude of police cars in the distance with their lights flashing. One block from the VFW post the police had blocked the road to divert traffic. I drove around the surrounding neighborhood until I found a parking place. Over a block away, I could already hear the angry chants of antiracist protesters. Once I arrived, I saw a hundred or more protestors blocking the entrance and thought, *Boy, is this going to be fun.*

As I pushed my way through the crowd, I was confronted by a black man nearly as large as myself. He yelled, "Where you going, boy?"

"To the VFW."

"No, you're not!"

A confrontation already. "I think you'd better get out of my way," I warned him.

He said nothing, but he took a quick step toward me and threw a punch. I ducked, avoiding a blow to the face, but his fist slammed against my shoulder. I responded with a strong elbow blow to the back, driving him face first to the ground. Someone grabbed me from behind. I jerked away and turned, finding myself face-to-face with a police officer.

"You're under arrest!" he screamed. "Turn around and put your hands behind your back."

"Why am I being arrested?" I wanted to know.

"Assault and battery." He cuffed one hand, but due to my size the handcuffs wouldn't reach my other hand. He yelled to another officer for a second set of cuffs.

"He hit me first," I protested, although I was sure he wouldn't believe me or wouldn't care. So much for my grand entrance into the skinhead concert. Instead, I was going off to jail. I wondered what Tym would think.

Then another officer stepped forward. "I saw the whole thing," he said. "The other guy swung first."

The arresting officer didn't take that well, but he reluctantly removed the handcuffs. As I rubbed my wrist, he said, "You have thirty seconds to leave the area or go to jail."

I looked around him to the black man who had accosted me. He was being helped to his feet, but blood streamed down his face. I decided that leaving was a good idea.

As I walked toward my car, I saw more police cruisers arriving. Several parked cars had been vandalized along the street and even mine, a rental, had the right-side mirror broken off. Feeling lucky, I headed back to the motel.

As I drove, it occurred to me that I might gain even more credibility with Jason and the others if I did get arrested, and I contemplated turning back. But then I decided that going to jail in Detroit on a Saturday night, branded as a white supremacist, might be a rather unpleasant experience. I called it a night.

I believed the trip had been a waste until I turned on the eleven o'clock news. The lead story was "White supremacists and protesters clash in Madison Heights neighborhood." There was videotape of police dispersing the crowd, which appeared to be larger than when I'd left. According to the report, there had been a couple of arrests and some property damage, and I took solace in the fact that the information I had provided was the reason the protesters had even been there. Jason and his skinheads could not have made much money, if any, from the concert. I turned off the TV with a smile on my face. For once, I had no difficulty falling asleep.

11

INFORMANT!

Tym Burkey

We were amused to learn that the organization had taken no profit from the concert, and we probably had Dave to thank for that. But as 1997 drew to a close, things were still stirring. I asked Dave to be especially vigilant about Dennis McGiffen.

I also realized that even as he was working hard for us, Dave was suffering from insomnia. As Christmas neared, the stress of his sleepless nights was coming to a head, and I was pretty sure it was exacerbated by several developments that gave him a scare.

Dave Hall

The private conversations among those in charge had increased, so I knew there was something in the air, but I still couldn't find out what it might be. At church one morning late in December, in a building as cold as a meat locker, Dan asked me what I thought about Bob Hill.

"I think he's got an overactive imagination," I said with a shrug, "but he seems harmless."

He didn't pursue it, but I wondered why he was asking.

Soon John Graham and a couple of his friends arrived from Cincinnati, followed by Kevin Burns and Bob. After Jason called the meeting to order, he stated that he was fed up with people arriving late, and from now on anyone late for meetings would be fined $10. He also informed us that on the weekend of April 19, 1998, there would be an Aryan Nations Youth Congress held at the AN World Headquarters in Hayden Lake, Idaho, a small community about ten miles north of Coeur d'Alene. He expected us all to attend. I wasn't keen about this, but I knew that the place was the AN center, the heart of it all, so I'd probably be going. I tried not to think too hard about that.

Dan then took over and stated that the heat and electric should be back on by the January meeting. We all applauded. John said that they had successfully recorded the skinhead concert on video and that he would have copies for everyone by the next meeting. I then submitted to Dan several copies of propaganda flyers for his approval, as per Pastor Ray's instructions before going to prison.

Just then, Bob stepped forward to say he had information about a former Aryan Nations member. Bob said that he was at a federal building in downtown Dayton when he saw this individual getting off the elevator as he was getting on. The implications were clear: Bob was suggesting this man was an informant.

Jason pulled Bob aside, and Dan joined them for a short private discussion. I strained to hear what they were saying, but as Bob's face grew redder and redder I figured that he was probably getting chewed out. Soon they broke it up and rejoined the group.

"If anyone has information about a current or former member," Jason said, "you are to report it to me or Dan in private."

Bob sat still, uncharacteristically quiet.

Dan and Jason resumed going over my flyers, which they approved for distribution. After Jason ended the meeting, when only

Dan and I remained with him, he pulled out his new .45-caliber automatic pistol to show us.

Seizing the opportunity, I asked, "Do you think what Bob said is true?" I knew for a fact that the person Bob had professed to see at the federal building had quit the Aryan Nations under pressure from his wife and family. I also knew he had no connection with law enforcement whatsoever, and I didn't want to see him pegged as an informant.

"He's an idiot" was Jason's response. "You can't believe anything that comes out of his mouth."

I was relieved that the matter seemed dead.

Tym Burkey

When I learned from Dave about the Aryan Nations Youth Congress slated for April 19, I told him that we had not heard about it. The truth is, we had.

It was my practice to reveal as little as possible to a source, for two very good reasons. First, you always want a source to develop information independently. Second, you never give information to a source that he might inadvertently reveal, letting the bad guy realize that the source knew things he shouldn't. This was for his own protection.

By this time in the investigation, I was in weekly communication with FBI headquarters and other divisions, so whatever Dave reported, I could check for accuracy or consistency with what was known in other corners. It was important to the investigation that I vet Dave, because this procedure helped me to know (1) when a source might be lying and (2) when we might have some serious holes in other areas.

"Jason expects us all to attend the conference," Dave said.

"So how would you like to vacation in Idaho in April?" I asked him.

"Spending four days with hundreds of extreme far-right maniacs isn't my idea of a vacation."

"Nevertheless, you should consider going."

He told me he'd think about it. That surprised me, because I didn't understand why a trip out west would concern him. I asked if he didn't like the idea of being there among so many radicals, and he said that didn't bother him. I suggested a few more things that came to mind, but he assured me he could do the job. Yet clearly something was wrong. I pressed again, but he wouldn't tell me.

Dave Hall

The truth is, I was terrified of flying. The mere thought of boarding a plane made me break out in a cold sweat. But I knew it was too great a distance to drive.

When I returned home, depression set in, clearly complicated by this new anxiety. I sat down and put my face in my hands, trying to ward off the waves of sadness that rolled over me.

Just then, Gary appeared in front of me with his Frisbee in his mouth and his tail wagging. I had to laugh. I took the Frisbee and we headed to the backyard for a game of catch. A good friend, Gary always made me feel better.

But soon Christmas Eve was upon me. I went to see my mother and a couple of close friends, then returned to a dark house. I woke up the next day, Christmas, and despite Gary's company I felt completely alone.

The next day, I woke up with severe chest pain. It wouldn't go away and I believed it was a heart attack, so I went straight to the emergency room. But after the doctors performed some tests, they assured me it wasn't a heart attack at all. I was having what they called a panic attack. In other words, the tension in my life had produced a reaction in my body that felt to me as if I might die, but it was actually just a collection of emotions that overwhelmed me. I could take some medication if I needed it, to alleviate stress, but it would eventually pass.

I was relieved at the diagnosis, but the incident made clear that this job was getting to me. We'd been at it for a year and a half now, with at least another few months to go. I hoped I'd make it.

After the holidays, I went out to distribute my flyers at the Salem Mall, a shopping center in the north Dayton suburb of Trotwood. The mall had been failing economically for months, largely due to crime in the area. An African American community surrounded the mall and these flyers were designed to enrage them, because I had written them in such a way as to blame the community for the mall's troubles. I arrived around noon and slipped the flyers under the windshield wipers of all the cars in the parking lot.

Just as I was finishing up, two young black men approached me. They started to harass me about the flyers but were probably too intimidated by my size to do much else. I held my ground and pretended to believe what the flyers said, but I just wanted to get out of there. After a while, they left me alone.

At home, in an attempt to calm my nerves, I made myself a cup of tea and put on some classical music. After about a half hour I was feeling much better when the phone rang.

"You've been at it again, haven't you?" Tym asked.

"What are you talking about?"

"You know damn well what I am talking about! I've had at least half a dozen calls, including calls from a Trotwood councilman and the chief of police. They weren't very happy."

I laughed so hard I almost dropped the phone.

"Thanks," Tym said. "Now I have to spend the rest of the day returning phone calls and doing paperwork."

"Well, why don't you just look at what I'm doing as job security for you?"

Tym finally let out a chuckle and told me to go fishing, preferably somewhere far away. He added, "And don't be in a hurry to get back."

For the rest of the month, I continued my Bible study, going over the Christian Identity doctrines about how God had created the two races and had cursed women with the pains of childbirth. I'd devised a tactic where I could let myself be partially brainwashed: I intentionally developed a split personality. My alter ego was the dedicated white supremacist, eager to learn the beliefs and ways of the Church of Jesus Christ Christian. I was even getting used to the foul language regarding other human beings. On the other hand, I tried to keep my true personality grounded firmly in reality. It was a dangerous mental game, and I constantly thought of my mother's favorite saying, "When you dance with the Devil, the Devil doesn't change, the Devil changes you." This job had taken me right into the devil's den and I wasn't sure I'd ever be normal again.

When I arrived at church one Sunday morning earlier than usual, I saw that Dan Rick was the only one there, and I realized I had an opportunity to dig for information. It had been my experience that without Jason Swanson's dominating presence, Dan was more apt to talk. I decided not to be inquisitive, but rather to show off some of my newfound biblical knowledge. I could tell that Dan was impressed. Then I asked him where Jason was, and he told me Jason was taking care of errands. He also revealed that Jason might be expelling one or two members. This got my interest, especially in light of the issues raised in December about informants. In fact, Dan admitted that someone had been leaking information about the group's activities over the past few months and they thought they knew who the traitor could be.

I could only hope I wasn't the one they suspected, but I had to wait and see.

After Dan called the meeting to order, I showed him a propaganda flyer that I had created to be distributed in the Oxford, Ohio, area, home of Miami University. Recently two white men had beaten two gay men with baseball bats on a street in downtown Oxford. The gay men had been hospitalized in serious condition, and their attackers remained at large. Since I was propaganda minister, it was my job to take advantage of such situations to create civil unrest. Among other inflammatory remarks, all of which offended me, I had also written in the flyers that when the two suspects were found they should be given medals. I included a poem by Rudyard Kipling that glorified the Aryan warriors. Dan smiled as he approved the material and remarked that the flyers "should really stir those faggots up."

Oddly, we ended the meeting without the issue of informants being raised, so I wasn't going to get an answer to my question any time soon. I also had gotten nowhere with Dan.

Tym Burkey

After Dave distributed his flyers in Oxford, I received the usual calls—in fact, more than usual, but as I read the contents of this flyer, which the police had faxed to me, I grew concerned. Even the fire chief had complained. In addition, my boss had gotten wind of the flyers and he called me as well, so I contacted Dave to discuss it.

"It'll be a miracle if they don't have rioting in the streets," I said.

"I guess I did too good a job, didn't I?" Dave responded.

I explained that he should do only the minimum needed to please the AN, and told him from now on to go to one car and place the flyer on it, then throw the rest away. That way he could truthfully say that he'd posted flyers. I then added, "I think that in the future it would be a good idea if I read all of your flyers before you pass them out."

"All right, that's fine."

"I realize you're just trying to do your best, but try to tone it down."

Dave was quiet for a moment. "Maybe I'm losing my focus. Sometimes it feels like this poison is seeping into my soul."

"Listen," I said, "don't worry about it. Just get some rest."

"I'm sorry for causing you so much grief."

"Hey," I assured him, "that's my job."

But I told Dave to check with me every few days. I knew that going undercover for this long could take a toll on anyone, no matter how mentally fit, and I wanted to be certain Dave was not losing himself. If he was ever really on the spot, he could save himself by telling the others that he'd been hired as an informant and then offering himself as *their* tool. Such things happen. After all, we'd been involved in this assignment for over a year and I'd seen informants do many unexpected things. But Dave seemed more solid than that. I had tested him, tried to catch him in a lie or exaggeration. But so far, his information had been dead-on and free of deception. He'd also asked only for enough money to cover his expenses. And who could blame him for that?

Dave Hall

It was mid-February, the next meeting was approaching, and I was certain that Jason would name the informant at this one. I drank my coffee, cleaned my pistol, made sure it was fully loaded, and prayed that I wouldn't have to use it.

In the church parking lot, I saw Jason and Dan talking at the rear of the building. I got out of my car and headed toward them. As I came closer, they both gave me the Nazi salute, which I returned.

Jason asked if I would watch the church while they ran down to the Quickie Mart for some coffee. I took the opportunity to give the place a quick looking over. I knew there were wall compartments behind the pulpit, hidden by the large Nazi and Confederate flags, where the assault rifles and other weapons were kept. But when I searched, I found the compartments empty. If there were weapons in the building, I needed to find them, but time was growing short and I didn't want to be caught alone inside, so I headed back out.

Soon Hoge Tabor drove in, accompanied by Bob. Then Jason and Dan returned. Bob didn't have much to say. Others came as well, and Jason called the meeting to order, asking five National Socialist members who had accompanied John to wait outside the meeting room. He wanted to address the AN members first.

After we discussed the progress of the cable TV programs, someone brought up the subject of Eric Robert Rudolph, the main suspect in the 1996 Olympic Park bombing in Atlanta, as well as in several abortion clinic bombings in 1997. John Graham added that Rudolph was supposedly a member of the Army of God, a far-right extremist group vehemently opposed to abortion.

"My cousin is a member of that," Bob said.

Suddenly Jason stood up and asked Bob and Dan to join him in the next room. After they closed the door behind them we all just looked at one another somewhat dumbfounded. A couple of minutes passed before Dan returned, telling us that he and Jason were going to give Bob a ride home and that no one was to leave until they returned.

Now this was an interesting development. After Dan left the room, Hoge took charge in a grandfatherly way, offering me advice about the flyers that I'd created, saying that commenting on current events was all good and fine, but maybe I should concentrate more on educating people about our beliefs.

I knew he was right, but I had my own agenda. So far, I'd created flyers that would potentially influence public opinion against the Aryan Nations. Through my flyers, I'd clandestinely been able to hold down the number of new members. But I thanked Hoge for his advice as if I meant to take it, hoping he wouldn't influence Jason, Dan, or even Pastor Ray to force me into compliance.

It had been a little over an hour since Jason, Dan, and Bob had left, and I was starting to get a sick feeling in the pit of my stomach. I knew in my heart that Jason and Dan probably had fingered Bob as the suspected informant, and I could only hope that they wouldn't do something stupid, like shoot him in the head. Finally we heard the rear door of the church open and close. With our hands on our sidearms, Kevin Burns and I went to investigate.

It was Jason and Dan. Alone. As they entered the meeting room I could see that Dan was visibly shaken, while Jason looked angry. After we all returned to our seats, Jason explained that Bob was cast out of the group and no one was to have any contact with him in the future. I relaxed. That had to mean that Bob was still alive. Jason went on to say that if Bob tried to call any of us, we were to hang up on him. We were no longer even to mention his name.

I felt sorry for Bob, but he'd done it to himself with his big mouth. Still, they now believed they had stopped the leak, which meant I'd bought some time. No one yet suspected me. And I still had a mission that day: I wanted to know what had happened to all the weapons. I decided to approach Dan, the easiest one to manipulate.

"I got myself an AK-47 assault rifle," I lied, "but the wooden stock is cracked and I'd like to replace it with a new plastic composite stock. Do you think you could show me with one of the rifles we have here how to change the stock?"

He couldn't, he said, because the weapons weren't there. He'd grown concerned about the security of the church, so he'd taken the weapons to his house.

"Well, then," I said, thinking fast, "could you just draw me a diagram?"

He was happy to do so. I was disappointed, but I did have a little something to pass on to Tym.

The stress of this meeting must have gotten to me, because that night I had one of my recurring nightmares. I was standing alongside a wide street with hundreds of Nazi storm troopers marching in goose step directly toward me. As they drew closer I could actually hear and feel their boots striking the pavement in unison. They passed me, and then all turned their heads to the right and shouted *"Sieg heil!"* As they raised their hands in the Nazi salute, I turned around to see if I could make out who or what they were saluting. I couldn't believe what I saw: right in front of the north portico of the White House, facing Pennsylvania Avenue, stood a larger-than-life statue of Adolf Hitler. Suddenly enraged, I turned and ran into the street to attack the soldiers, but they beat me with their rifle butts. That's when I woke up.

I sat on the edge of the bed, my hair soaked in sweat, and wondered why these nightmares were so damned real. I looked across the room at the clock. I had only been asleep for a couple of hours. Knowing it was useless to go back to bed, I went into the living room and spent the remainder of the night watching TV, trying to avoid thinking about the life I was living.

12

KEEPING COVER

Tym Burkey

As the McGiffen investigation heated up, approaching an arrest based on various sources of information, I was more convinced that Redfeairn had played a role. He was still in prison, and I told the Springfield, Illinois, agents I would like to see the investigation delayed as long as possible, to give us the best chance of catching Redfeairn in the net, too. They agreed, but we all knew that community safety outweighed our shot at Redfeairn, and McGiffen and his cohorts were dangerous in their own right. If they were planning some kind of attack, we had to stop them at once.

Finally, in February, after listening to incriminating messages recorded by an informant about the McGiffen cell's terrorist plots, the Springfield agents decided they could wait no longer. At the end of the month, they arrested Dennis McGiffen, along with Dan Rick and the other two cell members, on charges of conspiracy to sell guns. Searches were conducted by the Springfield and Detroit divisions. At the time, Rick was working at Jason Swanson's tattoo parlor in Detroit, and although the FBI executed a search warrant there, they were unable to find sufficient evidence to implicate Swanson in the cell's plans. He escaped the net.

Since Vince Reed, one of our sources, had dropped out of sight, the rumors were that he'd been busted for something and had ratted out the others to save himself. If only they knew.

Even though I was disappointed about Redfeairn, the Springfield agents had done the right thing. This so-called New Order had planned to bomb the Anti-Defamation League; the Southern Poverty Law Center, where Morris Dees worked; and the Simon Wiesenthal Center in Los Angeles. They were planning to assassinate a federal judge as well.

Yet I remained suspicious of Redfeairn's possible participation. I worked with Matt Meyer, a very good gang investigator at the prison where Redfeairn was housed. Meyer provided us with records of Redfeairn's telephone calls. On the day of the arrests, a very interesting call was recorded between him and Jason Swanson. Swanson had been shaken to the core over the FBI interview he'd endured earlier that day and the search of his business. His voice quivered as he stammered to Redfeairn that McGiffen and Rick had been arrested. Redfeairn said nothing for a long moment, but finally uttered, "I wonder when they will come for me." After another long pause, he recovered, as if he remembered we could be listening, and added, "But I didn't do anything anyhow."

Redfeairn, whom I'd nicknamed "Teflon Ray," was good, I had to admit, but he'd come damn close that day to admitting his role. This was some consolation for me, and I at least got a good laugh out of his near slip.

Dave Hall

Jason called me to tell me about the arrests, so I called Tym, and of course he was already aware of them. When I asked why this group had been arrested, Tym said that the only thing he would tell me was that they were up to no good. I laughed and said I had figured that much out on my own. "I guess they probably weren't out collecting money for the United Negro College Fund."

Tym thought it was significant that I was among the first people Jason had called about the incident, and he urged me to keep up the good work.

I spent the remainder of the morning reading *Mein Kampf.* I had read almost half of Hitler's book by now. Although I could understand some of his views, he still came across to me as a self-serving megalomaniac. I didn't like having to read this stuff, but I wanted to impress Pastor Ray, who would be out of prison by the end of the month.

Just after lunch, Jason called again. He told me that he had just talked with Pastor Ray and they both agreed that Vince Reed had ratted on Dan and Dennis. He also told me that when the feds had searched Dennis' home they found guns and explosives, among other things.

"What kind of other things?" I asked.

He would say only that he'd fill me in when he saw me at the next meeting. He added that Ray had warned Dan and Dennis about Reed, so they should have known better than to trust him. Then Jason asked me if the FBI or ATF had tried to contact me. I told him that I hadn't heard from anyone, not even Pastor Ray.

"He won't call you from prison because the FBI is keeping a list of people that he calls and who call him. Whenever I call him, I always use a pay phone."

That amused me. Apparently this idiot didn't realize that the FBI also recorded all of Ray's phone calls.

After hanging up with Jason, I gave Tym a call to fill him in. He let me know that thanks in part to my information, the FBI had been able to thwart the New Order's plans. But he still wouldn't tell me specifically what those plans had been. Nevertheless, I had a renewed sense of purpose. Up until then I'd thought I'd been spinning my wheels and taking risks for nothing. But now, at least, I'd had some tangible results.

At the next meeting, we learned a few details, but not many. There had been some sort of bombing plot that had precipitated the arrests, but Jason wouldn't say anything more. Instead, he changed the subject, announcing that on June 6, the Aryan Nations and the KKK would be holding a joint rally at Cincinnati's Fountain Square Park and we were all required to attend.

As the meeting ended and the others filed out, I lagged behind on the pretext of going through some literature to use in upcoming propaganda flyers. I was hoping that time alone with Jason would yield additional information. He'd always been suspicious of everybody, but over the past few months it seemed like he was beginning to trust me. I believe this was partly due to my close relationship to Pastor Ray, as well as the hard work that I was devoting to my post as a propaganda minister.

I told Jason that I liked Dan and hoped he'd be able to get out of this mess. Suddenly Jason opened up. He told me that after the feds had towed his car during Dan's arrest they found a handgun under the seat, but so far they hadn't charged him with anything. He also confided that had they searched his home rather than the tattoo parlor, they'd have found a lot more. He didn't elaborate on what "a lot more" meant, but I assumed he was referring to weapons.

I asked no questions as I shuffled through a stack of papers. I had learned early on about the inherent paranoia shared by most members of the various white supremacist groups, and had developed a technique where I would lead a conversation into a particular direction, then wait for information to be given voluntarily. Using this approach, I was usually able to get more information than if I had asked direct questions. You could say this was a type of passive intelligence gathering, and it had paid off again.

Jason then mentioned a meeting with the Michigan Militia, to be held sometime after Pastor Ray's release from prison. He added that this was to be an attempt to draw not only the Michigan Militia but also other state militias under the umbrella of the Aryan Nations.

When it was clear that Jason was ready to go, I packed the literature I'd gathered into my briefcase.

After locking up the church, we headed for the parking lot. Along the way, Jason told me that he was going to try to get Pastor James Wickstrom to come to the militia meeting. I had read and heard a lot about Pastor Wickstrom, who had strong ties to the far-right militia movement and was rumored to have been one of the founders of the infamous Posse Comitatus, a militant group that recognized no government above the county level. Pastor Wickstrom lived in Michigan and had many friends in the militia there. Jason and I both agreed that if a merger occured between the Aryan Nations and the Michigan Militia, this man would be a critical part of the equation.

As I drove home, I reflected on the militia's reported membership—in the thousands—and the thought of them adopting the beliefs of the white supremacist movement chilled my bones. Yet it was beginning to seem inevitable.

Tym Burkey

When Dave told me about the attempt to form a merger between the AN and Michigan Militia, I was alarmed. "We can't let that happen," I said. Dave was the first to report this potential merger, and it was a significant turn.

"How do you propose to stop it?" he asked.

I thought for a moment and then told him, "You just keep working your magic, Dave, and we'll figure something out. I'll let the agents in Detroit know about this news. They keep asking me how I know these things before they do. I just tell them a little bird told me."

"A little bird," Dave said with a chuckle. "I think that a giant pterodactyl would be a more accurate description."

I laughed and told Dave to keep in touch.

It wasn't long before he called again to tell me about another development. It seems they were going to prepare the church for Redfeairn's return. I'd just been going over the tapes we had of Redfeairn's prison conversations, which were frustrating because he knew how to communicate in a way that made him seem cooperative while he actually remained evasive. He surely knew what his cohorts had been planning, but he'd said nothing to implicate himself. I told Dave to be extra careful.

Dave Hall

On Saturday morning I arrived at the church with mop and bucket in hand. Besides myself, Jason and Kevin Burns were the only ones there. As we cleaned and made repairs in preparation for Ray's approaching freedom, others arrived to help. It was during this event that I picked up yet another important piece of information.

As I was putting away the cleaning supplies, I noticed Jason and Kevin talking in a secluded corner. I could tell from their faces and tone that it was about something serious. Kevin left without saying good-bye, which was unusual, so I asked Jason if Kevin was all right. He told me that ever since the arrests of Dan Rick and Dennis McGiffen, Kevin's wife had been pressuring him to resign from the Aryan Nations.

"That's too bad," I said. "We can't afford to lose any more members."

Jason put his hand on my shoulder and said, "It's times like this when you find out who the truly dedicated members are."

I just nodded.

As I headed for home, it occurred to me that if Kevin did in fact quit, I would become Pastor Ray's right-hand man. It had taken me more than a year and a half to get myself into this position, and I found myself hoping that Kevin would indeed quit. He was basically a good young man who'd fallen in with the wrong crowd. I knew that Tym would like to see every last Aryan Nations member behind bars, but I secretly hoped that Kevin would escape that fate.

At church that Sunday, Jason asked if I was planning to go to the AN Youth Congress in Idaho. He said he'd already made plane reservations for himself and Pastor Ray, and if I hurried, I could possibly get on the same flight. I got their flight information for Tym—Northwest Airlines out of Columbus, Ohio, 6:00 A.M., April 16.

Tym Burkey

When Dave called me with the information, I again noticed that something was bothering him. I urged him to get himself a seat on the flight, but he hesitated. I told him to call me back when he had his reservation confirmed.

But when he called he said that flight was completely full. He'd gotten onto the flight right after that, and asked if I could find out about their return flight. Then he seemed to want to say something else, so I urged him to.

"I've got a personal problem," he said.

"What is it?"

He was quiet for a moment. Then he confessed, "I'm scared to death of flying."

I just started laughing. I couldn't help it.

"I'm glad you find something funny in that," Dave said.

"I'm sorry," I responded, still laughing, "but for the past year and a half you've been making friends with some of the most dangerous people I've ever known, and now you tell me that you're afraid to fly."

He was defensive. "Everybody is afraid of something."

"Okay, I'm sorry for laughing. Is there anything I can do to help?"

"No, I'll just have to deal with it."

I reminded Dave that Redfeairn was leaving prison that day, and asked him to call me after Redfeairn got in touch with him. He said he would, but I heard nothing from him that day, so I called him on Tuesday. Dave said he'd been to Ikes on the outside chance Redfeairn would show up there, but so far he'd heard nothing. I assured him that Redfeairn would eventually call, and that he should be prepared.

Dave Hall

That afternoon, I finally heard from Pastor Ray. Lying through my teeth, I said, "You don't know how good it feels to hear your voice again."

"You don't know how good it feels to be a free man again," Ray responded. "Can you meet me tonight at Ikes?"

I arrived at 6:00 P.M. sharp, as Ray had asked, and as I ordered a drink I looked around, but there was no sign of him. I waited, and after a couple of minutes he emerged from the bathroom with a mutual biker friend of ours. Upon seeing me, Ray raised his right hand and shouted, "Hail victory, Brother Dave!"

"Hail victory, Pastor Ray!"

He hugged me, and I could see that he was drunk, undoubtedly celebrating his freedom. Apparently Ray had also been enjoying some cocaine, because he had forgotten to wipe the white powder residue from around his nostrils. A few moments later, this mutual friend invited me to the bathroom to do a couple of lines. I told him that I shouldn't do any cocaine with Pastor Ray around. He laughed and said, "Hell, we've been doing it all afternoon." So I agreed to do a line or two, but asked him to keep it to himself.

During the course of the evening, as Ray grew drunker and more stoned, he remained careful of what he said. Each time I raised the subject of Dan's and Dennis' arrests, Ray would only say that he had warned them about having anything to do with Vince Reed. He said that he hadn't trusted Reed from the first time they'd met. But he wouldn't elaborate.

After I'd abused my liver for a few hours, the best information I could get was that Ray had only a vague idea of what Dan and Dennis had been planning. So either he hadn't been part of their scheme or he wasn't going to tell me. The meeting had produced nothing.

But two days later Ray asked me to meet him for lunch at Maggie's, a small restaurant on Dayton's north side. He wanted to talk to me, but not on the phone.

I arrived at the restaurant ahead of schedule. As I was waiting, I realized that although this place offered the best shrimp dinner in town, I wouldn't be able to order it because shrimp was on the list of foods forbidden by the Bible. Ironically, the Christian Identity beliefs held by the Aryan Nations were the same as the kosher diet observed by the Jews. I cursed my luck and ordered something else.

A quarter of an hour passed before Pastor Ray walked in. As he sat down he said that he wanted to thank me for being so loyal to the church while he was in prison. He told me that Jason Swanson had said that I was among the only members who hadn't missed a single meeting while he was away. Then he began talking about Dan and Dennis. He said that Vince Reed had urged them to create the New Order. He repeated that he'd never trusted Reed and had warned Dan and Dennis to steer clear of him, but they hadn't listened and now they were paying the price.

Once back home, I called Tym. He agreed that Ray must have known more than he was admitting about what McGiffen had been up to, but that proving it would be very difficult.

"How do you feel about wearing a wire to record your conversations with him?" he asked.

"Let me remind you," I responded, "of my two stipulations: number one, I will not under any circumstances inform on the Outlaws, and number two, I won't wear a wire. Ray checks, you know. I don't want a bullet in my head."

"I remember, but I had to ask." Changing the subject, Tym said he would check out the statement about Troy Murphy and the planned assassination of Morris Dees.

Several days later, Pastor Ray called to tell me that Kevin Burns had resigned from the Aryan Nations. He followed this by saying that I was now his number one man and he had big plans for me.

It was what Tym and I had been waiting for, but it still made me nervous. "What sort of plans?" I asked.

"We need to get you ordained as a minister. I'm impressed with your progress in your Bible study. I think you can replace me as the leader of the Ohio Aryan Nations."

"Replace you?" I truly couldn't believe what I was hearing.

"I have my own plans," Ray went on. He then told me of his dream to move to Idaho to be closer to Pastor Butler, and one day to become the AN's national leader.

I sat there with the phone in my hand, thinking that if the good pastor was in the same room with me at that moment I surely would have shot him dead. I'd been desperately hoping for some event that would give me a way out, and now Ray was telling me that I was in line to succeed him. I could feel the noose tightening around my neck.

Ray was still talking, telling me that he was happy that I was going to the Aryan Nations Youth Congress in Idaho.

I recovered and said, "I'm looking forward to meeting Pastor Butler. That will be like meeting Yahshua himself."

"I'm sure you won't be disappointed," Ray assured me. He then described the beauty of the AN compound and the surrounding countryside. He said he'd stop by in a couple of days to help me with my Bible studies, and closed with "Hail victory!"

I sat for a few moments to absorb the quickly evolving situation. If Ray did move to Idaho, I wondered, would this absolve me of the promise I'd made to Tym? Or would Tym want me to remain on as the Ohio state leader? I could only hope that the answers would be in my favor, because the investigation was undoubtedly driving me insane.

As I suspected, Tym was elated with the news of Kevin Burns' resignation.

"Maybe now Ray will confide more in you," he said.

"Well, he wants to move to Idaho and put me in charge of the church here."

That seemed to take Tym by surprise. "How close are you to becoming a minister?"

"I could drag it out a few months, pretend I don't understand things."

"Okay. Try to slow it down a little. Hopefully, Ray will slip up and we'll be able to put him away."

"I hope he slips up soon. I don't know how much longer I can put up with this crap."

"Well, look at it this way," Tym said. "If Ray does move to Idaho, he becomes Idaho's problem, and after a short while we'll just shut down the Ohio chapter."

"That would be just fine with me."

Especially because my trip to Idaho was just around the corner.

13

IDAHO IMMERSION

Tym Burkey

I wanted to be in Idaho with Dave, but I couldn't be. By this time, I'd interviewed all of the Ohio AN members, so they'd know me on sight. I had a contact for him in Coeur d'Alene, in case he ran into trouble, but he'd be deep in the heart of the AN headquarters, and if they grew suspicious of him, there would be nothing any of us could do. But I didn't tell him that. My contact was Agent Tom Norris, a Vietnam War hero who had been awarded the Congressional Medal of Honor. One of his exploits in Vietnam had become the subject of a book and movie, *Bat*21,* which chronicled the rescue of Air Force Lieutenant Colonel Iceal Hambleton after his reconnaissance aircraft was shot down. Agent Norris had been instrumental in the rescue, so he was a good man to know. Even so, I realized I'd still be worried the entire time Dave was away.

Dave Hall

Before leaving, I'd seen my doctor to get a prescription for Xanax, to help with my anxiety. I didn't want a repeat of that hospital visit

I'd made at Christmastime. I also spent the evening before the trip playing with Gary and watching old movies—the best way I had of relaxing. Gary always had a way of getting me to laugh. I also talked with my mother and she agreed to watch Gary while I was away. She was the only one besides Tym with whom I could discuss my Aryan Nations activities. Mom usually made me feel better, no matter how bad things seemed to be. She is the type of person who could whistle "Zip-a-Dee-Doo-Dah" and knit a sweater during a category five hurricane.

Tym, late as usual and nearly causing me another panic attack, finally arrived, and I got into his car. As he drove, he told me the name of the contact agent and watched as I wrote it down, along with the emergency phone number. With a puzzled look on his face, Tym asked, "What the hell kind of language is that?"

"Phoenician," I told him.

"How do you know how to write in Phoenician?"

I looked up. "Doesn't everybody?" I started laughing and explained that this was the method I'd devised to make notes. Once I knew the thousand-year-old alphabetical symbols, it was just a matter of associating them with symbols from the English alphabet.

Tym looked at me and shook his head. "You never cease to amaze me."

After a car ride that would have made Mario Andretti's hair stand on end, we pulled up in front of the airport terminal in Columbus. As I was trying to pull my fingernails out of the car's dashboard, Tym asked me if I wanted him to accompany me to the plane. I told him no, I would be all right.

"Well, be careful, then, and don't take any unnecessary chances."

"You should have told me that before I got into the car with you."

As I walked into the terminal, an intense sense of dread came over me. I could feel the beginnings of a panic attack starting, so I made my way to the nearest water fountain and took a couple of Xanax. That eventually calmed me down. Before boarding the plane, I paused and took a deep breath. Feeling like a condemned man, I entered.

Once seated, I gripped the armrests as the plane began taxiing toward the runway. I closed my eyes tight for the takeoff, but once the plane leveled off, so did I. Fortunately, the first leg was uneventful, and when I changed planes in Minnesota, I felt more confident. But then the plane went into a thunderstorm. As it pitched to and fro, with announcements from the intercom to remain in our seats with our seatbelts fastened, I fumbled with the Xanax bottle. At one point, we dropped sharply, and a few of the passengers gasped out loud. Somehow this made me feel better, not being the only one a nervous wreck. Eventually the weather subsided, but as we were coming in to the runway at the Spokane airport, a sudden wind shear pushed us violently to the right. I thought I would pass out, but we finally landed. I disembarked on rubbery legs and went to collect my luggage.

After I rented a car, I went into a gas station to call Aryan Nations headquarters for directions. Then I got on my way. Despite what I faced, I was able to notice that the scenery along the way was beautiful. It was the middle of April, but there was still snow on the mountaintops. It was hard for me to imagine such ugly sentiments being nurtured in this scenic area. Yet I knew they were.

I found the compound easily enough. At the entrance was a sign on a pole with the Aryan Nations logo, bearing the words "The Church of Jesus Christ Christian." Near it was another sign, "White Kindred Only," along with a Confederate battle flag and a Nazi flag bearing a swastika.

At the guard shack, I was greeted by an armed Aryan Nations member in full uniform. After showing my driver's license and Aryan Nations membership card, I was allowed to enter the compound. For me, it was an ominous moment. I was finally here, the place where a quarter century earlier Pastor Richard Butler had first imagined founding an all-white nation. And I was entering as a secret agent of its destruction.

As I drove to the parking area I saw other uniformed Aryan Nations members and a large contingent of skinheads. Looming over the church was a fifty-foot guard tower draped with a large Nazi flag. These people were serious. After parking, I grabbed my camera—for photographs for the flyers, if anyone asked—and made my way through the compound to find Pastor Ray and Jason Swanson. Ray was talking with a group of young skinheads. Giving me the open-hand salute, he said, "Welcome, Brother Hall. I'm sure glad that you could make it."

"Me too." I tried to sound enthusiastic.

As we walked toward a building I believed was the church, Ray told me to make sure I got pictures of the compound. He was amused by my recent trauma on the flight, and as we were talking we rounded a corner and ran into Pastor Richard Butler himself. I knew what he looked like from pictures and newscasts, but it was startling to see him in the flesh.

"Pastor Butler," Ray said, "I'd like you to meet Dave Hall. He's one of my best men from Ohio."

I held out my hand. "It's a pleasure to finally meet you, sir."

"It's always a pleasure to meet a fellow Aryan," he replied as he gave my hand a vigorous pumping, "especially one of your size, and I can tell by your handshake that you must be a descendant of the Vikings."

"Well, I am of Celtic blood, so that's entirely possible."

Butler welcomed me to the congress and moved along to talk with others, while Ray escorted me around the grounds, introducing me to a few of the people in attendance.

But after a moment, one of the Aryan Nations security team members pulled Ray aside. They talked for a minute and I could tell it was about me. I tried not to sweat. What could they have discovered? Had they gone through my car or my suitcase?

Then I heard one of them say they had run the plates on the rental car, and my name wasn't Dave Hall but John D. Hall. In irritation, Ray said, "What do you think the *D* stands for? It stands for David."

The security guy hung his head and said, "Sorry."

If this is the kind of people I'd have to deal with, I thought, *maybe this wouldn't be so hard after all.* No one that I'd yet met had struck me as highly intelligent or clever. Jesse Warfield, the head of security, came across like a semiliterate hillbilly; most of the others seemed, at best, your typical Joe Six-pack blue-collar types.

The congress was set to begin the next day, so I drove back to town to get a motel room. All along, I wondered what the next three days would bring.

Tym Burkey

Richard Butler, who once had been an aerospace engineer for Lockheed, had taken over control of the Church of Jesus Christ Christian in 1973, moving its headquarters from California to Hayden Lake in northern Idaho, and since the 1980s he'd held annual congresses at this compound. From there, he ruled the Aryan Nations and nurtured his ties with other white supremacist organizations. He'd ordained Jim Wickstrom of the Posse Comitatus, Thom Robb from the Ku Klux Klan, and Ralph Forbes, former member of the American Nazi Party and an aide to David Duke. We believed he'd supported The Order, and there were even rumors that he'd allowed them to counterfeit U.S. currency on the grounds. As a result of Matthews' death and the incarceration of the surviving members of The Order, in 1988 several AN members were indicted for conspiracy to overthrow the government, Butler among them. Yet the trial in Fort Smith, Arkansas, ended in acquittals for all. Butler then prepared the compound to become the center of a five-state whites-only nation. These congresses were his way of whipping up enthusiasm and spreading his vision.

I knew that Dave would soon be exposed to the full force of his charisma.

Dave Hall

The next morning, I donned my uniform and stopped at a local restaurant for breakfast, wondering what reaction I might get. Much to my surprise, most of the patrons were cordial, bidding me good morning. The waitress, a pretty girl, came to my table and asked, "Are you in town for the Aryan Nations gathering?"

"Yes," I responded, "I just flew in from Ohio yesterday."

"We get a lot of Aryan Nations members in here to eat. We make hamburger gravy and biscuits if you'd like to try it."

So she was aware of the dietary restrictions that prohibited such items as pork, shellfish, and mushrooms. I ordered the gravy and biscuits and threw in some eggs.

At the compound, I saw two Chevy Suburbans and a van conspicuously parked across the road from the entrance. I don't know why they didn't just put FBI logos on the doors. With the morning sun at their backs, it was easy to see through the tinted windows to the silhouettes of agents with their cameras. I knew they were photographing and filming people coming and going from the congress, as well as writing down license plate numbers. At least I had some backup close by in case of trouble.

Inside, people were just beginning to stir. I heard women in a small building that housed the kitchen, and knew they'd probably been up for hours preparing breakfast. On the surface Aryan women were held in high regard, but in actuality it was their job to take care of and obey the men and to have Aryan babies. That's pretty much all they were thought to be good for, and I had yet to meet one who seemed to mind.

Jason emerged from the barracks and joined me as I walked to the church. Once inside we looked at all the Nazi memorabilia and some of the church pamphlets. Although Jason strictly observed the dietary restrictions, that was about as far as he went concerning the religious aspects of the Aryan Nations. He left me to go get breakfast, and I headed over to greet Pastor Ray. He was at a picnic table with some skinheads. I joined them and we talked for about an hour. During this conversation, I casually glanced around to gather information. I observed many small children running and playing, some dressed in paramilitary garb and others in KKK T-shirts. I wondered what chance they had of ever forming their own opinions. Having been brainwashed since birth, they were entering a life of hate.

Then I spotted a white Cadillac entering the compound. I watched as a couple of older men and women got out and began shaking hands with the people around them.

"Come on, Dave," said Ray. "I want you to meet somebody."

As we neared the car, one of the men turned to greet Ray, and he introduced me to Pastor Neuman Britton, the AN national pastor. The man had a round face like Santa Claus, a broad smile, and a strong handshake. He then introduced one of the women, Joan Kahl. After exchanging pleasantries, Ray and I excused ourselves and returned to the picnic area.

I would find out later that I had just met the widow of Gordon Kahl, who'd been a member of the Posse Comitatus. Kahl, a skilled marksman, had served prison time for refusing to pay federal income taxes, and shortly after his release he was involved in a shootout in North Dakota that resulted in the deaths of two federal marshals. After a six-week manhunt, Kahl was cornered in a remote farmhouse in Arkansas. The ensuing gun battle resulted in the death of a county sheriff as well as Kahl. The AN had then designated him as the first martyr of the "New American Revolution."

As we went in to hear Pastor Britton's sermon, I looked around at the packed seats. Pastor Britton took the podium and urged everyone to stand, give the Nazi salute, and say, "Hail victory!" Then he welcomed us to the congress and launched into his topic. Sometimes he spoke in a gentle voice with a warm smile on his face. At other times he would scream and show off a stern, fearsome look. His sermon was mainly anti-Semitic, containing warnings and condemnation of the Jewish-run press, movies, and television. He also warned everyone about ZOG, the Zionist Occupied Government. By the end of his sermon he had whipped most of his audience into a frenzy. We all rose to our feet, saluted, and shouted several rounds of "Hail victory!"

During lunch, I sat with Jason, Pastor Ray, and three skinheads. One of them told us they were going out and "booten." I asked what he meant, and he explained that "booten" was when you go find a fag or a nigger and you kick them and stomp them with your boots. That way you don't get their blood on your hands and get AIDS. I thought, *How charming*. Pastor Ray asked me if I would man the Aryan Nations booth that afternoon, and I agreed.

At the congress, they'd set up a small flea market. I visited the skinhead booth to see the racist hard rock music CDs and T-shirts, and moved on to the KKK booth. Then, of course, there was the AN booth, where I'd be selling T-shirts, flags, buttons, and books like *The Aryan Warrior* and *The Turner Diaries*.

It took just three hours to sell everything I had. With only an hour to go for the first day, it seemed like nothing much had happened, although I knew that I was being evaluated behind closed doors. I doubted that any newcomer got in here without some sort of scrutiny, so I didn't let my guard down. As we sat in the pew for the closing ceremony, Ray and Jason said that they wanted to visit a Christian Identity church in the town of Sandpoint, Idaho, over the weekend. Jason asked me to drive.

Now it was Pastor Butler's turn. He entered the church to rousing applause and took his place at the podium. As he explained his views on the government, Jews, and the "mud races," he displayed an uncanny ability to use verses from the Bible to validate these views. I could see where Ray had acquired his style of preaching, but Pastor Butler was even more persuasive. As he continued, I felt strangely drawn into his world. I thought, *Maybe this guy is right*. I couldn't help considering that many of his points made sense. But then, like a person who catches himself dozing off, I stopped myself, reminding myself not to be pulled into these twisted ideas.

Suddenly, everyone shouted, "Hail victory!" and I jerked into alertness and realized that I had daydreamed through the last part of Pastor Butler's sermon. I quickly rose to my feet and joined in another chorus of "Hail victory." Then it was over for the day.

The next morning, I noticed the FBI vehicles still at the entrance, while inside I saw several cars parked in single file, ready to exit. Several Klansmen appeared in their formal hoods and robes. I was beginning to wonder what the hell was going on when I ran into Jason. He said that everyone was preparing to go to Coeur d'Alene for a parade and rally at one of the downtown parks. As visions of the Hamilton, Ohio, rally filled my head, I thought, *God, not again.* But I shined up my boots and was squaring away my uniform when Pastor Ray approached me.

"Brother Dave," he said, "it looks like you've been chosen for guard duty at the main gate."

I was surprised but secretly pleased. That meant I'd stay here. Trying to look disappointed, I said, "Okay, if that's the order."

"I sure appreciate it," Ray replied. "We need someone that we can trust at the main gate. You'll have to keep a log of everyone entering and leaving the compound. No exceptions."

"I think I can handle that." Secretly I was hoping for a chance to look around undetected.

I was at my post when several vehicles loaded with KKK, skinheads, and uniformed AN members left for Coeur d'Alene. I sent each car off with the open-hand salute and a chant of "Hail victory!" With the exception of a few of the women and children and an armed guard in the watchtower, the compound was empty. But the presence of the guard with his assault rifle ready kept me from looking around, so I sat on the bench by the guard shack.

Late in the afternoon, the cars began returning from the rally. I stopped and checked every car. This annoyed some, but I explained that I was following orders. I even dropped the gate and inspected the Cadillac that contained Ray, Swanson, Pastor Britton, and Pastor Butler, who commended me on my professionalism. After being relieved, I attended the closing ceremony, in which Jason was promoted to the rank of major, thanks in large part to his help with the Ohio AN chapter while Ray was "held prisoner by the Zionist Occupied Government." Then Pastor Britton took to the pulpit to shout the same hate-filled rhetoric.

Finally it was over for the day and I went back to the motel. There I made several notes using my Phoenician system, placed the paper inside the phone book, and put it into the nightstand drawer. I stood in a welcome shower before collapsing on the bed, but after trying to get some rest, I finally gave up my battle with the echoing shouts of "Hail victory!" I sat on the edge of the bed with my head in my hands and prayed I could get through the rest of the conference.

14

SIDE TRIP WITH PSYCHOPATHS

Dave Hall

At the compound the next morning, I found Pastor Ray and Jason Swanson, now a major, waiting for me in the picnic area. This was the day scheduled for our trip to Sandpoint to see another church, so we got into my rental and drove away. The mountain air was cool and crisp, flavored with the smell of the previous night's fires from those camping around the compound.

"You know," said Jason, "I really like it out here. I was thinking of moving to Spokane and opening a tattoo parlor. I think I could do pretty well, with all the skinheads out here."

"I don't blame you," I said. "I'd move out here myself if I could."

The trip was a forty-five-mile drive and the scenery along the way was breathtaking. Ray asked me how I liked the congress so far. I said, "I really like it. It's nice to be around so many people who share the same beliefs, and the sermons of Pastor Butler and Pastor Britton were fantastic." Not much else was said during the trip, and we soon arrived in Sandpoint. I noted the small shops, cafes, and restaurants that lined both sides of the main street, but there was not much else here.

Ray had directions to the church from Pastor Butler, so we arrived quickly at America's Promise Ministries. The building, which resembled an octagonal log cabin, looked relatively new. Since it was early yet, no one was around. We'd already had breakfast, and there wasn't much to do but wait.

After a few minutes, a pickup truck pulled up and we met the church janitor. He agreed to show us through the building. We all went inside, and it was a lot bigger than it had looked from outside. In the rear of the building, on shelves, sat an impressive inventory of books and cassette tapes. I also noticed a large table piled high with items packaged and ready for delivery. From the labels I could see that these packages were going out to almost every state. The church also had a catalog that listed books and cassette tapes for sale on the Christian Identity movement. Clearly, Idaho was the place to be if you really believed in this stuff. Unlike ours in New Vienna, this church was making money. Seeing a place like this, I could envision a future for the white supremacist movement. It could grow stronger and stronger, undetected, striking out the way Timothy McVeigh had done, but in full force, causing greater damage.

Pastor Ray, Jason, and I gathered a few pamphlets and other literature that explained the Church's particular views on Christian Identity. I really didn't understand what we were doing here. We hadn't come to attend the service, and it seemed like nothing in this trip was worth leaving the congress for. I wondered if Ray might be up to something else. I decided to keep an extra-watchful eye out for any unusual moves. These two were the least trustworthy of the lot.

Finally Pastor Ray said, "We really should be getting back to the compound if we want to hear Pastor Butler's ten-thirty sermon." Thanking the janitor for his courtesies, we left the church and drove back through the town of Sandpoint. Pastor Ray kept looking behind as if watching to see if someone was following, and I was beginning to feel as nervous as he seemed.

About ten miles outside of Sandpoint, Jason and Pastor Ray both announced that they needed to relieve themselves. I thought this was strange, since we'd just been in a building with bathroom facilities.

"I know where there's a state park nearby," Ray said. He instructed me to turn right at the next crossroad. This proved to be a gravel road that wound through a thick pine forest. I couldn't imagine where we were going. Soon I spotted a road sign that read "Priest River, 12 miles."

Priest River. That name rang a bell.

I searched my mind. I'd heard of it before, I was sure, and I nearly drove off the road in my effort to concentrate on the name.

Then I realized: I'd heard about a couple of Aryan Nations members and a skinhead taking a suspected informant to the woods, where they shot him in the head. That had occurred right outside Priest River.

They're on to me, I thought. *Something tipped them off and they're going to take care of me.* I was too big for them to confront head-on, the way they'd done with Bob Hill. And this was an easy place to hide a body as large as mine.

I kept driving, hoping they wouldn't see me sweat, trying to think of a plan of defense. Luckily, the day was warm, so perhaps they wouldn't realize I was nervous. But the drive felt interminable, and I kept wondering when they would make their move.

Soon we approached a picnic area with bathrooms. Pastor Ray motioned toward a parking lot near the bathrooms, and I pulled in. As we all got out, I stayed close to Jason. He was a big guy, six foot one and 225 pounds, who regularly worked out, and I knew if anything went down I would have to take him out first.

I casually picked up a stick that I saw lying on the ground, which allowed them to walk ahead and kept them in front of me. The stick had one good sharp end—useful for jamming into someone's eye.

I thought about Gary. If I disappeared, who'd take care of him? My mother was with him now, thankfully, so at least he'd be fed. Then I wondered how Tym would ever know where to find me.

I waited outside while Ray and Jason were in the bathroom, and looked around for a better weapon. Soon they emerged, talking together. I watched them, wondering if they'd made a plan while alone together. If one of them made a quick move or even looked at me cross-eyed, I'd spring.

But they passed me and headed to the car. I followed and got into the driver's side, looked at Jason in the rearview mirror, and hoped he wasn't going to try something from back there. But I didn't see anything in his hands, like a wire or a gun. I knew that Pastor Ray was uncanny, and if he truly suspected me, he'd figure out a way to catch me in an unguarded moment.

I knew I'd have to remain calm. I couldn't reach for a Xanax here, and this kind of stress could trigger another panic attack. I had to relax.

I started the car and returned the way we'd come, putting the road to Priest River behind us. I continued to listen for rustling or any sound of sudden movement. Even though I was driving, which would put them at risk if I went off the road, I still didn't trust them. For all I knew, they could have planned to throw me off guard with this ploy.

But my real fear was that they were suspicious of me, had considered killing me, but then had decided to wait for more evidence. That meant I'd have to be extra careful from here on out, at all times, even home alone.

Finally, we were back on the main highway.

We arrived at the compound without incident, except to my nerves. I walked over to a picnic table, sat down, and lit a cigarette. Had I had a close call or had I just imagined the danger? Anymore, I just couldn't tell.

I saw Pastor Butler walking from his house toward the Aryan Nations office located in a building adjacent to the church, a large German shepherd at his side. It made me miss Gary. One of Butler's associates, Mike Teague, was nearby and saw me watching the dog. He told me that Pastor Butler used to have two dogs like that, but members of the Jewish Defense League had lured one away and killed it, leaving its disemboweled carcass draped across the fence down by the road.

"That's horrible!" I exclaimed.

Teague went on to say that during an interview at a Los Angeles radio station, Irv Rubin, the head of the JDL, admitted killing the dog himself.

I didn't want to hear this. I didn't really believe it. I excused myself and went to see if I might talk with Pastor Butler in private. I entered the office, noticing pictures of Adolf Hitler, Hermann Goering, and other Nazi figures. In one corner, under a large Nazi battle flag, Pastor Butler sat at his desk, surrounded by stacks of paper and books. I greeted him and said, "If you're not too busy, I'd like to talk with you for a couple of minutes."

"I'm never too busy to talk with one of my kindred," Pastor Butler assured me. "What's on your mind?"

I sat down and asked, "Do you think we'll ever be able to establish an all-white homeland here in America?"

"Well, Dave," he replied with a kindly tone, "when my wife and I moved here to Idaho twenty-five years ago, I knew that this would be the place to establish the last great white American bastion. The Pacific Northwest has traditionally been the home of the white supremacist movement, and with good Aryan Nations members like yourself, I can see this dream coming to fruition."

"I sure hope that you're right, Pastor."

A smile came across his face as if he knew something I didn't. "I am, Dave, I am."

Somehow, I felt sorry for the man. This was obviously a dearly held dream of his, and everyone deserves to have a dream. I thought, *All that energy and obvious talent poured into the white supremacist movement, when he could have used it for good.* Of course, that's what he believed he was doing. I said, "I'm looking forward to your sermon this morning, so I'll get out of here and let you get back to work."

Feeling somewhat renewed and a little calmer, I returned to the group in front of the church. Pastor Ray said he'd been looking all over the compound for me. I told him that I had gone for a walk to admire the snow-capped mountains.

For the sermon on this last day, the attendance was about 150 people. As Pastor Butler entered the church, people applauded and shouted, "Hail victory!" A hush came over the crowd as he began to speak. He thanked everyone for attending the 1998 Aryan Nations Youth Congress, then launched into his sermon. He explained why white Aryans were the true Israelites chosen by God and the Jews were the vile children of Satan, promoting "race mixing" in an effort to destroy the white race. The audience hung on his every word.

"God said to hate your enemies with a perfect hatred! A perfect hatred! Soon there will come the day when the streets will run bridle deep with the blood of our enemies. And on that day our Savior Jesus Christ will return to lead us to our victory. Hail victory!"

"Hail victory!" Some people were in a frenzy, while others sat mesmerized, seemingly catatonic. It was disturbing to see the influence this man could exert over such a large crowd, and I tried to occupy my mind with more pleasant thoughts while maintaining an expression of rapt interest. He went on for almost an hour about the need to exterminate all Jews on the face of the earth, and I found the repetition mind-numbing. He drew to a close, and the congregation applauded and cheered, but I thought, *I feel like going out and killing someone myself after hearing all this crap!*

Afterward at lunch, as I listened to the many conversations going on around me, I realized even more clearly the power that Pastor Butler had over these people. Indeed, if it weren't for the strength of my convictions, I could imagine myself sucked into his black hole of hate.

As the conference drew to a close and I faced the trauma of getting back on a plane (for the last time, I hoped), I pondered the information I'd picked up for Tym. There was nothing new from the sermons, but I now knew that three or four different skinhead groups from Idaho, Washington, Oregon, and Montana had responded to Butler's call. The general consensus was that their mission in life was to inflict as much pain and suffering on minorities and gays as possible, and they viewed this convocation as a way to strengthen their forces. They claimed as their mentor Tom Metzger, a former grand dragon of the KKK in California who had moved to the Pacific Northwest and formed his own group, White Aryan Resistance (WAR).

Metzger had recently been put on trial in Portland, Oregon, after a few of his followers beat an Ethiopian exchange student to death. Attorney Morris Dees, cofounder of the Southern Poverty Law Center—the same Morris Dees that Dennis McGiffen and Dan Rick had recently hoped to assassinate—had sued Metzger on behalf of the student's family. Dees successfully argued that Metzger was partially responsible for the student's death because he preached and condoned violence against minorities and gays, and he obtained a $5 million judgment against Metzger. He'd used the same tactics he'd used previously against other hate groups, realizing that hitting their bank accounts effectively crippled them. Ray had told me that Dees had actually bankrupted KKK organizations and seized their assets. White supremacist groups throughout the country hated Dees, and privately many expressed the view that the assassination of Dees would be the greatest achievement any white supremacist could accomplish.

Tym knew all this, but he'd be interested in the type of people who'd attended this event. He'd also want to hear about my little "side trip." As dusk drew near, I went to the field behind the church where they were preparing for the cross-lighting ceremony. A few of the men wrapped a twenty-five-foot-long wooden cross with kerosene-soaked burlap bags. As they hoisted it into position, I could see a wooden swastika nailed to the center.

We all gathered around, and Pastor Butler appeared with a flaming torch in hand. It shone bright in the encroaching darkness, adding warmth and drama to the event. The smell of kerosene and burning cloth filled the air, and the crackling flames drew us closer. There was complete silence as Butler recited a traditional prayer, which ended with the words "As we light this cross, we bring light to the darkness in tribute to our Lord Jesus Christ." As he reached up to touch the flame to the kerosene-soaked cloth, cheers of "Hail victory" filled the night. Then one by one, people posed in front of the burning cross for pictures, as if they were tourists. I even got a picture of myself standing arm in arm with Pastors Butler and Britton. I hoped I would survive to know that they would look back on that day with deep regret. I planned to view that photo with a sense of triumph—and not the kind they espoused that night.

As I drove back toward Coeur d'Alene, I turned the car stereo up as loud as I could, but couldn't drown out the cries of "Hail victory" that echoed in my head. I stopped at a liquor store and bought a bottle of vodka, hoping I could drink these voices into oblivion. I wished I could call my mother or even Tym, but I dared not. I had not forgotten my little side trip with the psychopaths, and I knew it would be better to believe they were watching me.

That night, I drank myself to sleep. It didn't stop me from having my usual nightmare, which left me panting and sweating at 4:00 A.M., but it seemed to me that I had to be on the downside of all this. The scare I'd had the previous day was probably the worst of it.

I was glad I didn't know then what lay ahead.

I hadn't yet seen the worst.

That morning as we prepared to go to the airport, I overheard Ray talking with Pastor Butler about Larry Wayne Harris, the microbiologist and Aryan Nations member who'd been arrested in 1995 for possession of bubonic plague bacteria he'd fraudulently obtained through the mail. Shortly after Harris' arrest, Ray had stripped him of his membership but allowed him to keep attending services. Back in February 1998, Harris and another man had been arrested in Las Vegas for possession of a dangerous biological toxin, believed to be anthrax. Ray said he and a couple of guys had gone through Harris' house while he was in jail and removed anything that linked him to the church and the AN. Ray described Harris' house as a big mess,

Pastor Ray Redfeairn and Dave Hall pose with a bust of Adolph Hitler at the Aryan Nations compound at the Aryan Nations Youth Congress in Hayden Lake, Idaho, April 1998.

Coeur d'Alene Lake

The AN compound.

Pastor Ray Redfeairn and Jason Swanson at the AN compound's front gate. Note the welcome sign's last line: "WHITE KINDRED ONLY!"

Pastor Ray Redfeairn at the pulpit inside the AN church at the
Hayden Lake compound.

Dave Hall holds a sword behind the pulpit at the AN church at the Hayden Lake compound.

Jason Swanson holds the same sword.

Dave Hall; Pastor Neuman Britton, National Pastor of the AN; unidentified woman; and Pastor Richard Butler, the founder and head of the AN, pose before a burning cross embellished with a swastika.

The burning cross/swastika that signified the close of the Hayden Lake conference.

Dave Hall in uniform and
on gate duty at the Hayden
Lake compound.

Nazi party emblem, hung
on a wall of one of the
compound's buildings.

Dave Hall and Jason Swanson standing on either side of the pulpit at the AN church.

Jason Swanson and Dave Hall in front of the AN church.

Pastor Ray Redfeairn and Jason Swanson in front of the Christian Identity church in Sandpoint, Idaho. This picture was taken just before the return trip to the AN compound. The stop at the Priest River State Park occurred approximately thirty minutes after this picture was taken.

Pastor Ray Redfeairn arrives at a white supremacist wedding, at which he will officiate, in Serro Gordo, Illinois, August 1998.

Dave Hall, Pastor Ray Redfeairn, and the couple about to be married,
all giving the Nazi salute.

The wedding ceremony, in front of a burning cross flanked by
two burning swastikas.

The newly married couple embraces.

Pastor Ray Redfeairn in his
hotel room at the Feast of
the Tabernacles in Athens,
Tennessee, October 1998.

Dave Hall, Pastor Neuman
Britton, Pastor Ray
Redfeairn, and attendees
at the conference.

The Warrior's Ransom Ceremony, performed by Pastor
Neuman Britton.

Jason Swanson and Dave Hall pose before a Confederate flag
at the Feast of the Tabernacles.

with cages stacked everywhere containing dogs, cats, and mice, and said that he and the others were afraid to touch some of the things, fearing contagion, an explosion, or worse. Nevertheless, they'd managed to remove a truckload of stuff from Harris' house. I knew that Tym would find this interesting.

Despite my fear, the flight went smoothly and after a few hours we descended into the Minneapolis–St. Paul airport. We had a six-hour layover, so Jason, Ray, and I went looking for something to eat. This seemingly simple chore became an enormous problem because Jason refused to eat anyplace where minorities worked, and we kept seeing blacks, Hispanics, or Asians at the counters. After an extensive search, we found a small sandwich shop where the staff was all white. After placing our orders, we were given a small plastic number to put on our table. Our food, we were told, would be brought to us. We talked as we waited, and soon a young Chinese man appeared with a tray of food. He stopped right in front of our table, which made both Pastor Ray and me burst out laughing, but Jason was furious with us. We apologized, and he calmed down enough to eat his food—although he clearly wasn't happy about the person who had touched his plate.

Later as we waited to board, Jason's pager went off. There were several pay phones right near where we were sitting, but he opted to walk to the other side of the waiting area to use a phone there. After about ten minutes, he returned and informed us that he'd just talked with Troy Murphy, the imperial wizard of the KKK in central Indiana. I'd met Murphy at the Hamilton rally and had assumed that he'd been arrested along with Dan Rick and Dennis McGiffen, but apparently he was out on bail. Jason said that Murphy had told him that the feds had been handing down more indictments connected with the Dennis McGiffen case. Murphy believed that the government's case was falling apart and that the indictments were merely an attempt to scare someone into talking. Ray told us not to worry and that he would do some checking into it when we got home.

We got home all right, despite some turbulence that scared the living daylights out of me, and Jason drove us back to Dayton. He wove in and out of traffic, mostly at speeds in excess of ninety miles per hour, and I was a nervous wreck when they finally dropped me at my house around 3:00 A.M. I opened the door and smelled bacon frying.

My mother, who'd stayed with Gary while I was gone and knew when I'd be back, had prepared breakfast. I hugged her as Gary went crazy, jumping on me and wagging his tail. I hugged him, too.

"How was the trip?" Mom asked

"Don't ask."

After she was satisfied I couldn't eat another bite, she left and I went to bed. Safe at home with my faithful dog breathing evenly by my side, I drifted off to sleep. A bad dream woke me, but I was able to return to welcome darkness for a couple more hours.

Tym Burkey

When Dave called with information from the weekend, he apologized for being groggy, as he hadn't gotten much sleep over the past few days.

"I didn't, either," I told him. "I'm just glad you're back."

He thanked me for being concerned and then told me what he'd learned. I stopped him occasionally to ask more questions and make my own notes. When Dave related the side trip into the state park, I grew concerned. "I believe I'd have been sweating bullets myself, Dave," I assured him.

"I wasn't far from it. At first I was nervous, but then an eerie feeling of calm came over me and I resigned myself to expect the worst. If I'd seen anything on their part that alarmed me, I planned to kill them both."

I wasn't sure what to say. Of course I couldn't sanction such violence, but I did understand how he felt. "I'm glad it never came to that."

"Me, too."

"The Bureau really appreciates what you're doing, Dave, and so do I."

"You could thank me best by putting these maniacs out of business."

"With your help," I replied, "that's just what we plan to do."

I told him to go get some sleep, but I worried about the impact of four full days of exposure to these hatemongers. I didn't tell him until later that two FBI agents from the Spokane office had been on the plane with him, Jason, and Ray, doing surveillance the whole time, even during their layover in Minneapolis. I suppose he could have used them to better effect on his side trip, but it was good to know that on this plane trip at least, Ray and Jason could not have touched him without agents jumping right in.

Still, I was worn out myself from the tension. Dave was getting us a lot of good information, but we had a long way to go, and if Redfeairn was suspicious, it would be even more dangerous for Dave. I had to get him more expense money so that he could see that we were backing him all the way. Perhaps the most valuable piece of information was Dave's contact with Butler. This was another step up in the ranks. I was as frustrated as Dave regarding putting these guys away, but Dave's actions were bringing the goal closer.

Around the same time, April 1998, I was fortunate to be able to interview Cheyne Kehoe with other FBI agents. The Kehoe brothers had finally been caught the previous July after a nationwide manhunt, and Cheyne had been convicted of the assault on a police officer, receiving a twenty-five-year sentence. Chevie, too, was convicted, but he would stand trial later as well for three counts of murder in another incident. He remained a suspect in a bombing in a courthouse in Spokane, Washington, and of killing an associate.

Cheyne was tall and lean, looking like any twenty-one-year-old. I found him likable, in fact, and he reminded me of a farm kid, like those I'd grown up around. He did not look or act like a cold-blooded cop shooter and proved to be open and willing to talk. In his prison blues, he seemed more a fit for a school dormitory than a prison.

During the discussion, it became apparent that Chevie, the older of the two, controlled Cheyne. As good-natured as Cheyne appeared, Chevie was the equivalent in being cold and calculating. Although the pair had traveled together, Chevie had kept Cheyne out of his business, using him when he needed him. Cheyne claimed Chevie would leave to conduct business, which largely involved selling firearms at various gun shows. He also said he did not know Redfeairn, but we weren't sure we believed that. "Willing to talk" does not necessarily mean "willing to tell the truth." We did learn that Cheyne and Chevie had previously traveled to various white supremacist compounds, including the Aryan Nations headquarters in Hayden Lake and Elohim City, a Christian identity sect in Oklahoma. Chevie, it seemed, was more involved with the AN than Cheyne.

Despite what Cheyne told us (and didn't tell us), it was my belief that on the day of the shootout that had gotten them into trouble, the Kehoes were heading to see Redfeairn to sell him some firearms. The timing was right: the Columbus rally had been scheduled for the next day, and we had evidence from the AN factions that Redfeairn had wanted to buy guns.

At any rate, it was an interesting experience to interview Cheyne. Even if he wasn't as violent as his brother, I was glad we had him locked up for a good long time. But there were too many others still out there, still plotting and arming themselves, still preparing for what they viewed as an inevitable uprising.

15.

NO RETURN

Dave Hall

Tym called to assure me of reimbursement for my expenses from the trip and to ask about the photos I had taken. He'd never seen pictures of the Aryan Nations compound and was anxious to do so. But after hanging up, my hands started shaking uncontrollably. Soon I began sweating profusely and hyperventilating, and a feeling of intense dread came over me. Confused, I struggled to the kitchen sink and splashed some cold water on my face. Leaning on the edge of the counter, I tried to control my breathing. I thought I might pass out, but after a few minutes I began to calm down. When the spell had passed, I made my way back to the living room and collapsed into a chair. I felt like I'd just run up ten flights of stairs. Gary came over and laid his head in my lap. He remained quiet. He knew something was wrong.

I'd suffered a couple of episodes like this in recent weeks, but not nearly of this magnitude. It seemed much worse than a panic attack. Fearing that something could be wrong with my heart, I called my doctor. He advised me to go to the emergency room and said he wanted to see me on Monday.

Although I was still a little weak, I was feeling better, so I decided to forgo the trip to the emergency room. Instead, I just went back to bed. As I looked at the walls of my bedroom, I realized it was no wonder I had stress and nightmares. They were adorned with Nazi battle flags and other memorabilia, including a large picture of Adolf Hitler given to me by Pastor Ray. I wondered if actors who played the same characters for a long time ever got lost in them like this.

Later that day, Pastor Ray asked if he could ride with me to church on Sunday, to inspect the electrical system and get the building ready for meetings again. This was potentially a good situation because it was an hour-long drive—two hours round trip—alone with Ray. He'd been showing more trust in me since he'd gotten out of jail, but I knew he'd never entirely trust anyone. And there was always the possibility that he really *didn't* trust me, and thus wanted to keep a close eye on me. I hadn't forgotten our side trip to Priest River.

It was raining on that last Sunday in April. I packed my Bible, Bible study course, and, last but not least, my .357 Smith and Wesson revolver. As I looked at the contents of my briefcase, I shook my head. Insanity.

I picked Ray up, and almost immediately he mentioned Morris Gulett. He said that Mo could be getting out of jail soon, and added that though he'd been denied pastoral visits, he and Mo had kept in contact through the mail and by telephone. Ray had made no secret of his disappointment with Mo over his last brush with the law, and I wondered if Mo would be allowed back into the Aryan Nations. I decided not to ask.

Soon the topic turned to my Bible studies. As we discussed the Aryan Nations views on the Good Book, Ray seemed impressed with the progress I'd made. He thought I'd be ready to become a minister in no time. Yet I had to remember that Tym wanted me to stall.

We stayed at the building for a brief time and then drove back to Dayton. Ray confided in me that he had gotten a letter from Bob H., who'd accused Dan Rick of being an FBI informant. Clearly upset, Ray said, "Here we have a brother sitting in prison for doing something that he believed in, and I'm not going to put up with this nonsense from anybody, especially Bob. I think we're going to have to pay him a visit."

"Just let me know when," I said.

I knew what Ray was capable of, and I figured that if I was along, maybe I could keep him from killing poor Bob. But I also realized that Ray might ask me, because of my size, to do the dirty work for him. I hoped it wouldn't come to that. I simply wasn't ready to face that kind of test.

When I told Tym the next morning that there was no news, he said it was time to "stir the pot" again. He used this phrase whenever he was going to interview Ray just to shake him up.

"Oh no," I said. "What are you going to do now?"

"Special Agent Bob Hlavac and I are going to spend the day traveling the area, interviewing Aryan Nations members. We'll go to three or four members, including you, and then move on to Ray."

"That oughta get everyone's blood pumping."

"It can't hurt."

It started quickly. About 11:00 A.M., I got a call from Kevin Burns, who had quit the AN back in March. He told me that the FBI had just left his place. I asked him what they wanted and Kevin said that they were trying to get him to say something about Dan Rick.

"Did you tell them anything?"

"No. I called Pastor Ray and he said not to say anything."

Kevin lived only about a mile from me, so I knew that Tym and Bob would be at my house soon. I decided to give them a surprise.

Tym Burkey

SA Bob Hlavac and I came up to Dave's house as part of the plan. If anyone was keeping an eye on him or might ask him, he could say that he, too, had been subjected to an FBI "home invasion." These visits also gave me a chance to spread disinformation, as well as getting the AN to focus on us or each other instead of on blowing things up. I pulled out my ID and knocked on the door.

I didn't expect anything more than a brief, pleasant conversation, but when Dave answered, I was speechless. He wore a black T-shirt with a large white swastika on the front and "White Power" printed in large letters underneath. At size 4XL, it made quite an impression.

"May I help you?" he asked.

Bob was smiling ear to ear, on the verge of laughing out loud. Dave just stood there grinning, and I clenched my teeth to keep from laughing. This was supposed to be a serious interview. I fought to keep my composure as I went through the routine questions.

"I'll get you back for this," I said through gritted teeth. I put my business card in his hand and we left. Once we were in the car, Bob roared, and I let it out, too. Dave was having his joke on us, but secretly I was relieved that he still had a sense of humor.

I knew that the phone lines between Redfeairn and the others would be abuzz that afternoon, and I looked forward to my visit with him. I interviewed him regularly and I knew it annoyed him, but it also gave me an advantage. If I ever did come to arrest him, he wouldn't expect it and I could take him by surprise.

Redfeairn was cocky that day, as usual, and full of himself. He even asked me if I was German.

"I'm American," I said.

"You have blue eyes, so you're Aryan." He added that I'd be welcome at his church anytime. It was a blatant and sloppy attempt to recruit an FBI agent to his cause. That man had a lot of gall.

Around this same time, I interviewed Kale Kelly just before his release from prison for the concealed weapon charge. During the interview, Kelly was clear he did not like federal law enforcement, especially the FBI. He was threatening but stopped short of making a direct threat toward me, yet he repeated several times, "If you're not for us, you're against us." I took his veiled threats seriously.

Dave Hall

When Ray called again that day, he speculated that the case against Dan Rick and Dennis McGiffen was falling apart, so the feds had been on a fishing expedition. He added that if the FBI ever came to see me again, I should not let them into my house unless they had a warrant.

"I know how to handle the feds," I assured him.

The next Sunday, I took Ray to the church again. He mentioned that the Aryan World Congress would be held July 17 at Hayden Lake, with a large parade of kindred carrying flags of various Aryan countries through Coeur d'Alene. The Aryan Nations had long been a thorn in the side of the good people of Coeur d'Alene, and I was sure they weren't looking forward to it. But I wasn't keen about another plane ride. I hoped I could think of a way out.

Then Kale Kelly was released from prison. Ray asked for a ride to church, where we were going to meet him. I recalled the first time I'd seen Kelly in February 1997, well over a year ago. He'd been the armed uniformed man on the church roof, scouring the surrounding area with binoculars. Barely a week later, Kelly was in jail, so I'd never gotten to know him. Over the past few months, Ray had mentioned him several times, declaring him a prisoner of the war against ZOG.

When Ray and I pulled into the parking lot, I saw a brown van at the rear of the church. It had distinctive markings and bumper stickers, and I instantly recognized it as a van belonging to old Joe Hobbes, a frequent visitor to the church. Joe's daughter Sandy exited the passenger side and greeted us. It turned out she was Kale Kelly's girlfriend. Kale then exited the driver's side and gave Ray and me the customary salute. Ray hugged him, saying, "It's good to have you back, Brother!" Then he reminded Kale who I was.

As we shook hands, Kale said, "It's good to see you again, Dave. Ray told me how you helped to hold the church together."

"It wasn't just me," I said, "we all worked at it."

Sensing that Ray wished to talk with Kale privately, I walked over to talk with Sandy. After about ten minutes Ray, Kale, Sandy, and I went into the church to get some of Kale's personal items from storage—mainly camping equipment. Kale said that he was so sick of being locked up that he was planning to camp out for a while. He added that he was contemplating a road trip out west to check out the Four Corners Militia, one of the largest in the country. I wondered what he might really be doing, but he didn't reveal any more details.

When others arrived, Kale and Sandy left, and we all went in to have a service. Ray asked me to give the traditional opening prayer. It was the first time I'd been invited to do this, and I was nervous. I walked up and stood behind the pulpit. I took a moment or two, looking into the faces of the parishioners. After collecting my thoughts, I called them all to their feet. I then said, "Welcome to the Church of Jesus Christ Christian, and in Yahweh's name we say 'Hail victory!'" I thrust my right hand up in the Nazi salute. "Yahweh, please bless those in attendance today as well as all our brothers and sisters everywhere, especially those being held prisoner in the gulags of the Zionist Occupied Government. Yahweh, we also ask that you give us the strength to endure and pursue your cause. We now ask that you anoint the words of Pastor Redfeairn as he delivers the message today. In Yahshua's name we say, 'Hail victory!'"

"Hail victory!"

I then said, "Kindred, I give you Pastor Ray Redfeairn."

As I took my seat at the front of the congregation Pastor Ray stepped to the pulpit. After thanking me for my introduction, he began his sermon. It basically consisted of the same crap I'd heard a hundred times before. As he slowly whipped the small group of followers into the usual frenzy, I recalled again his similarity to Pastor Richard Butler.

Afterward, most everyone discussed the arrests of Dennis McGiffen, Dan Rick, and the other members of the New Order. It seemed as if each person had his own conspiracy theory. It was clear that the arrests had created a heightened air of paranoia.

Then I learned that John Graham had quit. "He decided to go back to the National Alliance," said Ray, adding that John was an atheist at heart and just couldn't get into the religious aspects of the Aryan Nations. Ray went on to tell me that he believed that John's real reason was the arrests.

As Ray and I prepared to leave, another car pulled in. It was Jeff Courtney and four of his National Socialist followers. Jeff was a leader of the northern Kentucky branch. All of these men were in their early twenties, and the one named Mike was bragging about the FBI coming to his home to interview him for handing out hate literature. Jeff's friends laughed as they told us of a recent incident. Apparently they had been visiting friends in Cincinnati and when they left for home an Ohio state trooper started following them down the Interstate. One boy said that they were nervous as hell because they had ten AK-47s in the trunk, along with eight thousand rounds of ammunition. The trooper had followed them across the bridge from Ohio to Kentucky, then took the first exit off the freeway, which made them all laugh so hard they almost wrecked the car.

Tym Burkey

I was concerned when Dave reported this conversation. "We can't have these guys driving around with a trunkload of assault rifles and ammunition," I said. I asked questions, hoping to pin down their identities, but Dave didn't have much.

"I'm sorry I can't give you more to work with," he said.

"That's all right. The FBI should be able to ID these guys."

Dave added that Ray had gone up to Detroit, supposedly to pick up some carpentry work from Jason Swanson.

"Do you think he's telling the truth?" I asked.

"Your guess is as good as mine. He does go up there a lot."

I told Dave, who was about to go fishing, to keep his pager on. He seemed as disappointed as I was that nothing much had happened over the past few months. Perhaps the paranoia had cooled some plans, or perhaps they'd been taken deeper underground. I wanted to believe that Dave was a trusted member and would eventually be informed, but no one really knew that for certain.

Then we got a name—the young man with the car full of assault rifles was Mike. I had spoken with the special agent out of the Cincinnati office, who'd interviewed Mike for passing out hate literature in the area, and that led to Mike's associates. But we still didn't know if they were planning something.

Dave Hall

On Sunday morning I picked up Pastor Ray and headed for New Vienna. During the long drive, Ray confided that he had covert members in Toledo, Akron, Zanesville, and Cleveland. He said these individuals never attended the church because they believed the FBI had it under surveillance. He sent them videotapes of his sermons.

Ray added that the Idaho compound had been raided and Pastor Butler was sprayed with pepper spray. He thought the whole thing started when Butler kicked out two rowdies at the church. These individuals went to the police, telling them that people were being held at the compound against their will. Ray told me that the police tore the place apart but found nothing.

"It is a pitiful shame," I said, "when the police feel that they have to pepper-spray an old man in his seventies."

"That's okay," said Ray. "They'll pay for it when the final war comes. Yes, Brother Dave, there will come a day when the streets will run bridle deep with the blood of our enemies."

"Hail victory!" I shouted.

Ray said he felt guilty about Dan, Dennis, and the others being in jail but that he had warned them about his suspicions that Vince Reed was an informant. Changing the subject, he said, "Kale's a solid brother. He served in the Gulf War as a sergeant in the army. He's had explosives and sniper training. He can hit anything he can see. As soon as we build our membership back up and find a larger compound, I'd like you and Kale to design a military-style training program."

"That can be easily done," I responded. "Kale could handle firearms training and with my martial arts background I could handle hand-to-hand combat training. And you, Pastor Ray, can handle the spiritual training."

Ray smiled and said, "That sounds like a good plan, Brother Dave."

We were approaching the outskirts of New Vienna when I turned to Ray and said, "Maybe this is none of my business, but I know that Morris Gulett has been out of prison for two weeks now, and I was wondering why he hasn't been to church."

Ray shook his head and said, "The first thing Mo did when he got out of jail was grab a crack pipe and a liquor bottle."

"Man, I sure hate to hear that," I said.

"If it would have been anyone else, they would have been kicked out of the Aryan Nations long ago. But I've been friends with Mo since high school and I just keep hoping that he'll get himself straightened out. I know someday I'm going to have to put my foot down."

"When that crack gets a hold of you, you're in big trouble," I said. "I have a cousin that has been addicted to that poison for over ten years."

Kale Kelly was at the church, loading a box into his van. Apparently, he had his own key. As we started up the stairs, I saw him looking at my pistol.

"You ever seen one of these?" I asked. I handed the pistol and holster to him. "That's a .357 Magnum Smith and Wesson that comes with a little surprise."

"What's that?"

"Pop out the cartridge chamber."

Upon doing so, Kale said, "Wow, this holds seven bullets."

"Just when they think you've run out of bullets," I said with a smile, "you've got a little surprise for them."

Handing the pistol back to me, Kale said, "That's a nice weapon, Brother, but I prefer a nine-millimeter automatic because they hold more rounds."

"I like a revolver because at twenty-five yards I can shoot the buttons off your shirt, but I couldn't hit the broad side of a barn with an automatic."

After Kale left, Pastor Ray and I went back into the church. I was getting a couple of my recruiting flyers out of my briefcase when I saw Ray coming out of the storeroom. He handed me a thick envelope, which turned out to contain a large number of photographs, and said, "Can you find a safe, dry place where you can hide these for me?" he asked. "I wouldn't want the feds finding those here in the church."

It might be a real bonanza, but I had to act as if I didn't care. "What exactly are these?" I asked.

Ray smiled. "You are holding pictures of a map of the entire eastern United States power grid. Those pictures map out every nuclear plant, hydroelectric plant, steam-generating plant, and switching station east of the Mississippi."

"Wow, that's wild."

"Just put them somewhere safe," Ray said, "and don't lose them."

"Don't worry," I said, "I've got just the place for them." I turned my back and cracked a smile as I put the photographs in my briefcase and locked it. I knew I could convince Tym to protect them.

Tym Burkey

That first Monday in June, I drove to meet Dave. He'd said he had something to show me but wouldn't specify what it was. I'd agreed to meet him at our usual place behind the school. When I got there—after him, as usual—he handed me a packet. Inside were photographs. I looked at him.

"Go ahead," he said. "See what they are."

I pulled one out. It had been taken at a distance and showed a large map measuring, I estimated, about six by six feet. Across the top of the map was "Tennessee Valley Authority Eastern Power Grid." Whoa. I knew we had some good stuff here. The remaining photographs were close-up shots of each quadrant, showing in great detail the locations of various nuclear, hydro, and steam power plants, as well as all the routing and switching stations.

After I looked at several, I said, "Holy shit, Dave. Where did you get these?"

"Pastor Ray gave them to me," he said with a pleased look, "and told me to keep them in a safe place because he didn't want the feds to find them at the church."

I shook my head. He knew he'd made a real catch with this stuff. "Damn, Dave, these show the location of every power plant on the eastern seaboard."

"I know. I studied each and every one last night. How do you think Ray got hold of those?"

"I don't know," I said, "but I'm damn sure going to find out. Do you mind if I borrow these long enough to make some duplicates?"

"Go ahead, but return them as soon as you can, in case Ray wants them back."

"I can get them to you tomorrow."

"That'll work."

I truly was impressed. "This is good work. It's exactly what we need. Now we have some idea of what they may be planning."

I think Dave really felt proud of himself, as well he should have.

As soon as I could, I made some calls. Among other things, I learned that the Tennessee Valley Authority doesn't make copies of its power grid plan available to the general public.

Dave Hall

I went out to Ikes that evening, and when I arrived, there were more motorcycles than usual parked out front. I quickly learned they were having a birthday party for one of the Outlaws. The bar was filled with drunken bikers and, of course, bare-chested women. I had no sooner sat down when a well-endowed young lady came up behind me and wrapped her breasts around my head like a pair of earmuffs. I could see Tigger laughing at me as he made my drink. By the time he brought it the young lady had moved along, no doubt to warm up another pair of cold ears.

"Dr. Dave, this place is driving me fucking nuts!" said Tigger. "There's already been a couple of fights tonight. I guess I should be grateful nobody's gotten killed yet."

"The night is young," I replied.

"I appreciate your optimism."

As I looked around the bar it reminded me of the movie *Animal House,* only X-rated. It wasn't long before I was half-assed drunk myself and joining in the festivities, but I wasn't looking for trouble. I was sitting at the bar talking with a little sweetheart when a neighborhood crackhead walked up, grabbed my drink, and proceeded to chug it down. I was having a good time, so I just brushed it off and ordered another. Tigger set the drink in front of me, and again the crackhead picked it up and started to drink it. I excused myself with the young lady, then turned and snatched my drink from his hand. "Buy your own fucking drink, asshole!" I growled.

The crackhead said, "Fuck you!" then drew back to hit me.

I raised my right leg and came down as hard as I could with my combat boot right on the top of his foot. The poor guy let out a scream that got the attention of the entire bar. He fell to the floor and lay there for a few moments, clearly in pain, before struggling to his feet and limping out the front door. Everything returned to normal, and I hoped that would be my only unpleasant encounter.

But half an hour later, I was talking with my Outlaw friend Carl when out of the corner of my eye I saw the crackhead back in the bar and limping in my direction. I spun around on my barstool just in time to feel the barrel of a revolver firmly pressed against my forehead.

"Whatcha gonna do now, big man?" he said.

He had me. I didn't dare move.

Carl yelled, "Hey, asshole!"

As the crackhead turned to look at him, I grabbed the gun, which luckily wasn't cocked, and stripped it from his hand. I then grabbed his jacket collar and hit him with the gun butt two or three times across the face. He fell to the floor with blood spurting from his nose. I sat back down on the stool and looked at Carl. "That was a close one," I said. "Thanks."

"I'll take care of this worthless son of a bitch," Carl said. He got up and proceeded to kick the guy the twenty feet to the front door. There, Carl picked him up and said "This is an Outlaws bar, and if you ever show your face around here again, you'll be one dead motherfucker." He threw the guy out onto the sidewalk. With that, the party resumed as if nothing had happened. I turned back around and asked Tigger to make me a double.

"That was a nice move, Dr. Dave," Tigger said as he handed me my drink.

"Thanks. And here, you can have this." I handed him the gun. He took it and shoved it under the bar. I stayed for a couple more drinks, then decided I'd better head for home. I didn't need a DUI, and I figured that I'd used up my luck for the night.

16

SUMMER OF HATE

Tym Burkey

On June 7, 1998, in Jasper, Texas, three white men offered a ride to a forty-nine-year-old black man, James Byrd Jr., who was on his way home from an anniversary party. Instead of taking him where he wanted to go, they beat, kicked, and tortured him, then spray-painted his face black before chaining him by the ankles to the back of their truck. As they sped down an isolated logging road, dragging him for nearly three miles, he tried keeping his head up, but his skin shredded, his bones broke, and his elbows shattered. When his head hit a culvert, it was ripped off, along with his right arm.

What was left of his torso was dumped in front of a church for a black congregation to find. Investigators found parts of his skin, clothing, and body at more than thirty locations along the road.

Dave Hall

When I arrived at church, most of the parishioners were standing at the foot of the stairs at the rear of the building. They all saluted and said "Hail victory!" as I approached. John Graham was there with six or seven of his National Alliance and National Socialist buddies, and there were four older men I recognized as KKK members from Chillicothe, Ohio. As I joined them, John said, "Hey, Dave, did you hear about those boys that killed that nigger down in Texas?"

"Yeah," I replied. "What a drag."

They laughed. As I climbed the stairs, I heard them making their own disgusting jokes. After wiping my feet on the Israeli flag, I headed for the room at the rear to change into my uniform. The old wooden floor creaked, and when Pastor Ray heard it he yelled, "Who's out there?"

"It's Dr. Dave, Pastor Ray."

"Welcome, Brother," said Ray. "I'm working on my sermon and I'll be out in a few minutes."

As I put on my uniform, I thought about the members we'd lost. The arrests of Dennis McGiffen and Dan Rick had prompted Steve, Andy, and Kevin to quit. Gulett had become a crackhead. Kale Kelly, released from prison, never attended services, and Frank Johnson had left the Aryan Nations after a dispute of some kind with Ray. I knew that Jason Swanson was planning to move to Spokane. Through the process of elimination, I would soon be the number two man in the Aryan Nations east of the Mississippi. Just what I'd always wanted.

Pastor Ray began the service by calling our attention to the incident in Texas.

"No doubt all of you have heard the news out of Jasper, Texas," he said, "about three young Aryan men chaining a nigger to the bumper of their pickup truck and dragging him to death. I think this is a terrible, terrible thing." He paused for a moment and let the room swell with confusion. "I think this was a terrible thing because they had to have had at least enough room for six more niggers on that bumper!"

Everyone around me burst out laughing. I have to admit I let out a chuckle or two myself.

"I couldn't care less about a dead nigger," Ray continued, "but now we have three good young Aryan men going to prison, and they'll probably be put to death for killing one stupid nigger! As far as I am concerned, there aren't any ten thousand niggers worth one Aryan's life."

This statement drew cries of "Hail victory" and "Rahowa" from the crowd.

Ray went on ranting and raving for almost an hour. I didn't stay long afterward. That day, their celebration of wanton cruelty was too much for me.

A week later, I arrived at the church to find Ray in discussion with Kale Kelly and his girlfriend. As I joined them, Kale told us he'd been camping out in the woods near East Fork State Park down in Clermont County, Ohio, living off the land, fishing and eating turtles, frogs, and snakes.

"You know, you're breaking the Bible's food laws by eating that stuff," Ray commented.

Kale shrugged this off. "I don't know if I told you this, Pastor, but Tym Burkey came to interview me in jail just before I got released."

"Who's Tym Burkey?" I asked.

"He's an FBI agent that harasses white supremacists."

"Oh yeah," I replied, "I remember now. He's that guy that came to my house. There was another agent with him whose name I can't remember, but he looked like Peter Lorre."

"That's Bob Hlavac," said Ray.

Kale started laughing and said, "You know, I never thought about it, but he does look like Peter Lorre."

Ray asked me to keep Sandy company while he discussed something with Kale.

I kept my eye on them as they went to Kale's car. He opened the door and got something from under the seat. They both leaned inside, and Kale showed him what appeared to be a handgun. After a moment, Kale put it back under the seat and closed the door. That's when Sandy and I went down the stairs to join them. As we walked up, Ray was asking Kale if he was going to the Aryan Nations World Congress in July. Kale said he was thinking about making a road trip out to the Four Corners area in the Southwest to check out the militia, then continue up to Idaho for the congress. Ray looked at me and said, "Brother Dave, can you go to the congress?"

"At this point, I just don't know," I replied. "I'd like to go, but I don't know if I'll be able to afford it." But of course the truth was that there was no way in hell that I was ever getting back on another airplane.

Tym Burkey

I had wanted Dave to attend the World Congress in Idaho, but he was adamant that he would not. He used the excuse that he thought Ray would get suspicious if he was able to afford two such trips in a matter of months, but I knew his fear of flying was uppermost in his mind. I relented. I couldn't very well pressure him. Dave was doing well for us, and I'd always told him it was his call how he got involved. I'm sure that Redfeairn certainly might wonder how Dave could afford to travel to Idaho.

But a week before the July event, something happened in Idaho that would have major repercussions throughout the AN, and eventually for Dave.

A local woman and her son, Victoria and Jason Keenan, were driving by the front gate of the Aryan Nations compound when their car backfired. Apparently the guards believed they were under attack, so they pursued the pair and forced their car off the road. They then beat Ms. Keenan and her son with rifle butts before telling them, "We're going to let you live only because you're white."

That beating of innocent citizens had been a serious error of judgment. They'd left themselves wide open for arrest, negative publicity, and a damaging lawsuit. Paranoia was finally proving to be the organization's undoing.

Dave Hall

I received a message to meet Pastor Ray at Ikes during the late afternoon. This was out of the ordinary, and I was wondering what was on his mind. I had just ordered my first drink when he walked in. Ray walked past the dozen or so drunks and joined me at the bar, saying, "Hail victory, Brother Dave."

I returned his greeting. "So what's up, Pastor Ray?"

He shook his head. "It seems we have an infrastructure problem at the headquarters out in Idaho."

I pricked up my ears. "What kind of problem?"

"Do you remember Jesse Warfield?"

"Yeah, I met him at the Youth Congress."

"I don't know all the details yet," said Ray, "but it seems that a few days ago Jesse and a couple of the other AN security guards were drunk and they assaulted a couple of people down on the road in front of the compound."

"Why the hell did they do that?"

"I don't know," said Ray. "I tried to tell Pastor Butler when we were there that Jesse was going to be nothing but trouble, but apparently he didn't listen to me."

"Did they get arrested?" I asked.

"I guess the cops came to the compound looking for them, but they had already taken off. I don't know if they've been arrested or not."

"Sounds like a mess to me."

"I was going to go to Idaho on the fifteenth," said Ray, "but I may have to go sooner to try to straighten this mess out."

"Those idiots shouldn't be drinking on church property, anyhow," I retorted.

Then Ray changed the subject. "Do you know if Greyhound or UPS X-rays shipping boxes?"

I shrugged. "I don't know. Why?"

"Just between you and me, I was thinking about sending a gun out to Idaho."

Without thinking I said, "What for?" Then I immediately said, "No, don't tell me. I don't want to know."

Pastor Ray just smiled.

I gave the matter some thought and told him, "You know, you could disassemble the gun, then wrap all the individual parts in aluminum foil. This would disguise them so you could ship them in separate boxes. Once you got to Idaho you could then reassemble the gun."

"Brother Dave," Ray said, "you're a genius."

I took a sip of my drink and thought, *I can't believe I just told that maniac how to get a gun out to Idaho.* I could only hope that I didn't wind up getting somebody killed. I made a mental note to mention this to Tym, so they could keep a watchful eye on Ray.

Three weeks went by before I heard from Pastor Ray again, and when I did he asked me to meet him at the Outlaws clubhouse. It was only two blocks from my place, so I walked. I saw Pastor Ray's car parked in J.D.'s driveway, across from the clubhouse, so I figured they were probably snorting coke together. I walked up to the clubhouse gate, pressed the buzzer, and showed my face to the security camera. A voice came over the intercom saying, "Be right there, Dr. Dave." A moment later Carl unlatched the gate to let me in. "What's happening, Doc?"

"Not much. I'm supposed to meet Pastor Ray here."

"I ain't seen that maniac in a while," said Carl. "What's he been up to?"

"He's been working up in Detroit for the past few months," I said.

Walking behind the bar, Carl asked, "What'll you have?"

"How much vodka ya got?"

"Enough."

"Make me a double and Coke," I told him, "and keep them coming till I'm blind."

"You got it, Doc."

The clubhouse had a fully equipped commercial bar like you would expect to see in any public tavern. It also had video games, a pool table, and a large-screen TV. As I was talking with Carl, he handed me a stack of pictures that he and another Outlaw named Psycho had taken while on a trip to Brussels, Belgium, a few weeks earlier. The Outlaws had chapters in Brussels as well as England, Australia, and a number of other countries. While looking at the pictures, I heard the buzzer go off. I glanced at the closed-circuit TV and saw Pastor Ray. After Carl let him in, Ray gave me a Nazi salute with a vigorous "Hail victory!" He was wound up tighter than an idiot's watch, and the white powder round his nostrils betrayed his recent activities. His first question to me was about my progress with the Bible, so I told him I was halfway through.

"Brother Dave," he said, "I've been contacted by a couple from a small town in Illinois called Cerro Gordo. They asked if I would come and perform their marriage ceremony. Do you think you could pick up a rental car and drive me over to Illinois? I'll help you pay for it."

"I've got an ex-girlfriend who manages a car rental agency at the airport," I said. "I'm sure she'll give me a good deal."

"That's great," said Ray.

After we made plans for the weekend of August 15, I decided to get away with Gary for a while and go fishing, but it was harder to do than I thought.

One morning up at the lake, around 3:00 A.M., I was awakened by a knock at the door. I got up and opened it. Pastor Ray, Jason Swanson, and Dan Rick walked in. They immediately began to accuse me of being a federal informant. I repeatedly denied their accusations. Pastor Ray was out of control, screaming at me at the top of his lungs, while Dan and Jason stood behind him with their right arms raised in the Nazi salute. Suddenly Ray pulled out a .45-caliber automatic pistol and forced me backward into a chair. He put the gun to my forehead and yelled, "Race traitor!"

Then he pulled the trigger.

There was a blinding flash and I was enveloped in a bright white light.

Then I was sitting on the edge of the bed, sweating profusely, trying to catch my breath.

Another nightmare. Another reminder to me of what might lie ahead. It had probably come from the anxiety I felt over being alone on a long trip with Ray just around the corner. At least this nightmare was better, I thought, than the ones where I was crucified on a cross.

Tym Burkey

Dave informed me of the plan to take Redfeairn on a weekend trip, which would put them in a car together for a distance, there and back, of six hundred miles. I didn't envy him, but I saw it as a real opportunity to get information. I was appreciative of his willingness to do it. The World Congress had come and gone, and we'd had no one on the inside to find out anything. Since Redfeairn had been there, he might divulge some interesting details.

"By the way," Dave said, "did you happen to hear about the big disaster at the airport in Cincinnati?"

"Uh, no," I responded, "I didn't." I wondered how he could know about something like that before I did.

"From what I understand," he said, "somehow a big fat woman wandered out onto the tarmac, backed up into a propeller, and it dis-assed her."

"Spare me the levity, Dave," I laughed. "That's got to be the worst joke I've ever heard."

But as always, it was good to hear him joke around.

Dave Hall

Around 6:00 A.M., Gary got out of his bed and sat down at the back door, ready for his morning constitutional. I let him out and started to get his breakfast ready. About that time Mom showed up to watch him.

"Where's my granddog?" she asked.

"He's out back, Mom."

She went to the door and yelled, "Gary!" Then she wisely stepped aside. A second later, Gary came flying through so fast he slid all the way across the tile floor into the living room. After regaining his footing, he ran to where Mom had sat down in a chair and laid the front part of his body on her lap. She scratched his head the way he liked.

"So where are you off to this time?" Mom said.

"I'm going with Pastor Ray to Illinois to perform a wedding."

She looked concerned. "How much longer are you going to have to associate with these people?"

"I don't *have* to do anything," I said, "but I did promise Tym I would stay with it until Ray was either in jail or run out of Ohio."

In the beginning, I hadn't trusted Tym, but by the time I promised to stay with the investigation, I did trust him. And by that time, I had also come to realize just how dangerous Ray was. When this all started I thought that basically Ray and the rest were just a bunch of nuts who were an isolated problem. But the more I learned about the AN and the men connected to the AN—McVeigh, Robert Mathews, the Kehoe brothers—I realized what these guys were capable of, and it scared me to death. I couldn't walk away from the investigation and then have people die because I failed to try and stop these guys. That's not something I could have lived with.

"Well," Mom said, "I always taught you to keep your promises, but these people scare me."

"Heck, Mom, I'm bigger than any three of them put together."

"I still worry when you go on these trips."

Later that morning, I picked up the rental car and went to get Ray where he lived with his mother. We engaged in small talk, and as I pulled onto Interstate 70, Ray reached into the backseat and grabbed a box he'd brought. When he opened it, I could see it was filled with cassette tapes. "This is a nice car," said Ray. "It ought to have a good stereo. I brought some sermons and lectures by Pastor James Wickstrom to listen to on the way."

Damn it, I thought, *now I'm going to have to listen to this crap for three hundred miles.*

Ray put in one of the tapes and turned it up. It began, "Hello, kindred, children of Jacob Israel. This is Pastor James Wickstrom and this sermon is titled, 'Who Rules America? The Dangers of the Jewish-Dominated News and Entertainment Medias.' " Wickstrom went on and on about how the Jews were promoting abortion and race mixing as a vehicle to eliminate the white race. Pastor Ray turned the volume up pretty loud, and after about fifteen minutes, I asked him to turn it down. He spoke only when he had a comment about something said on the tapes. Then I realized that he was acting as if he suspected that the car was bugged.

After two hours, I asked for a break, and Ray decided to take a nap. It was a blessed relief, despite the fact that his sleeping failed to serve Tym's purposes.

A couple of hours later, I woke him up. Rubbing his eyes, he asked, "Where are we?"

"We're getting close to the cutoff to Cerro Gordo."

Ray looked at his watch and said, "Looks like we're making good time."

Much to my dismay, he began looking through his box of tapes. Soon I was listening to Pastor Wickstrom singing the praises of Adolf Hitler, and that went on for an hour and a half. When we stopped to eat and get directions, I smuggled a french fry in a napkin out to the car. With a smile on my face I jammed it into the tape player's front opening. It was a hot day, so I started the car and turned on the AC. Ray came out of the restaurant and got in. He looked at his watch and said, "We've got about a half an hour to wait." He then started digging through his tapes. I could hardly contain myself. Just when I thought I was going to burst out laughing I said, "I'm going to run in and use the bathroom, I'll be right back." When I got to the bathroom, I looked around to make sure I was alone. Then I let myself laugh uncontrollably. After a few minutes I regained my composure and splashed some water on my face. I returned to the car and a befuddled Pastor Ray.

"I can't get this tape player to work," he said. "It keeps rejecting the tapes."

Trying my damnedest to keep a straight face, I said, "It was working fine a little while ago. You better be careful that it doesn't eat one of your tapes."

Ray was disappointed as he put the box back on the rear seat.

A couple of minutes later, an older-model Chevy pulled into the parking lot. "I believe that's our man," said Ray, and he got out of the car.

He spoke briefly with the young man, who we then followed out of town. After about forty minutes, we arrived at a remote farm. The driveway leading to the house was decorated on both sides with Nazi battle flags. I was introduced to Bob Russell who wore a 9mm Glock on his belt. He was medium-sized and had a burr haircut. As we entered the house I saw an array of weapons, including an AK-47 assault rifle in a corner by the door. In the backyard was a twenty-foot wooden cross, flanked on either side by ten-foot-high swastikas. They had all been wrapped with burlap bags, and I could smell the kerosene.

Then the bride and groom pulled in: Kent Wilson and his fiancée, Christine. Kent was about five foot eight with a medium build, a dark complexion, and a military-style haircut identical to Bob's. He looked to be in his late thirties or early forties. By contrast, Christine was an attractive, petite girl with almost albino features. I would find out later in the evening that she was only nineteen. Later as I was talking with Kent, I learned that he ran an Internet business at AryanGraphics.com selling white supremacist paraphernalia. He confided that his fiancée was the daughter of a wealthy contractor in Chicago who vigorously opposed the marriage. I could believe it.

At dusk, as the time for the wedding drew near, three carloads of people pulled into the driveway. Pastor Ray and I went into the house to change into our uniforms. When we emerged, I overheard one of the young men tell Bob, "Wow, man, you really did get the Aryan Nations to come!"

By this time there were approximately thirty people in attendance. Most were in their mid-twenties, but there were a couple of older guys. They all claimed to be members of the National Socialist Party, with the exception of one older man who belonged to the KKK. Bob introduced Pastor Ray and me to his landlord, John McLaughlin. "John's the man who got in a fistfight with Geraldo Rivera at a KKK rally a couple of years ago," said Bob.

"I remember seeing that on TV," I said. "Didn't they wind up taking both of you to jail?"

"Yes," replied John. "I only wish they would have put us in the same cell."

As night fell, the cross and swastikas were set on fire. While they lit up the dark, Pastor Ray stood with Kent and Christine in front of the burning cross as everyone else gathered around. I took photographs. Kent offered to pay me, but I told him to consider them a wedding gift. Little did he know that the FBI would also get copies of their nuptials.

Soon Ray ended the ceremony by saying, "May Yahweh bless this union, and in Yahshua's name I now pronounce you man and wife."

I snapped a few more photos as the happy couple kissed in front of the blazing cross. With the wedding over, they broke out the beer and food. I continued taking pictures of the newlyweds from strategic positions so I could catch others in the background.

After using up all of my film, I grabbed a beer and a bite to eat. I was sitting at a picnic table with Ray, Bob, and Kent when a sheriff's deputy and a state trooper slowly cruised by the farm. "Don't worry," said Bob, "they drive by here all the time. They've been trying to pin a robbery on me where a bunch of guns were taken, but they ain't got no proof."

Eventually, Pastor Ray looked at his watch and said, "Brother Dave and I should head back."

This revelation made me feel like breaking the good pastor's neck: I'd been awake for twenty-one straight hours, and now he expected me to drive three hundred miles back. But as we started down the road, I smiled to myself as Ray tried unsuccessfully to get the tape player to work.

When we got to the interstate, I stopped at the truck stop and bought a couple of large cups of coffee. Ray decided to take a nap, and he stayed asleep the entire six hours home. As I dropped him off, he hinted that he might return to Idaho to take care of "some problems," but he wouldn't say what they were, just that they had to do with security issues. I could only hope that Tym would find something worthwhile in the photographs, because otherwise I counted this as a wasted weekend.

But fall was right around the corner, and the next trip I took for the Aryan Nations would move me deeper inside, into territory that was infinitely more dangerous.

17

THE FEAST OF THE TABERNACLES

Tym Burkey

Jesse Warfield had been arrested, along with John Yeager and Shane Wright, for their part in the fiasco in July in Hayden Lake. I was sure the incident had shaken up the organization, and in fact, Dave confirmed this when he said that Ray told him he'd have to travel to Idaho several times to assist with the "problem." We were aware, also thanks to Dave, that Ray was worried that the attorney Morris Dees might get involved. The AN wanted to avoid that at all cost, considering how successful Dees had been in bankrupting other white supremacist organizations.

In another conversation, which Dave related to me verbatim, Ray had mentioned that some members had been talking too much about the various arrests, and that he and Jason had tracked them down and made it clear that "their big mouths would cause them to have a fatal case of lead poisoning."

Redfeairn had also mentioned his concern about what was happening in Idaho. He'd been in touch with Butler and Teague, and they confided that the three young men who'd been arrested were talking too much, especially Jesse Warfield. Redfeairn said that if they had to take some drastic action, he knew a sniper who could take them out while they were being transferred from the jail to the courthouse. Even if he only killed one of them, he figured that would put a scare in the other two and keep them from saying anything more. Dave had surmised that the designated sniper was Kale Kelly, the only person he knew with that kind of training. Redfeairn also received a considerable amount of mail from correctional institutions, and he mentioned that a number of "good Aryan brothers" would be getting out of prison within the next two years. In addition, he was packing a pistol, which violated his parole, and which also made him armed and dangerous. Dave nearly had an opportunity to get the serial number so we could trace how Redfeairn had acquired it, but it slipped by. Again, we looked to arrest Redfeairn with the pistol, but he was extremely careful, and this would possibly burn Dave. We wanted to make sure that any charges we brought against Redfeairn would stick.

At the very least, I was able to alert law enforcement in Idaho to take extra precautions with the three inmates.

During the fall of 1998, Dave drove his own car to follow Redfeairn and Swanson to Athens, Tennessee, for the Feast of the Tabernacles, a Christian Identity celebration. Many of the Christian Identity religious holidays were based on events from the Old Testament. Since followers believed that whites were the lost tribes of Israel who had migrated to northern Europe, they actually celebrated religious holidays that were Jewish holidays as well. Also attending were Neuman Britton, the Aryan Nations national pastor, and James Wickstrom, a Christian Identity minister affiliated with the Michigan Militia.

I was deeply concerned about Dave's safety the entire time he was away.

Dave Hall

In order to be with these guys for long periods of time, I had to psych up, get into hate mode. I repeated over and over mantras such as "Niggers, greasers, chinks, nips, and filthy Jews, the children of Satan." One slip, saying something like "that black guy" instead of "that nigger," would not only upset Pastor Ray but might even cause him to suspect my loyalty to the Aryan race.

In anticipation of this next road trip, I'd experienced another panic attack and more nightmares. I'd dreamed again that Pastor Ray was waving a gun in my face, accusing me of being a race traitor. I ended up on the edge of the bed, trying to catch my breath, sweating. As I splashed cold water on my face, I saw my reflection in the mirror—my pale face, the bags under my blood-shot eyes—and said, "You know you're slowly killing yourself, don't you?"

I had told Tym that Pastor Wickstrom had ties to the Posse Comita-tus and the Michigan Militia. Jason Swanson was acquainted with him and had persuaded him to set up a meeting between the Aryan Nations and the Militia in November. I'd also passed along infor-mation that a guy named John, a Klansman from Chillicothe, had mentioned having joint rallies across southern Ohio.

When I got into Athens, Ray came to see me in my hotel room, and after he left, I noticed that as I was tying my tie my left hand was shaking uncontrollably. I thought, *Oh great, now what?* I shook my hand back and forth, then made a fist a couple of times until the trembling stopped.

Once I was ready, I went down to the conference room, where Jason and the two Michigan AN members, Steve and Mark, had congregated. When I reached Ray, he was with a middle-aged heavyset man with salt-and-pepper hair and a matching beard. Ray introduced me. "Brother Dave, I'd like you to meet Pastor Tom Wallace. He organized this meeting."

I shook Wallace's hand and said, "It's a pleasure to make your acquaintance, Pastor. My name's Dave Hall."

"Dave's my right-hand man," said Ray.

"He sure is a big one," Pastor Wallace commented. Then he let out a jovial laugh. With his rosy cheeks and beard, he put me to mind of someone who would play Santa Claus during the holidays. I later would learn that he raised Rottweilers and sold herbal remedies in a nearby town. He was also a nationally recognized expert shot with a pistol and the former head of security at Elohim City, the white supremacist enclave in Oklahoma. Elohim City had been a destination for numerous white supremacists, including Timothy McVeigh and members of the Aryan Republican Army. And also, of course, the notorious Kehoe brothers.

Pastor Wallace excused himself, saying that he had to get the meeting started. There were several rows of folding chairs, so Ray and I found a place to sit and were soon joined by Jason, Steve, and Mark. Pastor Wallace stood at the podium with a large Confederate flag on the wall behind him. I estimated there were about thirty-five people in the hall, and for the most part they seemed to be down-home country folk.

Pastor Wallace began by thanking everyone for attending the Feast of the Tabernacles. He then began to speak.

"This is not just the Confederate flag," said Wallace as he pointed at it. "This is the flag of Isaac and Jacob. The thirteen stars symbolize the thirteen tribes of Jacob. This is placed on a red field, purchased by our blood, and a blue background, which is the law, and thirteen white stars, which are symbolic of purity. This is what we are required to walk in. By the way, the purity depicted on this flag means honor coming to the house of Israel, when men are going to stand as men and women are going to stand as women, and we're going to march forward and do what the Father bids us to do. I've been informed that a lot of people don't like what we have to say, and I find that upsetting because it's not unscriptural. I've studied the scriptures, and I've studied them closely, because if they say something wrong and I'm involved with this feast, I'm going to have to say something. But the only thing I've been able to say is amen and sic 'm!"

The crowd laughed and shouted, "Amen!"

"So they haven't violated the precepts in the laws of our heavenly Father," Wallace continued, "so the only thing we can find them guilty of, and I've been thinking of this on this very afternoon, the only thing we can find them guilty of is not being afraid of men. I tell you that the glory in my crown is to associate with other men who aren't going to be afraid of what other men or the media or the Southern Poverty Law Center has to say about us. The SPLC—that happens to be run by a Jew that is a homosexual who has been going at it with a black woman." Wallace laughed. "I mean this guy, does it all in one spot. And he's our watchdog. He's the one who's going to notify the rest of the nation when we're out of order. Do you believe that! The only thing he isn't doing, and I believe that, is selling heroin, crack cocaine, and prostitution, but that's next! The man has obviously no basis for any moral sense on this planet."

Someone from the audience asked, "What's his name?"

"Morris Dees," Wallace replied.

He then introduced Pastor Wickstrom, who went on for almost two hours, giving his views on the Book of Genesis, going into the two seed line theory. When he finally called for a prayer, I felt like jumping up and shouting, "Hallelujah!" But my elation was short-lived. Wickstrom said, "I'll see you all back here for the evening service at seven-thirty." I could hardly believe I'd agreed to sit through so many hours of this repetitive, hateful nonsense.

It was early evening, and everyone was heading to local restaurants. Ray asked me to be Pastor Britton's bodyguard. I agreed, thinking this would place me in the inner circle should something important be discussed. We all decided to go to the Shoney's restaurant across the interstate from the motel. Ray and Jason rode with Wickstrom and Britton and Steve and Mark rode with me. Once at the restaurant, I was careful not to violate any of the biblical food laws.

As we ate dinner, Ray and Wickstrom discussed the upcoming

meeting between the Aryan Nations and the Michigan Militia. It sounded to me like it was a done deal and they just had to agree on a date.

The evening meeting was more of the same, but a special barb was reserved for Attorney General Janet Reno.

"And this lesbian of the Justice Department, Janet Reno," said Pastor Wickstrom, "this vile evil person who can't stay out of the backseats of cars with other women. She said the Christian Identity movement is the most dangerous threat to the government of the United States of America!" He paused for a moment, then continued, "I'd say what's more dangerous is Yahweh our Father!"

"Hallelujah!"

"This vile bitch that sits in the District of Columbia says, 'Anyone that reads the Bible is in the classification of a terrorist'!"

After more applause and cheers, Pastor Wickstrom ended the sermon with a prayer.

I declined to socialize and just returned to my room. There, I buried my head in the pillow and screamed as hard as I could. It was a great stress reliever that probably kept me from killing someone. After throwing cold water on my face, I got undressed, took one of the fifths of vodka out of my suitcase, and drank myself to sleep.

At breakfast the next morning, the subject of Morris Dees came up again.

"We think he is going to try to sue Pastor Butler and the Aryan Nations," Ray told me, "over that incident between Jesse Warfield and that woman and her son that he allegedly assaulted."

"That's not good," I replied, although I was of course very happy to hear of it.

"Just because Jesse and the others are members of the AN," said Wickstrom, "that snake thinks he can sue the whole organization."

"Isn't there anything we can do?" I asked.

"We can only pray he steps out in front of a speeding bus," Wickstrom replied with a tight smile, "or that some similar fate befalls him."

After another round of sermons and an hour of singing the praises of Yahweh and the white race, Pastor Britton asked Pastor Wickstrom to join him at the podium. I had the impression that something was coming.

"I've known this man of Yahweh for over twenty-five years," said Britton, "and I'm proud to call him my friend." After an embrace, Pastor Britton continued, "I'd like to make an announcement, and I'd like you all to celebrate with me." He stopped for a moment to look over the room. Then he said, "Pastor Richard Butler has named me as his successor as the world leader of the Aryan Nations."

I looked at Ray, who was visibly stunned. Ray had dreamed of succeeding Pastor Butler and probably had believed he would. I couldn't help feeling a little sorry for him.

After the applause, Pastor Britton said, "Thank you, my brothers and sisters. Now, while Pastor Johnson and his lovely wife sing us a song, we're going to pass the bucket around for love offerings to help pay for this rental hall. If anyone needs help for any health problems, Pastor Wickstrom and I will do the laying on of hands to heal through the power of Yahweh."

An older woman, whom Pastor Britton identified as his sister, stepped forward. He laid his hand upon her head and Pastor Wickstrom laid his hand on her shoulder. They both asked Yahweh to heal her.

I'm sure Ray was oblivious, even as others came forward.

Then Pastor Britton returned to the microphone and said, "All of us here have a job, and that job is to go out and find the lost sheep of Israel. I'm not talking about all of us here today, because we know who we are, don't we? We are the children of the house of Jacob Israel, are we not? It is our job to find and bring together lost sheep of the other twelve tribes of Israel! Only then will we be able to cleanse the land of the filthy Jews, niggers, and all of the other vermin that infest our nation!"

This statement drew a round of applause from the crowd. Pastor Wickstrom then stepped up to the microphone and said, "I started venturing into lower Michigan back in the early 1990s, making contact with members of the Michigan Militia, the largest militia in America. I'm proud to say that since then many militia men have become followers of Yahweh!"

This statement also drew applause. After a moment or two Pastor Wickstrom leaned over the podium and at almost a whisper he said, "At some of the militia meetings where I spoke, there were Jewry infiltrators." He paused and looked around the room, staring each person right in the eye. No one moved. Then Pastor Wickstrom yelled, "But we found them out! And we got rid of them!"

"Hallelujah! Hallelujah!"

I joined in but kept an eye on Ray. After the closing prayer, Tom Wallace stepped up to the microphone and said, "I don't want to alarm anyone, but an FBI agent just checked into the corner room on the second floor. I would invite him down to the meeting this afternoon, but he's black."

Everyone laughed.

When the subject of Morris Dees came up at dinner, Ray said, "I believe I've got just the right man for the job." I thought, *The right man for the job?* I hoped he wasn't thinking of me. But nothing more was said. I wondered if he wasn't trying to reassert himself and prove his importance. Still, I knew he wouldn't have said that if he didn't mean it.

There was more of the same the third and final day, although with one new element. Wickstrom lectured on the Jewish-run government and more about the Jewish usury system. After an hour, he announced that they were going to conduct the ritual of the Warriors' Ransom. This men-only ritual is rooted in the Old Testament. It consisted of warriors lining up and tossing thirty-three cents into a wicker basket to ensure Yahweh's protection in battle.

So we lined up, and when it came my turn, I tossed my coins into the basket, then leaned over for Pastor Britton to place his hand on my head. He said, "Brother Dave, do you pledge to be a great warrior for Yahweh and for our cause to overthrow ZOG and to end Jewish tyranny?"

"I do," I replied, hoping there would be no spiritual repercussions from that false pledge. I had to imagine God would understand.

"May Yahweh protect you and keep you," said Britton. "Now rise a warrior saint."

I lifted my head up and said, "Thank you, Pastor."

Britton raised both hands in the air and said, "Praise Yahweh!"

When the ceremony was over, it was late. Wickstrom, Britton, and Tom Wallace stood at the podium and thanked everyone for attending the Feast of the Tabernacles. Pastor Wallace asked Britton to say a prayer for Eric Robert Rudolph, so he added, "Yahweh, protect and keep Brother Eric Robert Rudolph, a young man following the path of Phineas and maybe even of the Phineas seed line. We ask that you hide him and provide for him. Amen."

I'd heard the doctrine that Yahweh had bestowed a priesthood upon Phineas and his seed line as a reward for slaying the race mixers. The AN believed the priesthood had existed down through the ages, with men even today acting as secret priests and guardians. Clearly, they thought that Rudolph might be among them.

Ray asked me, as the bodyguard, to escort Britton to his room. I went with Britton, Wickstrom, and Ray. When we got there, Ray thanked me and said he would see me in the morning. So I was excluded again. I stood outside the room and lit up a cigarette so I could hang around for a couple of minutes and maybe overhear something, but all that came through the crack was muffled voices. I decided instead to go finish the last of my vodka. The Feast of the Tabernacles was over, and I was aware that I'd gathered some important information: I believed these people meant to take action against Morris Dees, and that Ray would be central to that. In addition, it appeared I'd been accepted as a trusted member, since I'd been asked to protect one of their cherished leaders. I knew that Tym would appreciate all of this.

18.

AN MEETS MILITIA

Dave Hall

Ray decided to ride back with me, and during the drive, he quizzed me on my Bible studies and seemed impressed with my progress.

"Brother Dave," he commented, "as far as I'm concerned, getting you ordained is going to be a mere formality." He put his hand into his pocket and pulled out a large, crested Aryan Nations ring that was identical to the one on his hand. He handed it to me, saying, "Here, Brother. I believe you should have this."

I glanced at it. I was loath to accept it, which he probably read as humility, but he urged me to try it on.

"Shouldn't I wait until I've been ordained?" I was stalling.

"You've earned the right to wear that ring. Go ahead and put it on."

I couldn't think of any reason not to, so I put the ring on my finger. "It fits like a glove. Thanks, Pastor."

"You're welcome, Brother. Just don't let me down."

"I won't," I replied.

On the way back to Dayton we stopped at the church, where I saw old Joe Hobbes' van in the parking lot. "What's Joe doing here?" I asked.

"Kale Kelly's probably driving it," said Ray. "I told him to meet me here today because I need to talk to him."

Sure enough, Kale emerged from the van, followed by Sandy. Ray asked me to talk to her while he spoke with Kelly. It was half an hour before it hit me: he was probably talking with Kelly about the subject that had been discussed at the Feast of the Tabernacles. Kale Kelly was the only person I could think of whom Ray might propose for the job of assassinating Morris Dees. I had to let Tym know about this as soon as I could.

When they returned, they both had serious expressions on their faces. They shook hands, then Kelly said he had to head out.

"Dave and I have to get back to Dayton, too," said Ray. "Brother Dave, I want you and Kale to exchange phone numbers in case I can't get back down here next week. You two can get together and work on the church repairs."

We did as he asked. Ray then tossed me the keys to the church and said, "Here, Brother, you may as well have the keys. You'll probably be down here more than me." I couldn't imagine what it would be like to be a pastor in his absence, to try to lead a bunch of people in hatemongering, but I knew it could happen.

During the drive home, Ray said, "We're all going to have to get ready for the year 2000."

"Why's that?"

"Because if all the computer networks crash as they're expected to, FEMA can use it as an excuse to declare martial law and confiscate our weapons. We need to stockpile weapons now and find a safe place to hide them."

I thought, *Is this nut paranoid or what?* But he went on about how the federal government was out to put all of us—us white supremacists—in prison. When I was about ready to pull out my hair, we finally arrived at his place. He said he would call me the following Saturday, and we exchanged salutes.

On the way home I considered the idea of Kale Kelly killing Morris Dees. One minute I was thinking that maybe he had it in him, the next minute that maybe he didn't. He seemed like an okay guy, just a little misguided. Could he really be a cold-blooded killer? Hell, I didn't know. Between Pastor Ray's constant white supremacist brainwashing and the fifth of vodka I drank every night just to sleep, my brains were fried. I finally decided to keep my deductions to myself, at least for now. I would relay to Tym only what I'd seen and heard verbatim and let the FBI agents come up with their own conclusions.

Tym Burkey

When Dave called that Monday, I asked how his weekend had gone.

"Wonderful," he replied. "Spending over three hours alone in the car with Pastor Ray was such a joy."

I laughed. "I'm glad to hear that you're enjoying your work."

"Yeah, I'm enjoying it about as much as a stick in the eye."

"Just hang in there," I encouraged him. "I have a feeling that we're going to put these maniacs away soon."

"I certainly hope so. Some of the stuff Pastor Ray has been saying is starting to make sense, and that scares me."

Dave was wearing down from the constant exposure and the pressure to lose his identity in a role.

"Dave," I said, "you're stronger than that. You can't afford to let that maniac get inside your head."

"I know. But after almost two years of race sermons and twisted views of reality I find myself wondering what's right or wrong anymore."

"Anytime, day or night, if you need someone to talk to, you can call me. I mean that."

"I appreciate that, Tym. I just hope I can hold on to my sanity long enough to finish the job."

"You will." I did what I could to sound confident.

Although I was glad that Dave had gone to this event, I hadn't expected it to be all that significant. This changed after he reported what had happened. His attendance became a turning point in the AN investigation, not only in Ohio but nationally. No other FBI office had a source as trusted as Dave had become: He'd been appointed a bodyguard to the AN leadership; I knew Dave could now walk into any AN venue and be immediately accepted and respected. I had always had the goal of putting a source in the middle of the AN leadership; now I had that individual. I was excited, and I knew that Dave had gone beyond expectations.

All of the white supremacist heavy hitters had been there in Athens: Redfeairn, the Ohio AN leader; Neuman Britton, the California AN leader; Jason Swanson, the Michigan AN leader; August Kreis, soon to be the Pennsylvania AN leader; and James Wickstrom, a well-known Christian Identity leader from Michigan. Dave and Swanson were also elevated from the AN rank of "soldier saint" to "warrior saint."

As a bodyguard, Dave heard not only the public speeches by the leadership but also private planning sessions, including the attempts to bring the militias into the AN. The AN recognized the value of numbers and weapons to the movement. With Y2K looming, they wanted more in their ranks to prepare for the chaos that would allow the race war to begin. The biggest stumbling block to recruiting the militias was that the militias generally were not white supremacists. Although they were antigovernment, they had blacks, Jews, and other minorities in their ranks.

Then Dave told me about the meeting between Redfeairn and Kelly at the church. That these two had talked for an hour together concerned me. That indicated more than just a request on Redfeairn's part: it sounded more like the development of a plan. Kelly was looking more and more like the "lone wolf" we were watching for.

"I wonder what those two are up to," I said. Dave didn't speculate, but given what had transpired at the meeting he'd attended and the fact that things were moving forward for a legal suit in

Idaho, I imagined that Redfeairn wanted to prove himself by being instrumental in taking out a significant enemy of the AN. And we knew he wasn't just all talk. If he was determined to target Dees, he'd probably move forward without hesitation. We just had to be sure we knew what he was up to.

Dave had accomplished more at this event than I'd ever expected, and I was certain we were on the verge of getting something important.

Dave Hall

On Tuesday morning, the phone rang. When I answered it, I was surprised to hear a familiar voice—but one that I'd never before heard over the phone.

"Hey, Dave, it's Kale. How ya doin'?"

My heart nearly stopped. While I knew this could be good for the FBI, I also knew I might be getting cornered.

"I'm worn out," I replied, trying to keep my voice even. "I just got finished putting up a big-ass waterbed. What's up?"

"I just talked with Pastor Ray on the phone and he's not coming down this weekend. He asked me if I would meet you at the church to take down all the flags and stuff."

I recalled that I had suggested this myself to Pastor Ray, since building inspectors would be coming to observe the work we'd done. "I sure could use the help," I said. "Some of those things will need a ladder to get to. There's a couple of ladders down there, but they won't hold my three-hundred-fifty-pound body."

Kale laughed and said, "When do you want to get together?"

"Anytime is good for me."

"How about Saturday morning, then?"

"Sounds good to me."

We set a time of 9:00 A.M. As I hung up, I wondered if I should have tried to engage Kale in a little more conversation, but I figured I'd done the right thing by not being too inquisitive. I alerted Tym to the meeting, and he urged me to attempt to learn what Redfeairn had said to Kale.

I got up early Saturday morning, and after nearly breaking my neck by stepping on an empty vodka bottle, I let Gary out into the backyard. In the bathroom, I held my head under the cold water faucet for a few minutes. Then I got my coffee. Gary trotted into the kitchen for his morning head rub as the TV weatherman announced that it was going to be a crisp and cool day. I looked down at Gary and said, "You know what, Gary? How would you like to go to the church with me today?"

He started barking and jumping up and down. I knew the only word he understood was *go,* but for him, that was the best one. As long as he got to go, it didn't matter where.

At the church, I tied Gary to the stairs with a long piece of rope. It wasn't long before Kale showed up. When he looked at Gary, he seemed a little nervous. "Does he bite?" he asked.

"Only if he's in the car."

Kale walked over and patted Gary on the head. "What's his name?"

"Gary."

Kale smiled. "That's a funny name for a dog."

"It's the only name I could get him to answer to."

Kale laughed and said, "You're crazy, Dave."

It was at times like this I was convinced Kale couldn't go through with an assassination. He seemed too gentle. I put Gary's food and water bowls out where he could get to them and then went up the stairs to unlock the door. For about forty-five minutes we removed the flags and other paraphernalia, and I was careful not to ask any questions. Then I indicated I wanted to take a break to smoke, so we went out into the crisp autumn air.

Once outside, I saw an opportunity to get a little closer to Kale, so as casually as I could, I said, "Pastor Ray told me you were in the army."

"Yes," said Kale, "I served in Desert Storm."

"I did eight years in the Marine Corps," I said, to make him more comfortable with me, "but I got out before Desert Storm. However, I did a tour in Vietnam."

"Really?" said Kale. "What was your rank?"

"Staff sergeant. Yours?"

"Sergeant," replied Kale. "You know, Dave, we need to set up a paramilitary training routine for all these young guys that come to the church."

"I agree," I said. "But I'm too old and stove up to do much but teach."

Kale seemed to see me as a resource, so he asked me military questions. It was apparent that he didn't think I'd really been in the Marines, which of course I hadn't, but I had read many books on military conflicts and procedures, and I was especially interested in military aircraft. So I was able to field his questions. After about fifteen minutes of discussion, I knew I'd put his doubts to rest, even correcting some mistakes he'd made. Whether he made them to try to trap me, I'll never know.

Still, he hadn't yet offered anything that Tym would find of use. We went back into the church to finish our task. Inside, Kale told me that to make some extra money he'd been operating a bulldozer and was going to run a concession stand at the upcoming motorcycle hill climb rally in nearby Oregonia. I brought up Pastor Ray a few times, even asking Kale if he knew what plans Ray had in store for the church, but he didn't say much about that.

"I only know he wants to start having services again as soon as possible" was all I could get out of him. But I believed I'd made him feel more comfortable talking with me, so perhaps it was the start of something that would eventually pay off.

Two days later, he called me again.

"Hey, Dave, this is Kale. What's happenin'?"

"Not much," I replied. "Just hanging out."

"I talked with Pastor Ray this morning and he asked me to let you know he won't be back from Detroit until the first weekend in November."

That was two weeks away. Two blessed weeks.

"He must have plenty of work to keep him busy up there that long," I said. "What have you been up to?"

"I'm going to a KKK rally in Tennessee this weekend with some Klan buddies of mine," said Kale. "Then we're going to stop in Shepherdsville, Kentucky, for the annual machine gun convention."

"Machine gun convention?"

"Yeah," said Kale. "It's like a big swap meet. People come from all over the United States and they have demonstrations."

"That sounds pretty cool," I said.

"You ought to try to meet us there."

"I'd love to," I said, "but I'm running a little short on cash right now."

"I guess I'll catch you later then, Brother."

Tym Burkey

I was glad that Dave had some contact with Kelly, because after his release he'd disappeared from sight. I sent a warning and request to the other FBI offices to watch out for Kelly and report his whereabouts, but I heard nothing back. I never told my wife, but during this period, I would get up every morning and walk around the house with my pistol in hand. Kelly had been clear that he did not like federal law enforcement, especially the FBI. He'd stopped short of making a direct threat toward me, but he'd repeated several times, "If you're not for us, you're against us."

Also, I was extremely careful when driving in to work and leaving work. I was not about to let Kelly martyr himself "for the cause" at my expense. After several interviews with Kelly and information I had gathered about him, a clear picture emerged. After his arrest and court-martial in the army, Kelly was set adrift and had nothing to replace the regimented life he'd experienced in the military. The Aryan Nations had become his "new army," and the white supremacist movement provided him with a cause to believe in, to fight for, and even to die for. Later, Kelly's probation officer told me Kelly had been the perfect soldier. If you told him, "Take that hill," Kelly would either take the hill or die trying.

Unfortunately, Kelly's new commander was Redfeairn, who knew how to bend and manipulate him. And in a twist of irony, the same government that Kelly had once sworn to defend was now the government he vowed to destroy. I was a part of that government and the enemy. There was no doubt in my mind Kelly was a lone wolf and up to no good. Further, while he was out of pocket from May until October, I was sure I'd been on his list of potential targets. By October, I'd learned where he'd gone. During a drive-by of his girlfriend's father's farm, I found him living in a tent along the Little Miami River. I relaxed a little, but not much.

Dave was a bit frustrated over the fact that he hadn't been able to penetrate Kelly's guard, but he did have information that would be of use to us. He'd received a flyer from Michigan that gave the date, time, and place of the meeting between the Aryan Nations and the Michigan Militia: November 8, 1998, at the VFW hall in Portland, Michigan, from 10:00 A.M. to 3:00 P.M. The flyer gave directions to the VFW hall on Lillian Boulevard and stated that a $10 donation would be accepted at the door. Among the guest speakers were Neuman Britton, James Wickstrom, Ray Redfeairn, and General Davidson from the Michigan Militia.

"The last thing in the world we need is for these two groups to get together," I said. The idea the AN had of combining forces with the militias was sound and had merit in their distorted view of the world. Militias had been stockpiling weapons, food, and water for years. Both disliked the federal government, and while militia members, in the eyes of the AN, tended to be mainstream—in other words, they had jobs, which meant money—they were certainly ready to fight it out with the government.

"I agree," Dave replied. "Do you want me to go?"

"Certainly, if you want to."

"I don't necessarily want to, but I will. I'll have to rent a car."

"Don't worry," I assured him, "we'll take care of it. This is good information, Dave. I'm going to have to get in touch with the Lansing office."

Over the next few weeks, Dave told me about calls he'd received from Redfeairn, who was checking in from Michigan. We now knew that this meeting would involve uniforms, so it was not going to be clandestine. As the date approached, our office in Lansing prepared. Dave had no further information, so I waited with my usual concern as he drove up to Michigan on November 8.

Dave Hall

I rolled into Portland, Michigan, about 9:30 A.M. The VFW was easy to find, but as I pulled into the parking lot, I had to laugh. I'd never in my life seen so many pickup trucks with rifle racks over the rear windows. And most of them held rifles. I changed into my uniform shirt and was tying my tie when I heard, "Brother Dave! Glad you could make it."

I turned around to see Ray and Jason Swanson walking toward me. I saluted and said, "Hail victory!"

"How long did it take you to get here?" Ray asked.

"About five hours."

"Well, you're just in time. We're about to get started. Come with me and I'll introduce you to General Davidson."

As we rounded the corner of the building, I commented, "Have you ever seen so many pickup trucks with rifle racks on them?"

"These guys do like their weapons," said Ray.

When we got to the side entrance of the VFW hall, I saw three men sitting on a tailgate, completely clad in military camouflage fatigues and combat boots. They had patches on their upper arms that read "Michigan Militia Wolf Pack." It looked like they were preparing for war, and entering the hall felt like walking into an army barracks. Almost everyone there—around fifty men—was dressed like the three men outside. Across the room, I spotted Pastor Britton and Pastor Wickstrom talking with an older man of medium build, wearing military garb. Even from that distance I saw the four stars on his collar that set him apart, as did his age, which I assumed to be mid-sixties. I knew it must be General Davidson.

Ray seemed to know a lot of the people there. Although the majority of them were Wolf Pack members, I learned that some belonged to the Posse Comitatus and the NAAWP, the National Association for the Advancement of White People. The Aryan Nations was represented by myself, Pastor Ray, Jason, and two other members of the Michigan Aryan Nations, as well as Pastor Britton and the Indiana Aryan Nations state leader. I also saw one of the guys I had met at the Feast of the Tabernacles. He remembered me as well, and saluted in greeting.

Tables lined the room, covered with pamphlets and magazines on subjects ranging from how and where to buy military surplus items to white supremacist hate literature. After talking with a few others, Pastor Ray introduced me to General Davidson and his wife. She was in her mid-forties, much younger than he was, and both claimed to be former police officers. Ray fell right into a discussion with Wickstrom and Davidson as I stood by and listened. Finally Ray realized that since he'd initiated the meeting, he'd better get it started. No matter what, I knew that anything I learned here would be valuable to Tym.

Jason went up to the microphone and asked everyone to find a seat. Then Pastor Wickstrom stepped up to the microphone. "First of all," he said, "I would like to thank all of our friends of the Michigan Militia Wolf Pack for attending our meeting today, especially General Davidson. I would also like to welcome our brothers of the Posse Comitatus and the NAAWP."

Using passages from the Bible and examples of Jewish conspiracy, Pastor Wickstrom tactfully laid out several reasons for an alliance among all the groups represented. I looked around the room at the transfixed faces; he'd certainly caught their attention. In fact, I was concerned that this dangerous alliance might really happen, even given their differing opinions about religion.

Wickstrom ended his lecture with a prayer to Yahweh. Everyone rose and applauded. Then Jason sent us on a ten-minute break and I took the opportunity to wander around and listen to some of the conversations. I caught just a few phrases here and there, but it seemed that a majority of the militia members seemed to like what Pastor Wickstrom had said.

Next it was Ray's turn. His speech echoed Wickstrom's, but with Ray's own special panache. As usual, he railed against the Jews, at times screaming at the top of his lungs to fire up the crowd. Whenever he made a calculated pause, they applauded, and he managed to hold their attention for over an hour. Finally, none too soon for me, we broke for lunch.

Afterward, I saw Pastor Ray talking with Morris Gulett and a woman named Mary Williams, whom I knew from church. She was holding Mo's hand, which suggested a romance. I walked over to where they were standing and exchanged greetings. Before I could ask them anything, Jason announced the next speaker, Pastor Neuman Britton.

He, too, launched into a speech about how the Jewish media was corrupting our youth with TV shows and movies promoting homosexuality and race mixing. He also told how Alan Greenspan and the "Jewish usury system" were bankrupting American farmers and confiscating their lands, in many cases land that had been in the same family for generations.

"These vile children of Satan are infiltrating every facet of our government and they must be stopped," he insisted. "That's why we must join forces." Instead of yelling the way Ray had, he smiled and in a calm voice asked, "Can the Aryan Nations alone stop the unholy Jews? Sadly, I have to say, I don't think so. Can our brothers of the Posse Comitatus resist the children of Satan? I don't think so. Can our friends of the Michigan Militia defeat the Zionist Occupied

Government? I don't think so." He then paused for a moment and clasped his hands together before he made his point. "If we all join together and make a concerted effort"—he slammed a fist hard down on the podium—"we'll be able to send every last Jew on the face of the earth straight to hell, where they belong!"

There was silence until people realized he was waiting, then came applause, which encouraged Pastor Britton to continue for almost two hours, using the Bible and the Jews as reasons for an alliance between the groups. Then he, too, ended with a prayer.

I was decidedly weary of this stuff. I'd heard every version of it many times now, had seen all these men in action, and was thoroughly sick of spending my days being subjected to it. I had to remind myself of my promise to Tym.

As we all broke for refreshments I again wandered around, a spy among the wolves. The members of the Posse Comitatus seemed to be agreeable to an alliance, citing the Christian Identity doctrine as a common bond. However, the militia members seemed divided. I believe that Pastor Ray's and Pastor Britton's almost maniacal sermons may have scared a few of them, and they certainly weren't keen about the biblical angles. I noticed that the general didn't take the podium, and I could only assume that he was there simply to hear the arguments.

By the end of the day, as people filtered out, Ray surprised me. He stepped up to the microphone and said, "May I have everyone's attention, please?" There weren't that many of us still there, but we all looked at him, waiting.

"I've been asked to perform a marriage ceremony between Brother Morris Gulett and Sister Mary Williams," he said with a smile. It was an odd way to cap the day, but people applauded.

I thought about how it obviously wouldn't last, not with Mo's condescending attitude toward women and Mary's independent personality, and I felt sorry for Mary. I knew that Mo's first marriage had ended in divorce, due to domestic violence and his drug abuse.

But what I thought didn't count just then. This was supposed to be a happy moment for the couple. Ray positioned us around them, and as he began the ceremony, we stood with our arms raised in the Nazi salute, the whole thing feeling more like an impending train wreck than a love bond.

When I told this all to Tym the next day, he agreed with me. But even as we laughed about Mo we were both aware that if these various factions joined forces, they could strengthen the weaknesses of each and prove to be rather formidable. I knew there was more in store for me, as the FBI needed a resource inside. I knew I had to continue.

But then my whole world caved in.

19

TERRIBLE TIMES

Dave Hall

Tuesday morning, two days before Thanksgiving, I went outside to play with Gary. It was a crisp, cold morning, and I knew he'd be frisky and ready to have some fun. I had the Frisbee, his favorite toy, and I flipped it across the yard. He stood in place and watched it fly through the air and land on the frozen ground.

"Okay," I said, "if you don't want to play, I'm going back inside."

He didn't budge, so I went in. A few minutes later, Gary followed and went straight to his bed. Something was wrong.

"Don't you feel good, buddy?" I asked. I walked over to feel his nose and it was cold and wet, which indicated he wasn't ill, so I just figured he wanted to lie around for the day.

A couple of times, I tried to get him to go with me outside to play, but he didn't move, only got up to get a drink of water. I decided that if he wasn't better by the following day, I would take him to the vet.

On Wednesday morning, I made Gary his breakfast. As he gobbled it down, I said, "Well, it looks like you're feeling better." It was a huge relief. After all my losses, I couldn't lose him, too. But I still had the feeling he wasn't really back to his normal self. Usually after eating, he'd go right out and play. But this time he went back to bed.

Again I felt his nose and it was cold and wet, so I tried to put it out of my mind.

I worked for a while on my Bible studies until the phone rang.

"Hi, Dave," said Tym. "I just wanted to wish you a happy Thanksgiving. I'll be out of town for the weekend."

I returned the greeting and we chatted awhile. It felt good to have a friend call, just to connect. That I'd grown close with an FBI agent was against all expectations, but we'd been through a lot and Tym's genuine concern when I was with Ray and his sort touched me. I was glad he was getting time to spend with his wife and four boys.

Around five that afternoon, I let Gary outside to do his business. He didn't come right back, and after about twenty minutes I called for him to come inside because it was kind of chilly and I wanted to shut the inside door. When he didn't come running, I went out onto the deck to see what he was up to. He was just wandering around the yard.

"Gary, c'mon now," I called.

He just kept walking around as if he hadn't even heard me. I called him again, and again got no response. Finally I went out in the yard and grabbed him by his collar and led him toward the house.

"What's wrong, buddy?" By now I was feeling pretty nervous. When we got to the deck, Gary pulled back, like he didn't want to go up the stairs. But I had to get him inside, so I got behind him and pushed him up each step, one at a time. When we got to the top, to my utter surprise, Gary turned around and snapped at me.

That was when I knew for sure something was seriously wrong. Gary went into the house and started to pace from room to room. Despite the late hour, I called the vet. One of his assistants said he'd left for the day, and she suggested that I take Gary to the emergency animal hospital.

At the same moment, Gary fell down on the floor. I rushed to him just as he convulsed and began to foam at the mouth. I was freaking out, but for his sake, I knew I had to maintain control. I grabbed my wallet and keys and said a quick prayer of thanks that Gary had stopped convulsing. I picked him up and carried him to the car, then laid him on the front seat.

I took off for the animal hospital as fast as I could, running every stoplight, repeating over and over, "Hang in there, buddy, you're gonna be all right." I could only hope that was true. Gary was not just my dog, he was my best friend. He *had* to pull through.

I pulled into the parking lot at the animal hospital and ran inside. By the time I scribbled out a form and got a doctor with a gurney out to the car, Gary was standing up on the front seat. I looked at the doctor and said, "He must be feeling better."

"Bring him in," said the doctor, "and we'll check him out just to be sure."

I opened the door and hooked a leash onto Gary's collar. "C'mon, buddy," I said. He just stood there, so I lifted him out of the car and put him on the ground. As I led him into the hospital lobby, I saw that his legs were shaking. One of the assistants took us to an examining room and said the doctor would be right with us.

While we waited, Gary paced around the room, and he began bumping into walls as if he were blind. I was as scared as I'd ever been. Feeling a panic attack coming on, I fumbled for my pill bottle and downed a couple of Xanax.

The doctor entered and said, "So we're having some problems with Gary here."

"Yes sir," I said. "He's wandering around and walking into things like he can't see. He also acts like he can't hear me."

I tried to hold Gary still while the doctor examined him.

"Are there any chemicals or cleaning products he could've gotten into?" he asked.

"Absolutely not," I replied. "Why does he keep pacing around like that?"

"Gary's just confused because he can't understand what's happening to him."

"What can we do?" It was more than a question. I was begging the doctor to save my friend. I thought about how I'd raised him with that rubber glove, how we'd bonded so quickly. The image of his head on my lap whenever I'd been sad or stressed nearly made me cry right then and there.

"We'll take Gary into the lab," the doctor said kindly, "and draw some blood. Then we can run some tests and see if we can get him feeling better, okay, Mr. Hall?"

I couldn't speak, so I nodded. It occurred to me that this was no way to spend the Thanksgiving holiday.

The doctor patted me on the back and said, "Don't worry, Mr. Hall, we'll take good care of Gary."

I sat and waited for an hour or so, stepping outside occasionally for a cigarette. I wanted to talk to someone, I wanted to find some way to calm myself, but there was nothing to do. It went on forever, but each second that no one came was a second of hope; it meant Gary was still alive. Finally the doctor came out to the waiting room and sat down across from me. I could see he had serious news.

"Gary had another seizure," he told me "but we sedated him and he's resting easy now."

He was still alive.

"What could be wrong with him?" I asked.

"At this time I can't say," said the doctor. "You've been here for hours now, so why don't you go home and get some rest? We'll keep Gary here overnight for observation."

I swallowed and nodded. I knew he was right. There was no point in sitting here all night, especially if I couldn't be with Gary. I agreed to come back in the morning.

Thanksgiving came, and I found myself completely alone. I had watched the blank screen of the television all night, unable to sleep. I had smoked so many cigarettes that my chest ached. After splashing some water on my face, I called my mom to let her know what was going on. She tried to comfort me, but I had a bad feeling in the pit of my stomach. I couldn't eat anything, but I did manage to drink some coffee while driving back to the hospital. I prayed to God to give me something to be thankful for on this day.

I got to the hospital and told the receptionist I was there to check on my dog, Gary. She told me to have a seat and said she would get the doctor. A few minutes later, he came out, but it was not the same vet as the night before.

"Hello, Mr. Hall," he said. "We've been watching Gary and he did have two more seizures overnight. I've got him heavily sedated right now." He paused as if to give me a moment to prepare. "I ran a couple more tests on him, and I'm afraid that his symptoms are pointing to a possible brain tumor."

Stunned, I repeated the same helpless phrase as the night before. "What can we do?"

"First we'll have to know if that's what we're dealing with; then we'll have to decide if it's operable. However, we don't have a CAT scan here, and that's what it would take."

"Who does have a CAT scan?" I asked.

"The closest one would be at the university's school of veterinary medicine in Columbus. But this being Thanksgiving weekend, I can't say if anyone would be there."

"Gary's been my best friend for ten years," I said. "I've got to do something."

"I'll tell you what, Mr. Hall," he offered. "I just graduated from that school last year and I've still got some friends there. Let me make a couple of phone calls and see what I can do."

"I'd sure appreciate it, Doc."

About an hour later, he returned to the waiting room and told me he'd arranged for tests in the morning. He also said I could sit with Gary for a few minutes while he wrote down directions. I saw Gary lying on a gurney, with an IV in his leg and a big funnel-shaped collar around his neck.

"Why do you have that collar on him?" I asked.

"That's to keep him from pulling out the IV," the doctor explained. "I'll be back in a few minutes."

I pulled up a chair and began rubbing Gary's ears. He was sedated, but his eyes were open. "Gary is a good boy," I whispered, "and you're gonna be all right, buddy." He blinked his eyes as if he understood me. He loved to have his ears rubbed, so I sat there doing that and talking to him. Eventually he went to sleep, and I left.

On the way home I caught myself looking over my right shoulder, expecting to see Gary in the back of the station wagon. When I got home, I walked in and looked at Gary's bed. I could feel tears running down my cheeks, but I refused to let myself break down. I knew that if I did, I'd never stop.

I took a couple of Xanax and lay down. I tried but I couldn't go to sleep. I had vodka in the house, but I didn't feel like drinking anything. I just sat around. My mom called and asked me to come over for Thanksgiving dinner; I thanked her but told her what had happened and said that I needed to stay home in case the vet called. She offered to bring some food over, but I told her I couldn't eat anything right then. Mom told me to try not to worry so much.

As evening approached I couldn't stand it anymore, so I got in the car and went back to the hospital. The doctor let me spend more time with Gary. Even though he couldn't move, I could tell by his eyes that he knew I was there, petting him and talking to him.

The next morning, I got on the freeway with Gary and his dripping IV in the car and headed for Columbus. I talked to him all the way and after a couple of hours we arrived at the vet school. I found the entrance to the lab and knocked. A slender young man ushered me inside. He was expecting me. He grabbed a cart and went out with me to get Gary. Again I waited and finally it was over, but this young man was not allowed to read the results, so I still did not know. He told me it would be another few hours.

I headed back home. As we arrived back in Dayton, I notice that the IV bag was a little low, so I stopped by the regular vet's office. The doctor came out and replaced Gary's bag with a full one. At home, I carried Gary into the house and laid him on his bed. I made him as comfortable as possible and hung his IV bag from a nail above his bed. My nerves were shot, and I was so tired I just lay on the floor beside him.

Around 6:00 P.M. the emergency vet called and told me to bring Gary in. I asked him if he had received the test results and he said that we would discuss them when I got there. His voice sounded like a death sentence. I hung up and felt the approach of a panic attack coming on. No medication was going to cure this. I couldn't lose Gary. I couldn't. But I also couldn't lose control. I took four Xanax and grabbed a paper bag to breathe into. I began to calm down a bit. I took a deep breath or two. I carried Gary out and laid him down in the back of the car.

All the way to the hospital I talked to him. I don't know if it was for him or for me. Once there, the doctor saw me right away and told me that, as he suspected, Gary had a brain tumor. He'd contacted a specialist to ask about the possibility of operating, but he'd not yet heard back.

"I don't want to say anything until I hear from him," he explained, "so why don't you leave Gary here with us tonight and go home and try to get some sleep?"

"Okay," I said. "Just let me say good-bye."

I went back to the exam room and petted Gary, telling him quietly to be a good boy, and then I went home. I hadn't had a shower in three days, so I took a long hot one. I also hadn't eaten, and I still had no appetite, but I did force myself to drink a glass of milk. I tried to sleep. When I'd first gotten Gary, I had been suffering from severe depression, even contemplating suicide at one point. Suddenly I had this little puppy that was totally dependent on me. With each passing day, my depression had subsided and eventually I was able to flush the Haldol and Halcion that the doctor had prescribed for me down the toilet. I knew I had Gary to thank for that.

The next day, I returned to the hospital and the doctor took me into a room to discuss what he'd learned. "I've heard from the specialist," he said, "and I'm afraid the news isn't very good. He confirmed what I already thought. The situation is this: the chances are fifty-

fifty that Gary would survive the operation, and even if he did, he would never be the same dog again."

I looked at him. I asked him, "What would you do?"

"I can tell by Gary's records that you've taken very good care of him and it's obvious that you love him very much. But sometimes it's unfair to our pets to prolong their suffering. So I would let him go and end his suffering. You have ten years of memories to cherish. But, of course, the decision is yours."

By this time I had tears streaming down my face. "Can I spend a few minutes with him?" I asked.

"Sure," said the doctor. "Just give me a minute or two."

When he came back, he led me to the room where Gary was. The IV and cone collar were gone. Gary looked more like himself again.

"I'll be right outside when you've finished," said the doctor.

I thanked him, and after he left the room I pulled up a chair and sat down beside Gary. I laid my head on his furry shoulder. "How's my little buddy?"

He looked up at me as if to ask for my help, and I could feel my heart breaking in two. I stroked his head and said, "I'm sorry, Gary, but I've done everything I could do. I don't want to let you go, but it's not fair to make you suffer like this."

Gary licked my right hand, then looked into my eyes. He understood. This I knew. I hugged him the best I could. I had given up my life, my relationships, everything I loved in this world. I had spent two years in the presence of evil men, armed bigots who wouldn't hesitate to shoot me dead if they figured out who I was, yet this was my worst moment.

I said, "I believe in God and I also believe that we'll be together again, little buddy. Gary's the best buddy in the whole wide world." I rubbed his ears and said, "You be brave now, and I'll see you soon." I kissed him on the forehead, then stood up, took a deep breath, and walked out of the room. I was shaking, and the doctor asked me if I was all right.

"I guess," I said. "Just go ahead and do it."

"Would you like to be with him?"

"No. I want to remember him being alive."

"Have a seat in the waiting room, Mr. Hall, and I'll be out in a few minutes."

I went outside and lit up a cigarette. I had stopped crying. I felt empty. I looked up at the clear blue sky and said, "Please, God, take care of Gary until I can take care of him again myself."

I went back into the waiting room and sat down. The doctor finally came out. He sat down beside me and said, "It's over. I gave Gary a shot and he peacefully drifted off to sleep. You did the right thing, Mr. Hall."

I nodded. "Thank you for all your help, doctor."

"I know you'll want to keep this," the doctor said as he handed me a zip-top bag with Gary's collar, with its ten years' worth of dog license tags. "We'll keep Gary here in our refrigeration unit until Monday. Then we'll have him picked up and taken to Golden Acres Pet Cemetery. Do you know if you want a burial or cremation?"

"Cremation," I said "because when I die I'm going to have him buried with me."

After I made the arrangements, I went out and got into my car. I don't know how long I sat there. My mind had gone blank. I heard a voice saying, "Mr. Hall, are you all right?" I looked up to see one of the assistants standing beside my car. I rubbed my face and said, "Yeah, I'm okay. Thank you."

Then I started my car and went home. I sat there that day and night and stared at the walls. Occasionally I glanced at Gary's bed. I was lost. I didn't know how I could continue for Tym, or for anyone.

Tym Burkey

Although it had been a holiday and I knew Dave would have nothing for me, I called him anyway on Monday morning, just to check in.

"How was your weekend?" I asked.

"Not too good."

He sounded awful, so I asked, "What's wrong? Did something happen?"

Dave said nothing for a few moments, and then he told me the news: "Gary developed a brain tumor and I had to have him put to sleep on Saturday."

I hadn't expected this, and I knew it was more than just the loss of a dog; I knew Dave had lost relationships, his friends, even a few family associations. Gary had been his best friend. He had lost the one thing that meant the most to him.

"I'm really sorry to hear that, Dave," I told him, although I knew that was little consolation. "Is there anything I can do?"

"No. He's gone now. I guess I'll get over it in time."

Then I thought of something. "You know, my wife breeds border collies. Would you like to have one?"

"No. I don't think I'll ever have another dog."

I understood. It was too soon after losing Gary to even think of replacing him.

"If you change your mind," I said, "let me know. And if you just need someone to talk to, don't hesitate to call me."

"I appreciate it."

There was nothing more to say, so we said our good-byes and hung up. However, I knew that I'd have to keep close tabs on Dave. He'd once told me that taking care of Gary had pulled him out of a serious depression, and with the panic attacks, he could really wind up having a breakdown. He might even quit. We had no hold over him, and I guessed I wouldn't blame him if he gave it all up now. I could only hope he wouldn't. We needed him.

Especially with Dave on the sidelines, I tried to keep an eye on things. I'd learned from the FBI in Michigan that Ray had been working for a housing contractor in Rochester, so I didn't expect much from him for now, but I had little doubt that something was going down. I had worked enough criminal investigations to know when something was afoot. Redfeairn and Kelly were up to something.

20.

CONSPIRACY

Dave Hall

Losing Gary felt to me like the end of everything, and I had a hard time feeling motivated to do much of anything. I talked with Tym a few times but had nothing to report. I think he was afraid I was just pulling away from the investigation. The truth was I really hadn't heard from Pastor Ray. That was a welcome break, and Gary's death had given me a good reason to fully indulge in the time off. But that finally came to an end. It was time to go back to work.

On Christmas Eve, I decided to go down to Ikes. As I drove up the street, I saw Pastor Ray's car parked in front of my friend J.D.'s house. I pulled into the driveway and went up and knocked on the door. J.D. answered and said, "Hey, Dr. Dave. Come on in."

"What's happening, bro? I saw Pastor Ray's car outside."

"Ray's in the bathroom. Have a seat." J.D. handed me a mirror with a few lines of coke on it.

"Man, I better not," I said. "Not with Pastor Ray being here."

"Aw, fuck Ray. He's been snorting the shit all day with me."

Being on the spot, I went ahead, then put the mirror down on the coffee table.

"So, what're you up to?" J.D. asked me.

"I was on my way to Ikes to see what was going on."

"It's kind of dead there tonight."

"Well, you saved me a trip, then."

At that point Pastor Ray walked in the room. He was visibly drunk and had cocaine residue around his nostrils.

I saluted and said, "Hail victory, Pastor."

Ray looked a little surprised to see me. "Brother Dave, I was just going to call you. Can you give me a ride down to the church on Saturday?"

"Sure," I said. "I don't have anything planned."

"Great," said Ray. "I'll meet you at the mall at nine in the morning."

"Sounds good."

Ray sat down. "Brother, we've got a lot of good things happening."

"Like what?"

"The Michigan chapter is growing, and we've got a bunch of AK-47 assault rifles, some with fifty-round drums."

"That sounds great," I said. "Now we need to work on the Ohio chapter."

"I've got about two more weeks of work in Detroit and then I'll be back in Dayton for good," Ray assured me.

Gee, I thought, *I can't wait.* "How did you get ahold of so many assault rifles?" I asked.

"We've got our sources."

Clearly he wasn't going to reveal anything, but he looked at J.D. and smiled. That made me think that the Outlaws probably had something to do with it. I didn't want to get near that one.

Then Ray decided to head for home, so that was the end of my opportunity that evening. I spent the rest of it at the Outlaws' clubhouse, and when I woke up Sunday morning I had the mother of all hangovers. I couldn't even remember how or when I'd gotten home. I still had my clothes and shoes on. After stumbling into the living room, I looked out the window and saw that my car wasn't in the driveway. I figured I must've walked home. I headed to the kitchen for much-needed coffee, and as I passed the shelf where Gary's urn sat, I said, "Merry Christmas, little buddy."

Tym Burkey

Dave's catching Redfeairn at J.D.'s was extremely important. The AK-47 information was reported to our Detroit Division, where an aggressive agent, Mark Davidson, was assigned to it. (He would later make a gun case against Jason Swanson.) This chance meeting, when Dave reported it, confirmed my suspicion of how Redfeairn earned his money—dealing drugs—so we were one step closer, I believed, to bringing him and the Ohio AN down.

Dave Hall

When I got to the mall, I showed Ray my new flyers, which he approved for printing. During the drive, he quizzed me on the Bible, even trying to stump me, but I held my own. And when we entered the unheated church, Ray didn't let up as I'd expected him to.

"After Judas betrayed Yashua to the Jews for thirty pieces of silver," he said, "what did he do?"

"He eventually hung himself."

"That's good, Brother."

He entered a storage room and emerged with a .45-caliber automatic stuck inside his belt and a box of shells. He sat down across the table from me. "What happened to the thirty pieces of silver, Brother Dave?"

"Judas returned to the temple and gave back the thirty pieces, saying he couldn't accept it because it was tainted with blood. Then later is when he hung himself."

Ray ejected the clip. "What happened to the thirty pieces of silver?"

"The chief priest said they couldn't put money back into the treasury that had been tainted with blood. So the chief priest took the thirty pieces of silver and bought a parcel of land to bury strangers and the poor in. And they called it the potter's field or field of blood."

"Very good," said Pastor Ray.

Attempting to lighten the mood, I asked, "Got yourself a new weapon, Pastor?"

He looked at me. His eyes were sharp. He shook his head. "No," he said in a calm voice. "I've had this for a while now."

He picked up an ammo box and dumped some cartridges onto the table. He picked up a cartridge and looked it over, as if to assess its weight or shine. Then he slowly slipped it into the clip and said, "Brother Dave, today, just as in Yashua's day, we have to be very careful about informants like Judas." He reiterated again that he'd known all along that Vince Reed was an informant.

"I agree," I said.

Ray continued to slowly load the cartridges into the clip as I sat there. *What the hell is this homicidal maniac up to?* I wondered. I decided to remain cool, calm, but watchful. At the first sign the situation was going south, I was going to try my damnedest to kill the bastard.

Once the clip was fully loaded, Ray inserted the clip into the pistol and cocked it. With his finger fully on the trigger, he lowered the pistol down onto the tabletop and pointed it directly at my chest. I thought, *I'm fucked now.* I was hoping that even if he shot me I'd live long enough to take him with me.

He looked down at the gun that lay on the table between us, even as he continued to make some comment that I could hardly hear. By that time, blood was pumping in my ears, and the room was warming up despite the heat being shut off.

"Brother Dave," he said, "what do you think we ought to do about informants?"

I tried not to swallow. I had a sudden instinct to grab my side of the table, lift it, and turn it over on him, to crush him beneath it.

But somehow I kept my wits about me. If I were just another member of the Aryan Nations, I'd be assertive on this topic and ready to take action. I had to keep that in mind. I had to continue my role.

I looked at the ceiling for a moment and said, "I guess, first of all, I'd make sure the person was an informant. Then there's a couple of things we could do. We could use the informant to our advantage by feeding him or her incorrect information. Secondly, what I personally would prefer to do is to confront the person and demand they turn in their uniform and Aryan Nations ID card. I would then tell them to get out of the church and never come back, and then as soon as they turned to walk out the door, I'd shoot 'em in the back of the head."

A smile slowly came across Pastor Ray's face. He gently lowered the hammer on the pistol and said, "You're going to be a good pastor, Brother. I'm glad I'm going to have you to take over the reins of the Ohio church when I move out west."

"I'll try to never let you down," I said.

Ray stood up and stuck the gun in the belt behind his back, covering it with his shirt, then said, "Let's go visit Brother Kale."

"Sounds good to me."

I wasn't going to die that day. I stood up feeling like I had just pulled my finger out of a light socket. The old wooden floor of the church creaked under my weight as I walked toward the door. After Pastor Ray came out, I locked the door, then followed him down the steps. By this time my nervousness had turned to anger. As we walked down the sidewalk to the car, I fought off an overwhelming urge to pick up one of the bricks lining the walk and bash in Ray's head.

It had been such a simple test, but in that fragile moment, my life had hung in the balance. I couldn't have known for sure what was the right or wrong thing to say, but apparently I'd satisfied him.

During the drive over to Kale Kelly's place in Waynesville, Ohio, I managed to calm myself down.

"I gave Bob $120 to get the electricity at the church turned back on," said Ray.

"Bob?" I said. "I thought we kicked him out."

"He called me and explained how the incident with Dan and Jason was just a big misunderstanding. I finally told him he would be welcome to attend church services but not members-only meetings."

"Are you sure about this?" I asked.

"He's like a little puppy that wants to follow me around," said Ray. "I figured we could use him to run errands and stuff."

"I hope you're making the right decision," I said.

When we got to Waynesville, Ray directed me to a rural road just out of town. Soon he said, "Pull in here."

I drove into the driveway of a farmhouse across the road from the Little Miami River. There were three large wooden crosses in the front yard and a flagpole flying the Confederate flag. Both sides of the driveway were flanked by two large barns. Ray told me to park by the barn on the right, across from the house. Getting out of the car, I saw Kale coming from around the corner of that barn.

"Hey, Brother Kale," I said. "How ya doin'?"

"Pretty good, Dave." Looking at Ray, Kale said, "What're you guys up to?"

"We were down at the church, so we thought we'd pay you a visit."

"Come on upstairs, where it's warm," said Kale. We followed him around to the rear of the barn, where steps led to a second-story door. Inside, I saw that the second floor had been remodeled into an apartment. Kale invited us to take a seat in the living room. Looking around, I noticed a couple of handguns, a rifle, and a shotgun. Being a convicted felon, Kale was taking a big chance having so many firearms lying around, but it didn't seem to bother him. When Ray made it clear he wanted to talk with Kale privately, I went outside, over to the car, as they walked over by the woods bordering the backyard. After half an hour in which I saw Ray doing most of the talking, they came over to me and I heard Ray say, "Think about it, okay?"

"I will," Kale assured him.

On the way back to Dayton, thinking I might get Pastor Ray to tell me what just went on, I tried a circuitous strategy: I asked him what was going on out in Idaho.

"We expect that Morris Dees is going to sue Pastor Butler and the Aryan Nations," he said.

"What the hell are we going to do if that happens?"

"We'll have to take some drastic measures."

"Like what?"

"I can't say right now, but I do have a couple of irons in the fire."

When we got back to Dayton, I dropped Ray off at the mall and went home. The house was empty. When I couldn't take it anymore I decided to go to George's Tavern. It was my first visit to George's since Gary died, and all my friends were asking me where I'd been. I just told them I'd been busy. Soon I had about eight drinks sitting in front of me. It wasn't long before I'd forgotten all of my troubles, although I knew this was no way to deal with my situation on a regular basis. Still, for a day, it felt better.

The following day, Ray called and asked for another ride. This one was different. He wanted me to take him to Middletown, to see Bob. "I called Bob this morning," he said, "to remind him to go and pay the electric bill tomorrow. He told me that he fell down the stairs and had amnesia and couldn't remember anything about any money."

I started laughing and said, "Sorry, Pastor, but that has to be the lamest excuse I've ever heard."

"Well," Ray replied, "we're going down there and straighten his ass out."

"Okay. I'll pick you up in about twenty minutes."

In the car, Ray asked me to stop at Mary Williams' sign shop to pick up Morris Gulett. When we were on the freeway, I looked at Mo in the rearview mirror and asked, "How've you been doing, Brother Mo?"

"Pretty good, Brother," he replied. I could see him fidgeting, and when I looked over my shoulder, I saw that he was twirling a 9mm pistol around his finger like a cowboy.

"Mo," I said, "will you put that pistol down before you shoot me or Ray in the back!"

Ray turned around and said, "Put the gun away, Mo."

I knew Mo's rap sheet had charges ranging from domestic violence to drug possession, assault, and even attempted homicide, so the last thing I wanted was this idiot in my backseat with a loaded pistol. When we finally arrived in Middletown, Ray directed me to Bob's neighborhood. He instructed me to drive past Bob's house and park the car around the corner on a side street, so Bob wouldn't see us coming. I hadn't really thought about it until we got out of the car and I saw Mo stick the pistol into his belt. Suddenly it struck me why we were here. I knew Ray was really pissed off, and I was worried that he'd brought Mo along to shoot Bob. I tried to reassure myself that even Pastor Ray wouldn't kill somebody over $120.

The house was a duplex, and Bob lived on the top floor. Ray knocked but got no response, so he banged on the door hard with his bare fist. The lady who lived downstairs opened her door and inquired, "Are you looking for Bob?"

"Yes ma'am," said Ray, "we are."

"He must be home," she told us. "I just heard somebody walking around up there."

Ray knocked again, but still no one came. This made Ray even angrier, but he restrained it in front of the woman. "If you see Bob," he said, "would you tell him to call Ray?"

As we headed back down the steps, Ray said, "I've half a mind to kick that door in and drag that little coward out and beat his ass."

"He's not worth going to jail for," I pointed out.

On the way back to Dayton, we stopped at a computer store. When we came back out, I noticed that Mo had left his 9mm automatic in plain sight on the seat of my car.

"Pastor Ray," I said, "look at this."

Ray turned to Mo. "What the hell's wrong with you, Mo?"

"What?" replied Mo.

Ray pointed at the pistol and said, "If a cop had seen that, Brother Dave would be on his way to jail about now!"

"Sorry," said Mo. "I thought I'd put my coat over it."

After dropping him off, we headed for Pastor Ray's place. Along the way, Ray said he was going to stay in Dayton for a few days before returning to Detroit to finish up the job he'd been working on. As I pulled into his driveway, he added, "I'm sorry about Mo's actions today. I don't know what I'm going to do with that guy. I hate to give up on him."

"Hopefully he'll pull himself together, Yahweh willing."

"Thanks for the ride," said Ray. "Let me give you some gas money."

"No thanks, Pastor Ray. You bought lunch, that's good enough."

"If I don't see you or talk to you," said Ray, "have a happy New Year and hail victory!"

On the way home I started to feel some pain in my stomach, but I figured it was the spicy food from lunch. Stopping to get some Tums, I went on home. The Tums seemed to work and later that evening, I had a few stiff drinks and hit the sack.

On the Monday after Christmas, I called Tym to make my report. We then chatted about the upcoming holiday, and after hanging up the phone, I felt a sharp pain in my chest. Thinking it was just another panic attack, I took a couple of Xanax. An hour went by and the pain continued, so I drove myself to the emergency room. By the time I got to the hospital it was unbearable. I was nearly doubled over as I stumbled into the emergency entrance. Then everything became a blur. I remember a nurse giving me a shot in the arm and being hooked up to an EKG machine. After that, nothing.

Tym Burkey

When Dave called me on Tuesday, I was shocked to hear that he was in the hospital.

"What's wrong?" I asked, alarmed. "Are you all right?"

"I'm okay, I guess," he said. "Yesterday I started to have chest pains, so I drove myself to the emergency room. They sedated me and I woke up in the cardiac unit here at St. Elizabeth's. So far all my EKGs have been normal, but they're going to run some more tests today."

I offered to come, but he warned me that Ray might find out we'd been together, so I dropped that plan. Still, I knew he was alone, and I didn't like to leave him there.

Over the next two days, I checked in several times a day. Dave's heart seemed to be functioning normally, which was a relief. Finally they diagnosed him with a bleeding ulcer, scheduling an endoscopy. They also told him he was diabetic. He underwent the procedures, learned how to control his conditions (no alcohol for two weeks), and then went home. It began to snow. In fact, we were in for a snowstorm, and it wasn't long before the traffic officials declared a snow emergency. I wasn't about to let Dave lie there at home, without anyone to visit him, without a way to care for himself. Despite our protocol to keep a professional distance, I decided I had to venture out and brave the storm. It seemed unlikely that Ray or any of his spies would be out anywhere.

Anne packed some homemade soup and bread, and we got into the car with the boys. Shopping for more groceries so Dave wouldn't run out, we brought everything over to him. He was surprised and grateful.

For the first time, I went far enough into his home to see how he had decked out his bedroom with Confederate and Nazi flags to help himself stay in the role. Instantly overwhelmed by the hate paraphernalia, I just shook my head. No wonder he was having health problems. "Hopefully you'll be able to burn all this trash soon," I commented.

"It won't be soon enough," he agreed.

21

CLANDESTINE PREPARATIONS

Dave Hall

On the first Saturday of the new year, just before 5:00 P.M., I got a hysterical call from Mary Williams.

"Dave," she said through tears, "Mo's on crack and he's drunk and breaking everything in my sign shop. Can you get down here and get him under control?" I could hear what sounded like World War III in the background. She said something about wanting "all these guns out of here," and then hung up.

I called Ray, but his mother said he'd just stepped out, so I left a message for him to call at once. About twenty minutes later, he did, and I explained about the call from Mary.

"That damned Mo," said Ray. "This could be the final straw."

"Why don't you meet me at the sign shop and we'll try to do some damage control?"

"Thanks, Brother. I'll see you there in about ten minutes."

When I got to Mary's shop, I found a mess. It looked like a bomb had gone off inside. Mary had always kept the shop clean and tidy, with a place for everything and everything in its place, so it was a shock to see it in this condition. As I waded through the debris, I called out, "Mo! Mary!" From one corner I heard, "Over here, Dave." I turned to see Mary kneeling on the floor with her face in her hands.

"Are you all right, sweetheart?" I asked.

Mary wiped her eyes and stood up. "I'm all right. But that asshole Mo has destroyed everything I own."

"Where's he at?"

"I don't know and I don't care. He put a big box of guns in his van and left about fifteen minutes ago, after I threatened to call the cops."

"I'm sure sorry about this," I said.

"It's not your fault. It's my fault for marrying the asshole."

About that time, Pastor Ray walked in. He just stood there for a moment, shaking his head. Then he shouted, "Damn it! That does it. Mo is out of the Aryan Nations for good." He looked at Mary. "Don't worry, we'll help you clean up this mess."

"Don't bother," she told him. "I want everything to do with the Aryan Nations off my property by noon tomorrow, or it's all going into the Dumpster. And that includes trash like this."

She threw a copy of *The Warrior's Stand* at Ray's feet and walked away. I knew that it was a publication about how an Aryan warrior should act. One of its themes is that women are subservient to men and their primary function is to have babies. I could see why she wanted it out of there.

"Dave," said Ray, "you go home and I'll go find Mo."

"Do you want me to help look for him?"

"No. If I need you, I'll give you a call. Otherwise I'll see you here at seven o'clock tomorrow morning. We'll get our stuff."

"I'll be here."

On the way home I thought if all white supremacists were as stupid as Morris Gulett, the FBI's DT unit would be out of business.

The next day, I found both Ray and Mo in the shop. I noticed Mo's black eye and a split lip, but I didn't say anything. I suspected that

Ray had vented his anger. We cleaned out the place, and Ray took the literature to the church. We then went over to Kale's, and this time I managed to catch part of the conversation. It confirmed my fears.

"You know what happened to the KKK in North Carolina," Ray said. "We can't afford to let that happen to us, Brother."

"We won't," Kale replied.

I knew that had to be a reference to Morris Dees and his lawsuit against the Klan group on behalf of a black woman in North Carolina. That Klan group lost all of their land, houses, and other assets. I also knew that Jesse Warfield and the other two AN security guards were still in jail in Idaho.

As we took our leave, Ray shook Kale's hand. That was unusual, because he always saluted. I wondered if it had any special meaning. When I reported all this to Tym, he told me that Dees hadn't yet made a move, but he expected it. The waiting game had probably fried Ray's nerves.

A couple of weeks later, I learned from Kale that he'd been in Clanton, Alabama, a small town between Birmingham and Montgomery. I knew that the Southern Poverty Law Center was in Montgomery, so I wondered if he'd gone to check it out. He said that he'd attended a KKK rally.

"I would have ridden down with you," I said.

He shrugged. "I went at the last minute." He then asked me to have Ray, who was still in Detroit, give him a call whenever I talked to him next. Instead, I let Tym know about this development.

Tym Burkey

Dave kept me well apprised of Kale Kelly's movements now that he'd gotten closer to him. I also learned that Hoge Tabor, who owned the building that housed the church, was going to sell it. Apparently, he'd considered giving it to the AN but had then changed his mind. Ray had moved all of the AN paraphernalia to Kelly's place.

As expected, Morris Dees went ahead and sued the AN over the 1998 incident at Hayden Lake. I was certain this development would stir things up. Dees himself would have to watch his back, but with Dave in place, we'd certainly know if Kale Kelly had been selected as a potential assassin. It was our good luck, I thought, to have Dave so close to someone who might turn out to be as lethal as Redfeairn. We couldn't have planned it better.

I didn't say anything to Dave about Dees, letting him learn about it as if he were truly an AN member.

Dave Hall

In mid-February, Ray asked me to meet him at Ikes. He wanted to discuss something that he'd rather not say over the phone. I arrived at the bar in the late afternoon, but Ray wasn't there yet. Gwen was working, and when she saw me come in she came out from behind the bar toward me.

"Dr. Dave! Where have you been, sweetie?" She kissed me, then put my head between her breasts and rubbed my face against them.

"I'm going to have to stay away more often!" I said.

Gwen laughed. "The usual, Doc?"

"Yes, please." I had a couple of drinks before Ray finally showed up. To my surprise, Mo was with him. As they walked up, I saluted and said, "Hail victory, Pastor Ray. Hail victory, Mo."

Ray returned my salute and said, "It's good to see you, Brother. We need to talk."

Mo remained at the bar as Ray and I sat down at a secluded table. He looked around the bar, then turned back to me. "What I feared has happened. Morris Dees and the SPLC have filed a civil suit against Pastor Butler, Mike Teague, and the Aryan Nations on behalf of that woman and her son that Jesse Warfield, John Yaeger, and Shane Wright assaulted."

I acted surprised, but I was thinking that this could finally put the entire outfit out of commission. "That was way back before the

Aryan Nations World Congress in July 1998," I said. "Why would they wait so long?"

"They probably were slithering around trying to build a case against us."

"So what can we do?"

Ray looked down at the table for a moment, then looked into my eyes and said, "Morris Dees has to be killed."

I'd known it was coming, but to actually experience this moment was a bit of a shock. "What good would that do?" I asked.

"At the very least, it would make any other Jew lawyer think twice about taking over the case."

"You're probably right," I said, "but who's going to kill him?" After realizing what I'd just said, I added, "No, wait, I don't want to know." I'd learned over the past two years that the best way to avoid suspicion and still get information out of Ray was to pretend I didn't want to know.

"I've anticipated Dees filing this case," said Ray, "so I've been in touch with a good brother who has had military sniper training."

That remark clinched it for me. I knew in my gut that Kale Kelly was the "good brother" Ray was talking about.

"I've sent out to Idaho," Ray continued, "and have received legal documents containing names and addresses of some people we need to deal with. Tomorrow Jason Swanson is coming down and we'll go down to the church to discuss matters. We'll also take a load of stuff over to Kale's place."

"To put it bluntly," I said, "I guess the shit has hit the fan."

Ray smiled. "It hasn't yet, but it soon will."

We got up and went back to the bar, where Mo was standing. Ray said, "Brother Dave, we're going to head out, so I'll see you at the church around eleven o'clock tomorrow morning."

After they left I stayed for a few more drinks. I was just getting ready to leave when a couple of guys started fighting. Gwen yelled to me, "Dr. Dave, can you make those guys take it outside?"

I pulled the two apart and told them, "The lady said take it outside." One of the guys took a swing at me, barely missing my face. I reacted by hitting him hard in the throat and kicking him in the stomach. A good solid right uppercut to the face finished him off. I then looked at the other guy and said, "Are you going to leave or do you want to join your friend here on the floor?"

He started backing up. "I'm leaving, I'm leaving."

After he went out, I turned around and said, "See ya, Gwen."

The next morning in New Vienna, I saw Jason's car in the parking lot. Pastor Ray, Jason, and Mo were sitting on the stairs as I walked up. We exchanged greetings and then I unlocked the church. Ray had two or three manila envelopes with him, and he and Jason sat at a table going over what looked like legal documents. After loading up my car with flags, arm shields, and other AN paraphernalia (due to the pending building inspection), we all went over to Kelly's place, but no one was around, so we unloaded my car, putting everything in the lower part of the barn.

At lunch in Lebanon, Ohio, Jason looked out the window at a bank across the street and said, "We need to knock off a few of those."

"There isn't any money in jackin' up banks," Ray replied. "The real money is in armored cars." The conversation then shifted to the lawsuit Dees had filed. "Our biggest problem right now," said Ray, "is that damn Jesse Warfield. From what I've been told, he's singing like a canary trying to save his own skin."

"Can we get someone into the jail to shut him up?" I asked.

"No," Ray told me. "He's in protective custody."

After sitting there with them for over an hour, I still had not learned what Kale might be up to. There had to be a better way to get this information.

A few days later, I joined Jason and Ray at Kale's again, and Ray took him off into the woods for a private conversation. I found this frustrating as hell, but I listened patiently as Jason related tales of him and his boys going out and beating up niggers, Jews, "race mixers," and faggots. When Ray and Kale rejoined us we all went inside to warm up. I saw some computer components sitting on a desk and asked, "Did you get your computer working, Kale?"

"Almost. I need to pick up a few more parts, like a keyboard and a printer."

I looked around the room, but the only other thing of interest was Kale's .45 automatic sitting on top of his dresser. We sat around for a while just talking general bullshit. Kale told us about the KKK rally he'd attended in January in Clanton, Alabama. With delight, he said he'd worn camouflage clothing and tied an Israeli flag to his boot, dragging it through the streets as they marched. Finally, around three o'clock we headed back to Dayton. Ray put a cassette tape into the player for us to listen to. It was a sermon by Pastor Butler titled "The Jewish Threat." Once again, I found myself agreeing against my will with some of what Pastor Butler had to say. I had been inundated with so much of this propaganda, a bunch of it had seeped into my brain.

Tym Burkey

The information regarding Morris Dees was important. Anytime the FBI learns a threat has been made it's our responsibility to let the targeted person know. Threats were nothing new to Dees, but I knew he should be told about this one. I contacted the agent in Montgomery who was the liaison to the Southern Poverty Law Center and let her know. I followed up with a picture of Kale Kelly, as the SPLC already had photos of Redfeairn and Gulett.

Dave said something else about Redfeairn that interested me—his remark about armored cars.

"Damn it!" I said. "I knew it! That son of a bitch did it."

"Did what?"

I described an incident involving the holdup of an armored car, in which an eyewitness described a man who resembled Redfeairn.

Dave seemed to find this interesting. "That could be why Ray always has a pocketful of money," he said.

"It gets better. When we found the car used in the robbery, it had two different license plates on it. The front plate had been stolen from an apartment complex near where Mo lived and the rear plate from near Ray's neighborhood."

"Sounds to me like they did it."

"I agree, but so far all we have is circumstantial evidence. But we'll get those two idiots eventually."

Dave also told me that Ray had been packing a .45 when they'd visited the Air Force museum at Wright-Patterson Air Force Base in Dayton. That, he thought, was a way to get him back in jail, but I pointed out that it would only get him two years. We wanted more serious charges that would imprison him for a long time.

Dave Hall

I picked Ray up on Sunday morning to go again to Kale's place. Along the way Ray said, "Brother Dave, I'm sorry to say we can't trust Morris Gulett anymore."

"Why's that?" I asked. I was hoping for something good.

"Last week while we were in Detroit, Mo somehow got ahold of some crack. Then he stole the boss's work van and sold most of the power tools, probably for more crack."

"Where's Mo now?"

"He tried to make it back to Dayton, but about halfway there, he was running out of gas, so he stopped at a station and filled up, then drove off without paying. A couple of miles down the interstate, some troopers arrested him and took him to jail."

"He's in jail? Where?"

"I don't know," said Ray. "He called my mom and I told her to tell Mo to never call me again."

I knew that had been hard on Ray, after all his effort, but I was pleased to learn that Mo was out of the way. He asked me to sign a formal letter that stated that Mo was ejected from the AN. I complied, and he stuck it into the sun visor.

About that time Kale emerged from the barn and gave us a Nazi salute. He was followed by two other men who I learned were KKK members from Kentucky. Sandy came down from the apartment above the barn with a pot of hot coffee and some Styrofoam cups. Then once again, Ray went off with Kale. The other two men eventually left and Sandy went in, so I decided to take a chance.

I crept into the bottom part of the barn, going toward the rear, where I could see Kale and Ray through the openings in the slats. As I slunk down in a dark corner, I could hear parts of their conversation, which turned out to be a heated discussion. Ray said, "Those Klansmen are going to get you into trouble!"

"We know what we're doing," said Kale. "We've planned it meticulously."

Ray fired back saying, "If you go through with this Earl Cable thing, you're crazy and I want no part of it!" After a pause, Ray said, "We'll meet again next Sunday and talk more about it."

Kale shrugged. With that they turned to walk around to the front of the barn.

I moved as quickly and quietly as I could back outside. When they emerged, I was standing beside my car, lighting up a cigarette. I thought to myself, *I cut that pretty close.* But I'd succeeded. I had a name for Tym and a feeling that something was in the works that involved Kale and his buddies. When they got to where I was standing, Kale asked, "Why don't you and Dave come down to Kentucky with me to see Ron Edwards?" He looked at me and added, "He's a good friend of mine, and the grand dragon of the Kentucky KKK."

But Ray answered for me. "That depends on when. I've got a lot of things coming up and I'm going to be pretty busy. If nothing else, Brother Dave can go as my representative. I trust him completely and he's a good example of an Aryan Nations member."

"Thank you, Pastor Ray," I said.

"Well, let's just see when I can set up a meeting," Kale replied.

We all talked for a few more minutes before Ray and I got into the car and headed back to Dayton. Along the way, Ray said, "I'm afraid those Klansmen are going to get Kale into trouble."

"What do you mean?" I asked.

"I can only say that they're trying to get him involved in a hare-brained scheme and I don't like it."

I figured if Ray wanted to tell me what this scheme was, he would, so I didn't ask. But I knew that Tym would find all of this quite interesting. He might even know who this Earl Cable was.

Tym Burkey

This news indicated a plot of some sort. Kelly, our lone wolf, was planning something, but what? Who was Earl Cable? Did any of this relate to Morris Dees? I did not have the answers, so I sent a priority communication to FBI headquarters and all U.S. DT squads, providing the information I had and awaited a response.

22

EARLE CABELL

Dave Hall

I didn't hear anything from Pastor Ray until Friday morning. Mo had made bail, and Ray wanted me to help get him to sign the expulsion letter. When we arrived at the place where he was staying in north Dayton, we knew someone was inside, but no one would answer the door. Listening closely, we heard movement inside, which angered Ray.

"Mo's probably all cracked up," he said. "He always winds up at this damn crack house. We oughta just burn it down."

I managed to get him to leave with me. On the way back, I asked, "Do you still want me to go to Kentucky with Kale?"

"Yes, because I'm going to be busy in Michigan. The main reason I want you to go—and don't mention this to Kale—is to find out what kind of man Edwards is."

Great. Now I was working undercover for the FBI *and* the AN.

We decided to stop by Kale's place. He was home, so we went out for coffee at a local McDonald's. Ray once again raised the subject of the approaching millennium.

"You know," he said, "with the year 2000 just nine months away, we really need to be prepared. If all the computers crash, the government will use that as an excuse to confiscate our weapons."

"I don't buy all this Y2K crap," Kale said. "*Now* is the time to make something happen, and I'm not afraid to die trying. Hopefully it will have a domino effect."

"I'm not afraid to die, either," Ray replied, "if it's for the right reason."

"I have to agree with Brother Kale," I interjected. "I don't believe the computers are going to crash, either, so why wait until the government *expects* us to do something? Now is the time to catch them off guard."

Ray seemed to consider this. "Maybe you guys are right."

As we were leaving the McDonald's, Pastor Ray spotted a white Chevy Suburban parked across the street. "Guys," he said, "it looks like feds."

I looked over and saw four men in white shirts with ties and sunglasses sitting in the Suburban. I laughed and said, "Either the feds or used-car salesmen."

"Brother Dave," Kale said, "you're crazy."

"Now you sound like my mom," I replied. As I pulled out of the parking lot, I said, "Let's see if Janet Reno's little boys want to play follow the leader." I watched in the rearview mirror as we drove off. The Suburban remained parked until we were out of sight. When we got to the turnoff to Kale's place, I drove on by.

"Dave," said Kale, "you missed the turnoff."

"I know," I replied. "I'm just making sure that nobody's following us."

"Good thinking, Dave," he commented. I drove around out in the country for a while, then finally headed back to Kale's place. We all went behind the barn, where Kale had set up some targets. Ray pulled out a .45 automatic from under his shirt and handed it to Kale. "Try this," he said.

I'd had no idea he'd been packing that weapon around all morning, so I was glad the feds hadn't decided to approach us for a routine check.

Kale took aim at one of the targets and fired off three shots. "This fires pretty smooth, Ray," said Kale. Ray then handed the gun to me. I sensed another test and said, "You know I don't like automatics. I'm a revolver man myself."

"Give it a try," said Kale.

I shrugged. "Okay." Without aiming, I fired off three shots from the hip, hitting the bull's-eye twice, with the third shot just to the left.

Kale smiled and said, "Damn, Brother! I'd hate to have you shooting at me with a revolver."

I handed the gun back to Pastor Ray, and he shot it until the clip was empty. Then we went inside, and Kale raised the subject of purchasing guns.

"I'm thinking about going to a KKK rally on April seventh in Center City, Kentucky," he said. "I've got about five thousand dollars and I might be able to get a deal on some weapons."

I thought this might finally be my opportunity to get a specific illegal plan, but Ray cut him short: "You know Pastor Britton is going to be at the Feast of the Passover in Tennessee that weekend."

"That's right," said Kale. "I guess I'll be going down there instead."

The conversation soon fell off, and I was left wondering why Kale cared where Britton was.

On the way back to Dayton, Ray said, "Brother Dave, I'm going to tell you something that you must keep secret or it could cost you your life."

I didn't like these moments. While I might get important information, making all my work among these lunatics worthwhile, I simply couldn't stomach the sense of dire threat.

"Is it necessary for you to tell me this secret?" I asked. I knew that would give him even more reason to tell me, as well as waylay suspicion.

"Well," he said, "you're moving up in the organization and I already consider you a pastor, so there are a few things you need to know."

"Okay," I said. "I can keep a secret."

"Here it is. I'm a member of the Order of the Phineas Priesthood."

He let this sink in, knowing I was aware of the idea of a secret group of men who supposedly worked as enforcers for the Aryan Nations.

"When Mo got into trouble this last time," Ray went on, "the Order was going to kill him, but I talked them out of it. That's why I drew up that letter you signed stating he was no longer a member."

"I thought the Phineas Priesthood was just a story out of the Bible," I said.

"Yahweh bestowed a priesthood upon Phineas and his seed line," Ray replied, as if he were launching into a sermon. "A priesthood that has existed down through the ages, even today. Members of the Phineas Priesthood are known only to one another. The reason I'm telling you is that once you're ordained, you'll have to walk softly and be careful of what you say and do, because the Phineas Priesthood, by a majority vote, could eliminate you. And I don't mean by excommunication."

I glanced at him. "I believe I get what you mean, Pastor. Thanks for the heads-up."

"You're welcome, Brother. But remember that even revealing this secret—to anyone—can get you killed."

"I'll remember."

After dropping Ray off at his mom's house, I thought about this Phineas Priesthood stuff. If and when we put Ray away, would I have to forever watch my back because of some secret society? I wondered if it was true. I mean, how could they be watching all the AN members? And wasn't Tym aware of them? Even if they were for real, maybe Ray had just heard about them and invented himself a fantasy. I finally decided that Ray had told me the story just to keep me on the straight and narrow. Either way, it was a reality check.

I'd grown so comfortable in my role as a dedicated white supremacist that I'd nearly forgotten how dangerous these people were. Especially Ray.

In fact, the next time we went to Kale's, I had a chance to see his computer area. I spotted an e-mail lying on his desk from someone with the screen name of Eagle1. I could see that this person had mentioned the Feast of the Passover. I didn't have time to read it all, but I saw that one of the speakers would be a bioweapons specialist.

I then asked Kale if he and Sandy might like to ride with me to Sweetwater, Tennessee, next month, where the feast was to be held. He declined, because they were leaving early, but he revealed the date of an upcoming Klan rally—April 24—arranged by Ron Edwards. Ray mentioned that Jo Kinder of the Confederate Society of America, the woman who had spoken to us at church some time back about her racist newsletter, had invited us all to a party at her house in Cincinnati. He urged me to go. There was nothing I wanted more than to spend a whole Saturday at a white supremacist party.

Tym Burkey

I called Dave on Monday, and he told me about the various meetings. He also mentioned Ray's habit of carrying a .45. I was most curious about the e-mail from Eagle1 and the bioweapons expert scheduled for the Feast of the Passover.

"Now here's something that just doesn't sit right with me," Dave said. "Kale, who is not that religious to begin with and doesn't even follow the Bible's food laws, is going to drive hundreds of miles to Sweetwater, Tennessee, to spend three days at a religious event. I don't know why he'd do that."

"That does sound a little fishy, doesn't it?" I replied.

"I offered to drive, but Kale said he and Sandy were leaving a day early so they could stop and spend the night with an old friend in London, Kentucky. From some things that Sandy's told me, I believe the old friend's name is Steve Anderson."

"Slow down," I said, "my crayon is starting to melt."

"There's more."

"Okay, go ahead."

He told me about Kale's plans to take a trip out west in May, stopping in Kentucky, Tennessee, and at Elohim City before ending up at Hayden Lake for the Aryan Nations World Congress.

"Is that it?" I asked.

"There's one more thing," Dave said. He stopped for a moment, as if to prolong the suspense. "Ray told me a secret, but I can't tell you about it because if I do, members of a secret society will kill me."

I started to laugh. I couldn't help it.

"You wouldn't be laughing," said Dave, "if the boogie men were after you." Then *he* laughed. After we brought ourselves under control, he told me about the Phineas Priesthood and their role as enforcers. Supposedly, Ray was a member. He added that this group of enforcers had considered whacking Mo.

I think Dave was surprised that I already knew about it. "The Phineas Priesthood information has popped up before," I told him. "Personally, I think it's just a myth."

"I hope you're right," he said.

"How are you doing on money?"

"I could use some after all this driving around."

"I'll get some expense money together this week."

"Sounds good."

I was interested in this communication from Eagle1, but I thought for a moment about Ray's supposed membership in the Phineas Priesthood. He could certainly be using such revelations to keep people in line, but it wasn't that farfetched to imagine some members of a splinter group that took it upon themselves to maintain the organization's integrity. It took only one person with experience in explosives or weaponry who decided he had a mission to blow up buildings or assassinate "enemies." Ray was the right type of person.

Later that week, when I gave Dave more expense money, we agreed that spending time with Kale, without Ray around, might produce some effective leads.

Dave Hall

While Pastor Ray was in Michigan, I decided to drop by and see Kale. He showed me some stuff he'd downloaded off the Internet, mostly about Elohim City, the white supremacist mecca. At the top of one page were the words *"Bruder Schweigen."* I asked Kale what it meant.

" *'Bruder Schweigen'* is German for The Order," he told me. "I want to go out there to meet Pastor Miller, the leader of Elohim City and the Aryan Republican Army."

I asked if he was planning to attend Ray's special services at the church on April 18, a Sunday coming up, in honor of Hitler's birthday on the 20th. He said he had other plans, but didn't elaborate.

We talked for a while about the Jews and the government, and occasionally I'd tell Kale a joke just to keep him off balance. As tactfully as I could, I tried to get some information, but it was like trying to get blood from a turnip. Finally, afraid I'd make him suspicious, I quit trying. Just as I was about to leave, I learned that Kale didn't have a way to get to Jo Kinder's party, so I offered to pick him up. That seemed like an opportunity in the making.

Later that evening, after a few stiff drinks, I hit the sack. In the middle of the night, I heard a low-pitched voice.

"How does it feel to be a race traitor, Brother Dave?"

I couldn't breathe, and when I opened my eyes I realized I was inside a coffin. Panicked, I began pushing on the lid, then beating on it to get out. I was sweating, screaming, then the next thing I knew I was sitting up in the middle of the bed, hyperventilating.

After I caught my breath, I said out loud, "Oh boy, that was a good one!" I looked over at the clock: 4:00 A.M. There was no way I was going back to sleep after that nightmare, so I got up and watched some old movies on TV.

In the morning, exhausted but ready to continue with this madness, I picked up Kale. Before I could pull out of the driveway, a pickup truck drove in and parked beside me. Kale got out to talk with the driver, then asked me, "Do you mind if my friend Larry tags along?"

"Not at all," I assured him. "The more the merrier." Especially if the company of this man might loosen some tongues.

We stopped for coffee and sandwiches, then headed for Cincinnati. During the drive, I learned that Larry was a KKK member, and plenty of old stories went back and forth between these two, but nothing of any use to me. I was beginning to regret that Larry had happened by.

We were soon at Jo Kinder's house. As she invited us in, I saw that her home was immaculate. She led us through the living room, where about ten people were watching the silent film *Birth of a Nation*. We went to a large room at the rear of the house, into her office. I noticed that the walls were covered with Civil War–era pictures and memorabilia.

"This is where I write *The Copperhead Update*," said Jo. "Feel free to look around."

I spent the better part of an hour taking advantage of her invitation. One picture was of Jo and several women wearing 1880s-style dresses and hoops, standing under a banner that read "Daughters of the Confederacy." From the Spanish moss hanging from the trees behind them, I figured it was probably taken somewhere in the Deep South.

As I looked around, I noticed the house getting crowded, and many of the people who'd arrived I already knew from church. I was talking with a few people in the dining room when Jo brought out several large platters piled high with hors d'oeuvres and tiny tea party sandwiches. But try as I might, I didn't overhear any clandestine conversations or notice any people in corners with others, whispering in secret.

Kale, Larry, and I finally left, and as we were driving through Cincinnati, we passed the Jewish Hospital, located at the corner of Galbraith and Kenwood streets. I saw this as an opportunity, so I said, "The things you see when you don't have an Uzi."

Kale laughed. "You'd need something better than that."

"Like what? A rocket launcher?"

"No, about two tons of ammonium nitrate and a Ryder truck."

We all laughed. Then the subject of James Byrd Jr. came up, because one of the men involved in that vicious dragging murder had recently been convicted. Kale said, "The boy that killed that nigger is a hero; it was the will of Yahweh."

As we got closer to Kale's place, I once again brought up the subject of getting together to celebrate Hitler's birthday.

"I'd like to, but I've made other plans," said Kale. "Besides, something is going to happen on the nineteenth."

"What?" I asked.

Kale just smiled and shook his head. I decided it was probably better not to pursue the matter any further. Changing the subject, I said, "Have you been able to set up that meeting with Ron Edwards yet?"

"As a matter of fact, I have," said Kale. "Are you free this weekend?"

"I don't have anything planned."

"I was thinking about going down Friday morning and coming back Saturday or Sunday."

"Sounds good to me," I said. "You know, I've got an ex-girlfriend who works at a car rental place. She's given me a free rental a couple of times before when Ray and I went out of state. If you want, I'll give her call."

"Yeah, go ahead," said Kale. I was satisfied. Although I'd just wasted a day, I figured this next trip would be just me and Kale. Little did I know that we would not be entirely alone.

Tym Burkey

The communication regarding Earl Cable had paid off, in a big way. One of the analysts working the DT program in another state gave me some information that changed the direction of the AN investigation. He called and told me that "Earl Cable" might actually refer to the Earle Cabell Federal Building in Dallas. He added that McVeigh had originally targeted that building but then switched to the one in Oklahoma City. My heart sank from this news. I hung up the phone and put my head in my hands. It all made sense now. They were planning another bombing, and they had a definite target. I called my boss, Roger Wilson, and broke the news. On the phone, he maintained his usual cool demeanor, but within minutes he called back and said the boss wanted to talk and I was to get down to Cincinnati as soon as possible.

We'd been nervous that something was being planned for April 19 or 20, and Dave's information confirmed our hunch—especially Kelly's reference to ammonium nitrate, an ingredient in the bomb that McVeigh had used four years earlier. When he told me that he was going to get a rental car to take Kelly to Kentucky, I decided that we needed to keep minute-by-minute tabs on them.

"Do you have any plans for this morning, Dave?" I asked.

"I was going to get my brakes fixed," he told me, "because they're getting really bad."

"Where are you taking the car to?"

"A friend of mine manages a brake shop out in Trotwood, so I'll probably take it there. Why?"

"We need to talk, and not on the phone. Tell me where it is and I'll meet you there."

I knew I was making Dave nervous, especially when I arrived before he did. It was my habit to always come late. I'm sure he was pretty curious about what we needed to discuss. Bob Hlavac was with me.

Dave approached my car, spotted Bob, and said, "Well, if it isn't the Bobbsey Twins."

I smiled, but then I got right to the point. "We think these guys are planning something that could turn out to be deadly," I said.

Dave nodded. "I have the same feeling. Do you have any idea what it could be?"

"I can't tell you," I said. "You'll just have to trust me on this."

We needed Dave to come up with the plot on his own. Also, we did not want Dave to have too much knowledge of a plot that he could inadvertently reveal to the wrong person.

He shrugged. "What do you want from me that I'm not already doing?"

I looked at Bob. We both knew that Dave wasn't going to like this, but it was important that we convince him. "Dave, we need you to wear a wire."

He took a step back from the car, probably to remind me of one of his two conditions again, but I rushed right in. "I know I agreed from the very beginning that you'd never have to wear a wire, and I'm not going to try to force you to wear one now—"

"You know I've been checked for a wire several times."

"Yes, I know, Dave, but we've only got a month before April nineteenth and we have to get something on Kelly to prevent the possible loss of life."

Dave didn't say anything. He bit his lower lip and stared at me. I knew he was weighing the consequences against the benefits.

"If you wear a wire," I said, "you could be compelled to testify in federal court and possibly end up in the Witness Protection Program."

"Yeah," he replied. "But leaving my family and friends behind and starting a new life somewhere else would be pretty hard."

I recognized that I was asking a lot from him but we had no other option. He was the only person we had in the perfect position. He took a deep breath and asked, "Can I have some time to think about it and maybe discuss it with my mom?"

"Sure, Dave."

I knew that he had one foot in already, and he told me, "I'll call you this evening and let you know one way or the other."

I realized this would be a difficult decision for him and that he'd get nothing out of it except the satisfaction of knowing that he'd helped to stop these guys. That might not seem like much up against what he risked—his life, and possibly his home and family. Nevertheless, later that day, he called and said, "Okay, I'll do it."

"I don't know how to thank you, Dave," I told him, "but rest assured that we'll do everything we can to protect you. Let's discuss it further in the morning."

By that time, we'd decided to rig Dave's rental car with digital audio recorders and a global positioning system. That way, Dave wouldn't have to wear a wire on his body. He was grateful for the information. Even if someone found our equipment, he could still credibly pretend to know nothing about it. For all anyone knew, the FBI had been following him as an AN member, saw him at the rental agency, and made sure he got the car that we'd rigged.

Dave Hall

When I got to the airport the next morning to pick up the rental car, they didn't have the car I'd reserved, so they gave me a free upgrade to a luxury car. When I went to get in, I noticed it had Michigan plates. At the time I didn't think anything of it. There was no way to know that these plates would nearly get me killed.

When I arrived at the school, Tym was waiting. I pulled alongside him and he said, "That's one hell of a car, Dave."

"They didn't have the one I reserved, so they gave me this thing."

"Follow me," said Tym.

"Try to keep it at least thirty or forty miles above the speed limit, will you?"

Tym laughed and agreed. I followed him to the interstate and we headed south until we got to the Waynesville exit. I was wondering what the hell Tym was doing, because we were dangerously close to Kale's residence, although Kale wouldn't know this car. Tym led me through Waynesville to a park on the outskirts of town. Although the park was on the opposite side of town from Kale's place, it still made me nervous as hell. Tym drove to the rear of the park, out of sight of the main road. When we parked our cars, I got out and said, "Why didn't we just park in Kale's driveway?"

"Don't worry," said Tym. "I've got agents watching the entrance to the park, so we're safe."

"I sure hope so."

While we waited for the FBI technicians to arrive, we discussed what tactics I could use to extract information from Kale. I finally told Tym, "I don't think I should go into this with any set plans. I do better when I just wing it. I know Kale well enough to know when to back off."

"You've done an excellent job so far," Tym agreed, "so I'll just let you work your magic."

Two white vans came speeding toward us, and it turned out to be the FBI technicians. Two guys emerged from each van and immediately began installing the equipment. One went under the hood, one crawled under the car, one got into the car and disappeared under the dash, and one got into the trunk. In less than ten minutes, they had the car wired with microphones and a digital recorder, and they showed me how to make it all work. I thanked them, and they shook my hand and said, "Good luck, sir. And by the way, try not to play the radio. That could affect the microphones."

It was quarter of twelve. I was picking up Kale at noon. I looked at Tym and said, "Do you think we could've cut it any closer?"

"No," he said, "you'd better get going."

As I got in the car, Tym said, "Be careful, Dave, and don't take any unnecessary chances."

"Believe me, I won't."

I drove out of the park and a few minutes later I pulled into Kale's driveway. Kale and Sandy came down the stairs, and Sandy was visibly shaking. She hugged me and said, "I'm sorry, Dave."

I looked at Kale. "What's going on?"

He shook his head. "If I hadn't stopped her, you'd be sitting in that car with a bullet hole in you."

"What?"

"Her ex up in Detroit has threatened her life, and when she saw those Michigan plates, she thought you were him."

I looked at Sandy, who was still shaking, and said, "Now, nobody's got a bullet hole in 'em, so all's well that ends well."

"But if Kale hadn't stopped me . . ."

"If a frog had wings, it wouldn't bump its ass on the log," I said. "Don't worry about it." This remark brought a smile to Sandy's face. After she and Kale said good-bye, we were on the road to Kentucky.

Along the way I tried every trick I knew to get Kale to tell me what was going to happen on April 19, except for asking him directly, of course. Every time I sensed that he was getting uncomfortable with what we were talking about, I'd make a joke to loosen him up. But I was growing frustrated, and I figured that when Tym listened to the tape, he would be, too.

We had gone through Louisville and had been heading south on Interstate 65 for a couple of hours when I looked around and said, "Where are we supposed to turn off?"

"The Western Kentucky Parkway," Kale responded.

"I think I saw that sign a ways back."

About that time, we passed a sign that said "Cave City, next right." Kale started laughing and said, "You saw the sign all right, about sixty miles behind us. That's okay, though. I know a back way to where we're going. Turn off here."

He said he knew most of the back roads in the area from when he'd worked for the Tennessee Valley Authority. I recalled the map of the eastern seaboard grid and wondered if that was what all the secrecy was about. After a couple of hours of twisting and turning through the Kentucky backcountry, we finally arrived at Ron Edwards' place.

23

THE GRAND DRAGON

Dave Hall

The trailer and outbuildings sat on the corner of two roads. At the head of the driveway was a guard shack with flagpoles flying the KKK and Confederate flags. As we pulled onto the property, a middle-aged man about five foot eight and built like a bear exited the trailer. He motioned for me to park at the back of the property—to hide the car from the road, he said.

Kale introduced me to Ron Edwards, and after shaking hands, Ron said, "That's quite a grip you have there, Brother Dave."

"My grandpa always told me when you shake a man's hand, shake it like you mean it."

He invited us into the two-bedroom trailer and went into a built-on addition that he used for an office. The usual KKK posters adorned the walls, and on one side of the room, a rack held various KKK pamphlets. There were a few filing cabinets, and in one corner stood a gun rack loaded with two shotguns, two AK-47 assault rifles, one SKS assault rifle, and a .30-06 hunting rifle.

Edwards described his Internet network of white supremacist

groups, as well as his childhood in a rough neighborhood in Chicago. He'd been illiterate until his wife taught him to read and write. A couple of times during our conversation, Edwards winced and grabbed his head, then pulled a bottle of aspirin from his pocket. He took not one or two but a handful, and chewed on them. I just figured that he suffered from migraines.

Over the next few hours, Ron and Kale drank beer and surfed the Internet. As I watched over their shoulders, they jumped from one white supremacist website to another. At one point, I left to go to the bathroom, and when I returned, I opened the door just in time to hear Ron say, "They'll be surprised when the windows blow out."

Yet my entry into the room put a gag on their conversation. After a couple more minutes of online cruising, Kale said, "Brother Dave, why don't you go ahead and turn in. I'll be along in a little while."

"You guys can bunk in the guard shack," said Ron. "There's clean sheets and blankets already out there." He handed me a flashlight and a shotgun, saying, "You might need this just in case there's any trouble." I couldn't imagine what he meant.

With flashlight and shotgun in hand, I headed for the shack, which stood about 150 feet from the trailer. When I entered, I saw a set of homemade bunk beds and a small table with tools on it. With the flashlight, I scanned the walls and saw several KKK posters scattered about. Sitting on the lower bunk, I removed my shoes, then lit up a cigarette. After lying down, I took a deep breath and tried to relax. I'd been up for twenty hours and was worn out.

When I finished my cigarette, I turned off the flashlight. Then I heard a car in the distance, driving toward me. As it crested the hill and its lights hit the guard shack, the whole place lit up like a planetarium. I sat up to look, recognizing all the little holes in the walls as the result of local boys using the building as target practice. No wonder Ron thought I should have a gun! That did it for any sleeping that night—I'd never know which car contained the potential for "fun." Kale did not come to bed for nearly four hours, and I wondered what those two had been up to.

In the morning, Ron and Kale asked if I would drive them out to visit a couple of buddies. I hoped they might let something slip, so I was happy to do so. Following Ron's directions, we drove out into the country, to an old, dilapidated farmhouse. It struck me that, aside from Butler, a lot of these guys just didn't have much. The first thing that came into my head as I drove up the driveway was the theme song from the sixties TV show *Green Acres*. We parked in front of the barn and got out. Two guys in patched overalls emerged. Both were tall and skinny, but one had a scruffy black beard and mustache, while the other's hair and mustache were red. The black-haired guy actually wore one of those black hillbilly hats like they sell at the interstate souvenir shops.

After Kale and Ron shook their hands, Kale asked me to wait there. They all disappeared into the barn. About ten minutes went by, and Kale came out carrying two PVC pipes approximately three feet long and four to six inches in diameter. They'd been threaded and capped on both ends.

I opened the trunk, and he looked around as if to see whether anyone was watching before he carefully placed the pipes inside.

"If that's something illegal," I said to Kale, "tell me now, so I can be careful not to be pulled over by the cops."

He smiled. "There's nothing illegal in there."

As we left, I took note of the address on the mailbox, 2728 Good Acre Road. Ron asked me if I'd mind driving into nearby Madisonville to get a gun he'd left to be repaired.

"No problem," I replied. Along the way I thought about the idea of asking what the PVC pipes were for, so we'd have it on tape, but decided it was probably best not to. Tym might be frustrated with that decision, but Tym was not here. Soon we were in Madisonville at the Top Guns shop.

I turned the engine off to save recording time. This extra driving around was eating up the time without providing any real information. I could only hope that Kale would open up on the way back.

But to my disappointment, after we dropped Ron off and headed back to Ohio, Kale picked up the large leather pouch he always carried, unzipped it, pulled out a book on biological warfare, and began to read. So much for the digital equipment.

About fifty miles south of Cincinnati, Kale finally put that damned book away. I realized that the recorder had probably run out of time, but I engaged Kale in conversation anyway. I once again asked him about Hitler's birthday. Again, Kale wouldn't commit, but he said, "We all have things to do. I promise you this will be a spectacular one."

About that time we reached the crest of the hill that overlooked Cincinnati. Kale looked at the city and said, "I'd like to see one of those buildings fall."

When we arrived at his place, he directed me to back up the car to the barn. I got out and opened the trunk as he fetched a piece of orange carpet. After looking around to make sure no one was watching, he wrapped the two PVC pipes in the carpet and took them into the barn.

Tym Burkey

I was relieved when I received Dave's call to tell me he was back. That side trip they'd taken down the back roads, which had registered on the GPS, had worried me.

"Dave!" I said. "Am I glad you're back. I haven't slept all weekend."

"Well, that makes two of us," he replied.

"Where are you?"

"About halfway between Kale's place and Dayton."

"I'll meet you at the high school."

We arrived at about the same time and went to the rear of the building, out of sight. When we got out of our cars, I said, "How are you holding up, Dave? You look pretty tired."

"I'm beyond tired," he said. Then he opened the car trunk.

I removed the spare tire to retrieve the digital recorders as Dave gave me a brief rundown about the trip. When he got to the PVC pipes, I said, "Sounds like that son of a bitch is building bombs. Dave, you're going to be a hero! I mean it."

He shrugged. "Well, this hero is going to stop for a couple of drinks and then go home and get some sleep."

"I don't know how we can thank you enough."

"You can thank me by stopping these guys before a lot of people get killed."

Dave didn't go straight home. He stopped for a drink at a bar owned by a friend of his. Then he had another one. After he got drunk, he tried to drive. He wound up pulled over in the rigged-up rental, double-cuffed, and taken to the police station. I got a call and went down to get him.

As they turned him over into my custody, Dave apologized profusely. He said he was usually able to handle that much liquor, but he guessed the combination of alcohol and little sleep had done a job on him. He was sorry he'd gotten me out in the middle of the night.

"That's okay," I said. "I had the pleasure of waking up Bob Hlavac to go and pick up the rental car from the tow yard."

We got into my car, and Dave began to cry. I couldn't believe it. Tears streamed down his face. "I don't know what's wrong," he said. "I think I'm having a nervous breakdown. What if these guys pull off another Oklahoma City? I couldn't live with that kind of blood on my hands, especially the children, and it would be my fault, all my fault, for not stopping it."

This outburst probably had been coming for quite a while. The stress of undercover work is insidious, and the need to live a double identity can eat away at your nerves.

"First of all," I said to him, "you're not in this alone. Second, we're simply not going to let these idiots blow anything up. Put this on my shoulders, Dave."

Dave nodded and took a couple of deep breaths. "Maybe I just need to get some rest. I'm totally worn out."

At his house, I made sure Dave went inside, but I continued to worry. He was showing a lot of strain, and we couldn't have him taking chances like this. Of all times to get drunk and arrested, when he had our equipment in the car was not one of them. It had been poor judgment on his part, and he'd even told the police he was helping the FBI. I understood, especially with all that he'd been through and with the increased stress of an approaching incident, but he needed to find a way to get steady. In addition, we'd need to get him a good lawyer to deal with this DUI. A very good one.

Dave Hall

With the anniversaries of Waco, Ruby Ridge, the Oklahoma City bombing, and Hitler's birthday less than a month away, I was a nervous wreck. I was totally convinced that Ray and possibly Ron Edwards were trying to persuade Kale into doing something on April 19 or 20. To prevent it, I'd pondered the thought of killing Kale and Ray in an "accident." In the end, my conscience wouldn't let me, and I decided that the only thing I could do was keep my eyes and ears open and hope the FBI could stop something terrible from happening. There was so little time left.

Around ten that morning, Ray called for a pickup. Before I left, I touched Gary's urn and said, "Wish me luck, buddy." After I picked up Ray, we headed for New Vienna, and along the way Pastor Ray said, "So what do you think about Ron Edwards?"

"He's a nice enough guy," I replied, "and he's definitely dedicated to the KKK. He also has this computer thing down." I described what I'd seen.

"Sounds like he's got his act together," said Ray. I was sure he was pondering how he could exploit it.

When we got to the church, Ray borrowed my keys and said, "I just have to grab something. I'll be right back."

A few minutes later, he got back into the car and laid two large manila envelopes facedown on the seat. He instructed me to drive to the post office and suggested we then go see Kale. I was all for that.

When Ray went inside the post office, I took the opportunity to look at the front of the envelopes. One had "Klan Procedures" written on it, and the other read "Russian Mafia." I was careful to put the envelopes back in their original position, but I thought, *Russian Mafia? What the hell's going on here?*

At Kale's place, Ray got out of the car but then reached back in and grabbed the two manila envelopes, which he folded and put in his back pocket. By the time I got out, Kale was coming. We all talked for a few minutes before Ray said, "I've got to be in Idaho on April twenty-eighth to help Pastor Butler with this Morris Dees lawsuit." He looked at me and said, "Dave, will you excuse us for a minute?"

After Kale and Ray walked off into the woods, I decided to take advantage of the situation: I went into the barn for a quick look around. I saw various tools, the army ammo boxes, and the orange carpet Kale had wrapped the PVC pipes in, but no sign of the pipes, so I went back outside and lit up a cigarette. A few minutes later, Ray and Kale returned. The envelopes that had been in Ray's back pocket were now in Kale's back pocket.

After dropping Ray off at home, I got to thinking. The trips to the church had been a cover for the meeting with Kale, and Ray's time in Michigan was his way of distancing himself from any trouble Kale might get into. No matter what, he'd figure out a way not to go down with the others.

The next morning, I returned to Kale's on my own, at his invitation, to do some fishing. We ended up at McDonald's for breakfast, and the conversation turned to the subject of the Phineas Priesthood.

"Personally," I said, "I find the myth of a bunch of guys running around killing race traitors hard to believe."

Kale gave me a hard look. "Believe me, the Phineas Priesthood exists and you can take that to the bank."

I wanted him to explain, but he wouldn't, so I said, "I've been wondering where the Aryan Nations is headed. It seems like the last few months we've just been spinning our wheels, and now with that Morris Dees trying to sue us, I just don't know what's going to happen."

"Time's getting short," Kale stated. "I wouldn't worry too much about Morris Dees. A lot's going to happen."

"Kale, if you have something planned, first of all, I don't want to know anything about it. But having said that, you know you can count on me if you need any help. All you have to do is ask."

"I appreciate it, Brother, and I'll keep it in mind." He then changed the subject, inviting me on another trip to the Edwards farm. I accepted, swallowing my dread of that guardhouse.

For the next trip, with Kale driving this time, Tym asked me to purchase a jacket or windbreaker with a lining, and two three-ring binders.

"Okay. Anything else?" I asked.

"You already have a copy of that Bible study course printed up, haven't you?"

"Yes."

"Okay, go out and pick up the jacket and the binders and call me when you get home. Then we'll meet somewhere and I'll let you know what's going on."

I took a trip to the Harley-Davidson shop, choosing a size 4X leather vest with a small HD logo on the front and an inside pocket. Then I stopped and bought two identical three-ring binders.

Back behind the high school, I waited for Tym. When he came, he took one look at the vest and exclaimed, "Damn, Dave! How many cows did they have to kill to make this thing?"

"It does look like a dust cover for a Volkswagen, doesn't it?" I laughed.

"They should have plenty of room to work in."

That remark made me curious. "So what exactly is going on?"

"Bob is going to take this stuff to Cincinnati and the boys are going to work their magic. Then if everything goes as planned, you won't have to worry too much about them finding a wire on you."

I wasn't quite as confident about that, but I gave him the rest of the things he'd asked for.

On April Fool's Day, I was awakened by yet another nightmare. I was lying in a hole, and Kale and Ron Edwards were dumping shovelfuls of dirt on me. I sat up on the edge of the bed, startled by how real it had felt to be buried alive, and started laughing. I thought, *Well, it's finally happening. I'm starting to lose my mind.*

Tym Burkey

Once the items were ready, Bob Hlavac and I met Dave again.

"Watching those guys work on this stuff," said Bob as he handed over the vest, "was like something out of a James Bond movie." He showed Dave how they had created a way to wire him while protecting him from discovery. It involved a tube into which a pin was placed to make it record. Dave seemed impressed. So maybe he would feel safe wearing it.

Bob pulled out one of the three-ring binders. Dave opened it and noted that the Bible study course had been hole-punched and inserted into the binder. He leafed through the pages, looked over the binder, and asked, "What does this do? Shoot poison darts?"

We laughed, and Bob told him how it worked. Dave accepted these "gifts" and said he was going to go pack so he could meet Kale early the next morning. We wished him luck. I could feel the momentum building.

24.

APRIL FOOLS

Dave Hall

At Kale's, I put my cigarettes and lighter in the vest's inside pocket. That way, if I needed to turn on the recorder I could do so while getting a cigarette. When Kale came out, we headed for the interstate.

At Edwards' place, we found several more vehicles in the driveway. Ron and a tall red-haired guy emerged from his trailer, carrying a large ammo case marked "U.S. Army." I could tell it was heavy. Ron greeted us, and then he and the other guy hoisted the box into the trunk of a car. "Take this out and bury it with the rest of them," Ron instructed. I wondered how many were already out there in preparation for the Y2K chaos. He shook our hands and added, "There goes five thousand rounds of AK-47 ammo. C'mon, let's go into the house."

Our conversation was mostly mundane at first, but at some point the subject of Morris Dees came up and Ron said, "I'll be glad when that son of a bitch is dead." I noticed that he'd said "when."

As if he wanted to change the subject, Kale said, "Let's go for a ride to the license bureau. I want to get my van registered here."

That task led us on a wild-goose chase, because it was Good Friday and most places were closed. Ron suggested a restaurant for lunch, and as Kale pulled out, a black-and-white Chevy Blazer fell in behind us. I watched through the side mirror for a while before I said, "Excuse me, fellas, but I think we have company. See that Blazer behind us? He's been following us since we left Powderly."

"Are you sure?" Kale asked.

"Absolutely."

"It's probably the feds," said Ron. "They follow me all the time."

After a couple more turns, we saw that the Blazer was still with us. Kale nodded. "I believe you're right, Dave."

Just before we got to Central City, the Blazer turned onto a side road. Once we got into town, Ron directed Kale to the restaurant. About half an hour later, as we were eating, I tapped Kale on the arm and said, "Take a look."

The black-and-white Blazer was parked outside, and two men stood beside it. I now doubted they were feds. They looked more like local cops. One wore jeans and a flannel shirt and packed a sidearm. The other was wearing a white shirt, tie, and dress pants. He was talking into a portable radio. Kale turned back around and said, "Damn feds. I don't like anybody following me around."

I agreed. "A couple of feds came to my house asking questions. They'd been at Kevin Burns' house, and he called me to warn me. The one asking all the questions was named Tim or Tom something."

"Tym Burkey?" Kale asked, suddenly alert.

"Yeah, I think so. Burkey or Brickey, or something like that."

"It's Burkey. He came to interview me in jail. I can still remember those piercing green eyes."

Tym would love that. His eyes were blue, but he'd like the description. I decided to keep going. "I remember him saying, 'Now's the time to help yourself out,' so I asked, 'Help myself out of what?' Then he asked if we had anything planned for the month of April."

Upon hearing this, Ron cried out, "They know! Damn it, they know!"

Kale gave Ron a hard look as if to say, *Shut up*. Satisfied, but thinking fast, I said, "Of course they're gonna know about the rally on the twenty-fourth. You guys have passed out a bunch of flyers. They're bound to have gotten hold of one."

Kale played along with this, falling into talk about the rally. I had the impression he was covering something, but Edwards' little outburst had been telling.

When we returned to the trailer, Kale left the engine running. He asked Ron for directions to what sounded like the farm where we'd picked up the PVC pipes, then got back in the van. "I'm going to run some errands," he said.

When he was gone, Ron invited me into the trailer. I watched a videotape with Ron and his wife of a Klan gathering. Just then I remembered that the recorder was still on. I took out my cigarettes and lighter. After lighting up a cigarette, I put the lighter and pack back into the vest pocket, but when I went to pull out the pin, the plastic head came off. This meant the recorder was using up recording time on worthless material. I hoped the FBI would enjoy listening to it.

When the tape ended, I told Ron I was tired from the drive and excused myself to take a nap. Once inside the guard shack, I took off the vest, held it upside down, and shook it, but the pin wouldn't drop out. Knowing the vest was still recording, I said, "A note to the designers of this vest: do not use straight pins with the little round plastic heads because the head of the pin can and *did* come off, leaving the pin in the on position. Thank you!"

I found some tools and, holding the tube upside down, I began gently tapping on it with a screwdriver. After a few seconds, the tip of the pin slowly emerged from the tube. I carefully set the screwdriver down and picked up a pair of needle-nose pliers. Steadying myself, I grabbed the pin and pulled it out. Then I used the pliers to bend its top so it couldn't slide into the tube again.

After my nap, I went back in with Ron and watched him put together a survival kit for the approaching Y2K catastrophe. He had gun belts, cartridge belts, and U.S. and Israeli gas masks. His comment was that he wanted to be prepared for the approaching race war. When he came out of his office carrying several camouflage jumpsuits with thin red lines that formed a checkered pattern, I asked, "What kind of outfits are those?"

"They're infrared blocking suits so they can't see you at night." Ron looked at me with a serious expression. "You'd better make sure you have extra batteries for your blood tester and stockpile all your diabetes medicines. When the computers crash, you might not be able to get your supplies." This guy was even more paranoid than Ray.

When Kale returned, he and Ron went off to talk privately, so I looked in the van for the Aryan Nations shield and the binder with the Bible study course. As I rummaged around, I noticed that the zipper on my overnight bag was partially open, so I looked inside. It was obvious that Kale had gone through my stuff. I didn't think too much about it, because if I were Kale, I'd probably have done the same thing. In fact, this was possibly a positive development, because now he knew that I carried nothing to implicate me as an informant.

Soon Kale left again, supposedly to get some food.

In the early evening, three guys in camouflage gear drove up, took out their AK-47 assault rifles, and asked if they could shoot. Ron gave permission, so we were treated to a long period of incessantly loud gunfire. At one point during a brief respite, I commented, "I've got to get me one of those AK-47s."

"I've got plenty of weapons up there," replied Kale. By "up there," I assumed that he was referring to Ohio. That was interesting. And highly illegal.

I took out my cigarettes and lighter and lit up a cigarette. When I put them back into the inside vest pocket, I placed the pin into the tube. With Kale and Ron both drunk, I figured this would be a good time to start recording.

Ron said to Kale, "You need to hide or bury the bulk of your weapons, just in case the feds start confiscating them." Kale shrugged and nodded. I hoped the FBI would note this, because they might need to expand their search.

I then asked Kale if he thought Dees would win the lawsuit he'd filed against the AN.

He smiled. "I seriously doubt it."

Ron was smiling, too, and he added, "I've been monitoring the SPLC website and that asshole Morris Sleaze is full of shit. I'll be glad when that bastard is dead."

Good. Now I had that on record.

"I've already got everything I need down there," said Kale.

Ha! This, too, was on tape, and it made sense of Kale's recent movements in Alabama. I was feeling pretty pleased.

Ron immediately cleared his throat and gave Kale a meaningful look. Obviously they weren't too drunk to be careful. They were both silent for a couple of minutes, just sitting there drinking their beers. I tried some small talk, but it didn't go anywhere. Since we were leaving before dawn, at nine o'clock I decided to turn in.

I went into the guard shack as Kale and Ron walked toward the trailer. I set the alarm clock for 2:45 A.M. After turning off the vest recorder, I laid it on the floor and stretched out on the bunk. Shutting my eyes, I tried to relax, but Ron's remarks nagged at me. I believed that Ray and Ron had persuaded Kale to kill Dees, and I wondered how he was going to do it. He'd already gone down to scope out the situation and had been preparing. I assumed he meant it would take place on the nineteenth.

About fifteen minutes later, Kale and Ron appeared in the doorway. Kale flipped on the switch, nearly blinding me from the single overhead bulb. I could see they were both very drunk, and Ron was holding a pump shotgun in one hand and a Bible in the other. I wondered if I might be having another nightmare. I rubbed my eyes, pretending to have been deeply asleep, and asked, "Is it three o'clock already?"

"No," said Kale. "It's only nine-thirty."

"I didn't think I'd been asleep very long." I sat up on the edge of the bunk. I didn't know why they were there, but I tried to act natural. This was real.

"You've been studying the Bible," said Ron, "so I want to read you part of it and tell me what you think."

"Sure," I replied, "go ahead."

Ron then held up the Bible and began reading the passage pertaining to Judas' betrayal of Jesus. *Here we go again,* I thought. Occasionally he would stop and look at me. After finishing the part about Judas hanging himself, Ron looked at me and said, "So what do you think about Judas?"

Here I had an extremely intoxicated lunatic with a loaded shotgun hinting that I was an informant.

"Well, as you know," I responded, "Judas is arguably the most infamous informant of all time, but in my opinion, that passage is about Jesus *letting* Judas betray him. You know the old saying 'Keep your friends close to you and your enemies even closer'? Well, Jesus knew in advance that Judas was going to betray him. Jesus also knew that it was our Father Yahweh's commandment that he would be crucified on the cross and ultimately die for our sins, so to Jesus, Judas was just a means to an end. In other words, it was the will of Yahweh that Judas betray Jesus. Nowadays, we have to be constantly on the lookout for informants. I'll tell you guys the same thing I told Pastor Redfeairn. If you suspect someone of being an informant, you can use that to your advantage by feeding them false and misleading information, but if you're sure that this person is an informant, tell them to get the hell out, and when they turn to walk away, shoot 'em in the back of the head."

Kale's expression softened into a smile, while Ron merely looked like a confused drunk. After a moment, he handed me the shotgun—for my protection—and said, "You sure know the Bible, Brother Dave."

"Thanks, Ron, but I've got a whole lot more to learn."

Ron said good night, and Kale crawled into bed. Within fifteen minutes, he was snoring . . . but I remained wide awake. I wondered just how close I'd come to getting my head blown off. I couldn't help but wonder what had brought that on, and I recalled that Kale had searched my bag. I had to figure it had been more than liquor-fed paranoia.

The next morning, Kale drove. He was mostly quiet, apparently deep in thought, and at one point he exclaimed, "We gotta make it happen!"

I looked over at him. "Make what happen?"

He just smiled and shook his head back and forth. I figured I had more than enough time left on the vest wire to let it record all the way back to Kale's place. Again I lit up a cigarette, and when I put the pack back into my pocket, I turned on the recorder.

At another point, a gasoline tanker truck passed us and I said jokingly, "We ought to pay some wino to park one of those tankers in front of the federal building in Cincinnati, then watch everybody panic and run around."

"I've got a better building down there," said Kale.

"Down where?"

Kale just smiled and shook his head. A moment later he said, "I shouldn't have said that." Apparently he was still a bit drunk.

I wanted to act disinterested, so I said, "I don't know about you, but I'm so hungry I could eat a horse."

"Yeah, I could eat something," said Kale.

He got off at the next exit, and we grabbed some sandwiches and coffee. As we were eating, I said, "You know, it's tough to stick to the Bible's food laws. An egg-and-cheese biscuit without bacon or sausage is like a day without sunshine."

Kale smiled. "Or like the AN without the FO." By that he meant ammonium nitrate without the fuel oil. It didn't take much to figure out what he'd been pondering all this time. Kale was obviously overexcited about something. He shouldn't have been talking, but he couldn't contain himself, so these loose comments burst out of him. I'd let Tym and the FBI piece it together, but it sure seemed significant to me. And it wasn't over.

As we got close to Cincinnati, Kale gripped the steering wheel and rocked back and forth in his seat. A couple of times, he pulled himself right up to the steering wheel to bite down hard on it. Then he said, "We gotta make it happen!"

I just sat there quietly watching the road in front of us and praying he wouldn't drive off it. "Brother," I said, "you've got to cut back on the coffee."

Kale laughed a little. "You're probably right." A few minutes later he said, "I've been in touch with a friend out in California via the Internet and there's going to be some good things happening."

"Isn't that dangerous, sending e-mails over the Internet?"

"No. We've been using a code that even the FBI would have a hard time breaking."

"Oh yeah?" I was glad I'd already thought to turn on the recorder.

"Yeah, it's virtually unbreakable. The way it works is that if the document is dated in words, such as 'April 3,' that means it's not in code, but if it's written with the date in numbers, such as '4-3-99,' then it's in code. The next step in reading the code is to read the salutation. If, for example, the document says 'Hi, Tom,' then you take the two letters in *hi* and the three letters in *Tom* and multiply them together to get six. This means there are six words in the communication that are code words. Each receiver already has his own code number set up. My code number is five. That means that every fifth word in the communication is a code word."

"Wow," I commented, "that's pretty wild."

"What I do is work out what I want to send in code, then I write the communication around the code."

"That's pretty clever, man." To throw Kale off getting nervous, I changed the subject. I figured I'd gotten quite a nice piece of information for Tym, and it seemed clear to me that Kale had decided I could be trusted. At least a little.

When we got back to Kale's place I said good-bye, got into my car and headed for home. Along the way, I pulled back the left-hand side of the vest and said, "Before I start screaming and pulling my hair out, this is Dave signing off." Then I pulled out the pin. Once I arrived home, I called Tym.

Tym Burkey

"Once again the prodigal son has returned." It was Dave on the phone, ready to tell me about his latest adventure.

"I've been worried sick," I told him. "I'm glad you're back. How did it go?"

"I don't think I have to worry about having a nervous break-down anymore," he replied, "because I haven't got any nerves left to break."

I urged him to describe what had happened, and he told me about the incident in the guardhouse. More bizarre was Kale Kelly's be-havior in the car.

"He was so agitated," Dave said, "I just sat there praying he wouldn't cause an accident and kill us both."

"I can't imagine how stressful that must have been, but at least we know that you're back home and safe."

"I believe I've got some good clues on the recorder, as well as some that I wasn't able to record."

"I'll meet you over behind the high school."

Face-to-face, Dave described his problems with the pin and the recorder. So much for James Bond. "It figures," I said. "With all that high-tech equipment and everything that could have gone wrong, it came down to the head of a pin."

Dave handed over the vest and added a few more items to the list of what he had for me, notably Ron Edwards' remark—"They know, damn it, they know"—as well as his apparent belief that Morris Dees would soon be dead. I surmised that his later appear-ance in the guardhouse, armed, may have been the result of his rethinking how loose-lipped he'd been in front of Dave. He was probably just ensuring that Dave knew what was in store should he betray them.

"We've given Dees a heads-up already," I said, "but we'll reinforce that." I was aware that Dees was planning to make a speech soon at Baylor University in Waco, Texas, and if Kelly or anyone else from the AN managed to kill him there, that shooter would be immortalized in the movement. It was almost too rich an opportunity to pass up. Dees had guts.

I told Dave I'd better head to Cincinnati so we could download the contents of the recorder. I thanked him for all his work.

"I'm going to go home," he said, "park my car, and put vodka on the endangered species list."

The problem for us was that this information confirmed our belief that something was up for April 19, and Kelly and Edwards were probably at the center of it, but there was no hard proof that would allow us to act. We were working hand in glove with an aggressive assistant U. S. attorney, Ralph Kohnen, and he needed more information for an indictment or arrest warrant. Kelly was clearly being very careful, meeting people face-to-face, avoiding using the phone or even talking to himself in his Spartan barn loft. And we were running out of time.

Dave Hall

Tuesday morning I packed my bags for the trip to Sweetwater, Tennessee, to attend the Feast of the Passover. I was not looking forward to it. As I folded my clothes, I pondered the events of the past few weeks. I believed Kale was going to kill Dees, but I did not know how, when, or where. And how did this Earl Cable fit in, whoever he was? It was only two weeks until April 19. Tym had been urging me during the week to be more aggressive in my intelligence gathering, and the pressure to learn something to stop a potential assassination was getting almost unbearable, for me and for Tym.

After checking into the motel in Sweetwater, I looked for Kale and Sandy and spotted them with another couple at a table by the pool. Kale introduced them as Robert and Lynn Baker. Robert worked at a California nuclear power plant and Lynn had authored several books on the far right favorable to the AN. I wondered if one of them could be Kale's Internet friend Eagle1. After Kale and Lynn excused themselves to talk in private, I figured it was her. Kale made it a point never to discuss anything of importance inside a room or a car, because they could be bugged.

The rest of the day involved meetings and prayers that reminded me of the old-time hellfire tent revivals I used to attend as a kid with my grandmother, where the preacher would start out fully dressed and by the end would be wearing only his pants. My grandmother would just sit there, and eventually we stopped going.

For the life of me, I couldn't figure out why Kale Kelly would travel all this way to attend prayer meetings. He'd never shown any interest in the religious aspects of the church, being content just to be a member of the Aryan Nations' political arm. This fact, and the private meetings with Baker and others, confirmed for me that Kale had ulterior motives in coming to Sweetwater that had nothing to do with prayer.

Back in my room early that evening, I looked out the window and noticed Kale and Lynn together again, walking in the field adjacent to the motel. I would have given anything to know what they were talking about. They walked around for about twenty minutes before they disappeared back into the motel. I suspected that Lynn was involved in this upcoming project, whatever it was—possibly to document a significant AN event.

The next morning I attended the sessions, though they bored me to tears. When they ended at noon, Kale asked, "How would you like to go for a ride through the mountains with me and Sandy?"

In the car, Kale informed me that Robert and Lynn Baker would be following us in their pickup truck, adding that we'd be driving to Andrews, North Carolina. Lynn was thinking of writing a book about Eric Robert Rudolph. One of the last places he'd been seen was Andrews—also the field headquarters for some two hundred

FBI agents who'd been searching for Rudolph for months in the surrounding mountains. He'd become a folk hero among white supremacists, in part because he was reputedly an accomplished survivalist.

"You think Rudolph is good enough to keep eluding the FBI?" I asked Kale.

"He's either real good or real dead."

The drive took us through the breathtaking scenery of the Blue Ridge Mountains. Since it was early April, many of the wildflowers were in full bloom. Kale and I engaged in general conversation, but then he surprised me with a question.

"If anything happens to me, would you take care of Sandy?"

"Happens to you?" I replied. "What could happen?"

"You never know. Just promise."

I looked back at Sandy, in the backseat, and saw that her eyes had welled up with tears. Obviously, he'd told her something serious.

"Sure, man," I said. "I'll do my best."

Baker took a photo of Lynn in front of the sign for the town city limits, and then they led us to the Main Street Cafe. She hoped to contact a waitress who worked there with whom she'd developed an online connection, but the waitress was off for the day. Then we headed to the outskirts of town.

Kale followed the Bakers down a gravel road to a field near some railroad tracks. About a hundred yards away was the FBI compound, a large building on an acre of land surrounded by an eight-foot chain link fence topped with razor wire. Lynn took pictures from the front and both sides. Then she said something to Kale and we all got back into our vehicles.

This time Kale took the lead. As we drove back down the gravel road, Kale looked at me and grinned. "Are you ready for some excitement?"

"What the hell are you up to?" I asked.

He remained silent, so I steeled myself for whatever was coming. After a few turns through the neighborhood, we found ourselves on the street that dead-ended into the main gate of the FBI compound. Kale, with the Bakers tailgating us, showed no sign of slowing down as we approached. I thought, *This maniac is going to crash the gate and get us all killed.* I gripped the seat, like I was on a plane taking off, but just then Kale slowed down. He stopped about thirty feet from the guard shack. I tried to breathe evenly, hoping I wasn't going to land in jail over these hijinks.

Two large black corrections officers exited the shack, wearing full body armor and carrying MP-5 assault rifles. I looked at Kale and said, "Are you trying to get us killed?"

"They won't shoot at us. Lynn just wanted to get some close-up pictures."

I turned and looked at Sandy, whose eyes were as big as saucers. I could also see Lynn behind us, quickly snapping photos through the windshield.

A guard approached, his rifle at the ready. When he got ten feet from us, Kale stuck his head out and yelled, "Get the hell back over there, we don't need to talk to you!"

I rolled my eyes back into my head and thought, *So this is how it's all going to end. Shot to death by the very people I've been helping.*

The guard stopped short, probably aware of the potential for a standoff, and started backing up slowly. He yelled something to the other man and then stepped into the shack and picked up the phone. Ten seconds later, several more agents emerged from the main building and headed for the gate.

I grabbed Kale's arm and pleaded, "Now can we get out of here?"

"That sounds like a good idea, Brother." He signaled for Robert to start backing up, and I let out a sigh of relief. As we drove away, I looked back and saw the FBI agents and the guards just standing there. They seemed confused.

When we were a block from the compound, Kale and Robert backed into a parking lot and headed for the highway. I said to Kale, "The next time you plan on doing something like this, will you promise me something?"

"What?"

"Drop me off on the corner."

Then we both just started laughing, but there came an angry voice from the backseat. "I don't find any humor in this," said Sandy.

Kale tried to allay her fears, and soon we were all laughing as we reviewed the incident. Kale said, "Did you see the size of those two niggers?"

"I sure did," I told him. "They must have been six foot eight!"

"They were two of the biggest niggers that I've ever seen."

But the incident wasn't yet over. We were about ten miles outside of Andrews when a Suburban with government plates passed both of our vehicles at a high rate of speed. It pulled into our lane and stayed about an eighth of a mile in front of us. Kale soon noticed another Suburban following close behind. We were unsure of what was going to happen next. A couple of times, the Suburban following behind would pull up alongside us. Through the tinted windows, we could make out the silhouettes of four to five men. Then the car would fall back and resume its tail. I didn't know why they didn't just stop us. This cat-and-mouse game made Kale nervous. He was no longer smiling. I thought he might start biting the steering wheel again.

But then, as suddenly as they had appeared, they were gone. We'd reached the Tennessee border.

Back at Sweetwater, Pastor Britton had arrived and we went to the evening prayer meeting, largely subdued. I'd seen Pastor Britton talking intensely with Kale for a while and wondered if he, too, was part of this upcoming event. His ever-present smile was gone, and I doubted that Kale would stand still for long in a conversation about religion. At the meeting, I spotted Pastor Britton with Lynn. This triangle meant something.

I tried to deduce the connections among them, along with Ray and Ron Edwards. The same theme kept coming up: Morris Dees. Ray wanted to regain status by planning it, Pastor Britton wanted the AN free of the lawsuit, Baker hoped to document it, and Kale would carry it out. Edwards was probably just a facilitator, supplying the weapons.

With time growing short, I was desperate to learn any details of what they were planning. I'd originally believed that Kale was being prepared to use his sniper training to take out Dees, but from his numerous references to AN/FO bombs and his collection of PVC pipes, I was worried that Kale was going to try to blow up the SPLC and kill a bunch of people.

That night, after I'd heard Pastor Britton say that Morris Dees "needed killing," I couldn't sleep. It was a nice April evening, so I set a chair out on the second-floor walkway to sit outside and drink some vodka. Then I saw none other than Kale Kelly and Pastor Britton strolling out from behind the corner of the motel. Even though it was dark, I could tell from the constant hand gestures that Pastor Britton was doing most of the talking. They strolled along the parking lot toward me, and I knew that soon I would be spotted. I leaned forward in my chair and said, "I see that I'm not the only one that couldn't sleep."

I could tell I'd startled them as they looked up at me, so I said, "Nice night, isn't it?"

"It certainly is, Dave," replied Pastor Britton.

"Well, I guess I'm gonna turn in. I'll see you all in the morning."

They bid me good night, and I retired to my room.

As I lay in bed, I ran the images of the past few weeks through my mind, like an internal movie projector, until a pattern developed. It began with a remark from Pastor Ray that Kale would do anything he told him to, followed by his comment "It's nice to have an ace in the hole." The intense private conversations between them had begun just afterward, as the subject of the Dees lawsuit was on everyone's mind, and there had been many comments about the need to assassinate him. The handshake between Kale and Ray instead of the Nazi salute. The PVC pipes from Kentucky, and Kale's bizarre behavior on our second trip back. Edwards' repeated statements that he would be glad *when* Dees was dead. The meetings between

Kale and the author Lynn Baker. And now the private meetings be-tween Kale and Pastor Britton.

Kale was going to try to kill Dees, and it was going to be timed to coincide with the closely related April anniversaries of Waco, Ruby Ridge, Oklahoma City, and Hitler's birthday—in other words, soon. In my gut, I believed that Kale really didn't want to do it, but he'd gotten in over his head and couldn't back out without losing face. I was sure he'd carry on for the cause. I could only hope I'd given Tym enough information to stop him.

25

MELTDOWN

Dave Hall

Before going down for morning prayer and more vicious name-calling the next morning, I grabbed a pillow from the bed, pushed my face into it, and screamed as loud as I could. With that, I was ready to tell Pastor Britton with a straight face that I'd enjoyed his sermon. He mentioned that he'd be flying back to California that evening, which struck me as odd. Why would he fly all the way from San Diego to Sweetwater and then leave almost immediately? If Kale and Sandy left, too, I'd know that the Feast of the Passover had merely been a cover for some secret meetings. That afternoon, I learned that Robert and Lynn would exit before the services were over.

In the evening, Kale invited me to join him and Sandy for a beer. As a diabetic, I wasn't supposed to drink beer, but I believed it was my chance to gather more information. I grabbed what was left of the vodka, hoping that I could get Kale to drink some, because I'd previously noted that liquor loosened him up.

When I arrived at Kale's room, he and Sandy were on the couch holding hands. He gave me a beer, and as we talked about the past few days, it was evident that these two had already had a few beers. Soon I had Kale as well as Sandy sipping the vodka with me. Then he said what I'd been expecting.

"Sandy and I are leaving in the morning."

And a little later, he insisted again that I take care of Sandy.

"Man," I said, "there ain't nothing going to happen to you."

"How do you know?"

"I don't know," I replied. "But what I do know is that I could walk out that door right now and I might get run over by a beer truck. But I don't dwell on things like that."

Kale then forced a smile and shook his head. "We gotta make it happen."

"What?"

He continued to just shake his head. After a while, Sandy drifted off to sleep and I couldn't get anything else out of Kale, so I said good night and returned to my room. I thought I had plenty of significant material for Tym. And I was glad that I, too, could leave as soon as the others were gone.

The next morning, I saw Kale and Sandy leave, so I waited a while, then started my trip back. About an hour into the drive, I felt so drowsy I decided to pull over and get a nap. As I checked into my room at a Red Roof Inn, I turned the television on to CNN. Then I turned away to unpack something. Just at that moment, I heard the voice of a female reporter.

"Reporting live from the Earle Cabell Federal Building in Dallas, Texas," she said.

I snapped to attention to watch. She was standing beside a low brick wall with lettering that read "Earle Cabell Federal Building."

The blood drained from my head and I sat down hard on the edge of the bed. Visions of the Oklahoma City bombing and the firefighters carrying out the bodies of children flashed through my mind. I grabbed the phone and called Tym.

Tym Burkey

When the phone rang, I knew it was Dave. I'd been even more nervous for him this time, because I anticipated that the meetings taking place at this event, given how close it was to April 19, could be volatile. Should Dave happen upon a private conversation or even be suspected of overhearing information not intended for his ears, he would have been in big trouble. So it was a great relief for me to hear his voice. To my surprise, he was still on the road.

"I just saw a report on CNN," he said, nearly out of breath. "Remember Ray's reference to 'Earl Cable' a few weeks ago? Well, I just heard the name. It's the federal building in Dallas. I think they're going to blow it up!"

"Take it easy, Dave," I said. "We already put that one together, thanks to your information. We're on top of it. No one's going to have an easy time getting explosives in there."

He seemed relieved, and I'm sure he felt good as well that he'd made that contribution. That was at least one potential disaster averted. He then told me about the various meetings he'd witnessed between Kale Kelly, Pastor Britton, and Lynn Baker, the writer. All of it was potentially important, so I took careful notes. When Dave related the events at the FBI compound, I had to laugh.

"It wasn't funny at the time," said Dave. "I thought we'd all be shot."

"Okay," I responded. "Anything else?"

"No, that's about it. Unless you want to hear about the sermons."

"No, thanks. Let me get this information typed up so I can send it to the SAC in Cincinnati as soon as possible."

"I just hope it's good enough to stop whatever they're up to."

By the time Dave got home, I had another assignment for him, but this one involved the vest in which we'd hidden a recorder. We just didn't have enough information to implicate Redfeairn in whatever Kelly might do, and we wanted to be certain we could arrest him, too. I believed that it had been Ray's master plan and the others had agreed to it. I asked Dave to put the vest back on, which I would give to him behind the school, and see if he could get Red-feairn to talk. It was a risky venture, I knew, but if it worked, Dave would see the net result of all his hard work. In addition, if Kelly did move forward with an assassination attempt, then after his arrest Dave's cover would be blown. They'd have a pretty good idea who had tipped us to all these things. I wanted the risks he'd taken over the past two years to pay off as significantly as possible.

Dave Hall

I woke up early Sunday morning after only three hours of sleep. I was stressed out and my nerves were shot. I called Kale but got no answer. My mom arranged for me to meet her for lunch, and I used the opportunity to let her know where things stood and that I might have to go into the Witness Protection Program. She didn't like the situation but she told me that she understood and was very proud of me. I didn't like the thought of leaving Mom and my family behind, but this thing had gone too far now and there was no changing it. If I stayed, I'd put us all at risk.

After lunch, I spoke with Ray and asked if I could come over and talk with him privately. When he agreed, I put on the vest and went to his mother's house. We met out back.

"Maybe it's none of my business," I told him, "but Kale has been acting crazy lately." I described Kale's bizarre behavior on the trip back from Kentucky and his repeated comments about making something happen. "Kale isn't getting ready to do anything that's going to kill a lot of innocent babies and children, is he?"

Ray put his hand on my shoulder in a fatherly way and said, "There won't be any children hurt, I can promise you that." Then he turned and walked to the front of the house. I followed him and tried again, but he said he was returning to Detroit. Soon it was obvious that I wasn't going to get anywhere, so I went home to report to Tym. Oddly, Ray hadn't asked me a thing about the Feast of the Passover.

I spent the day preparing to make a hasty exit. I had arranged with a family member to retreat to a remote cabin deep in the mountains of West Virginia. The day had passed painfully slowly, and I was glad to see nightfall come. My attempts to contact Kale had failed, and I wondered if Ray had told him about my concern. I thought that Tym would surely call if they'd arrested anyone. It was nearing midnight when I drank a half pint of vodka and took a couple of sleeping pills, but it didn't keep the nightmares away.

I knew in the back of my head that this thing had to be bigger than just Kale Kelly. I knew that Kale had strong ties to the KKK, an organization that Morris Dees had vigorously attacked with crippling lawsuits, so I figured he'd have little reason to hold back. It bothered me, because deep down I thought Kale was essentially a good person. They'd picked him because he had skill, not because he was full of hate. The others were exploiting him.

The next day, Pastor Ray called. I was surprised, but he said he wanted to hear about how things had gone in Tennessee. I told him that everything had gone just fine. He then asked if Pastor Britton had been there. I said yes, and that he had given several good sermons. I remembered something I hadn't told him about Kale and thought it might give me an opportunity to get Ray to say something, even if it wasn't on tape. I described what had occurred at the FBI compound in Andrews. He didn't comment but only asked if I'd heard from Kale.

"No," I said, "although I've called him a few times. I know that he and Sandy stayed with some friends on their way back, but I thought he'd be home by now."

Ray told me that he'd be back in town this weekend and would get in touch then.

On April 14, with only five days to go, I was more anxious than ever. I kept popping Xanax to get myself through the day. I missed Gary terribly. He'd always been able to comfort me, and at the very least, he could wear me down by playing Frisbee. I missed him terribly.

I'd been up since 4:00 A.M., unable to sleep, despite drinking myself into unconsciousness the night before. Nothing I did—not a shower or coffee or aspirin—relieved the tension that felt as if it was about to explode in my head.

I waited for Tym to call, which he'd been doing every morning for the past two weeks, but eight-thirty came and went, and the phone remained silent. A half hour dragged by, then an hour. I called Tym's cell phone, but he didn't answer it. Growing desperate now, I left a message on his voice mail, asking him to call me back as soon as he could. An ache in my gut told me that this was too unusual. Something had happened. I prayed that he was okay. Then I prayed that they had stopped Kelly in time.

I tried watching television but couldn't pay attention. Nothing on CNN alerted me to anything unusual. Lunchtime came and went, but I couldn't eat. By one in the afternoon, I was a mess. I needed to know what was going on. I got up and looked out the window. I wished again that Gary was there.

When the phone finally did ring, I was so caught up with images of what could be taking place that the shrill sound startled me.

Tym Burkey

On the morning of April 14, we arrested Kale Kelly at a subdivision near Waynesville, Ohio, where he worked. He'd surrendered to our agents without incident. In fact, I had the impression that he was expecting this to happen. Maybe he was even relieved. At his residence, we executed a search warrant and confiscated three pistols, a shotgun, and other items of interest. The weapons seized were exactly the makes, models, and calibers of the weapons that Dave had reported seeing there. It would support his credibility if the case went to trial.

Once we had Kale under wraps, I called Dave. I knew he'd soon be in danger because even if his name was not mentioned in any official capacity, he'd come under suspicion as an informant. He had a matter of a few days at most to get his things together and get out. I knew he'd already been packing in preparation, but the situation was now urgent. Once Redfeairn knew about Kelly, he'd be furious. Then he might put two and two together, especially after Dave's recent comments to him.

"What the hell's going on?" Dave demanded. He sounded as if he was under great strain. I assured him that everything was all right and we'd just arrested Kelly, but that he only had a day to rent a van and prepare to leave. He wasn't happy about it, but he was prepared. He already had a cabin lined up in West Virginia where no one would know to look. Once he was safe, we could see how things developed.

Dave Hall

I spent the bulk of Thursday morning calling my mother and a few close friends, explaining that I would be out of town for a while. I also called Tym and asked him to find out from his buddies in Michigan if Pastor Ray was still there. I then called the people who were going to help implement my plan of escape.

When Tym called later that day, he said that Ray was indeed still in Michigan, but the FBI had no idea if he had gotten wind yet of Kale's arrest.

"Well, I'm heading to West Virginia early tomorrow morning," I told him.

"I'm sorry, Dave. I realize the sacrifice you're making. We appreciate your help. We couldn't have done it without you."

"Thank you, but the ball is in your hands now. Just don't drop it."

"I can assure you, the FBI has shattered any plans that Kelly and his friends may have had."

I felt better. It seemed at least that I'd done something worthwhile with my life. But my family and friends were a hell of a lot to give up. Tym asked me to call him daily.

My mom came over, and we spent some time together that evening, not knowing if or when we'd see each other again. It was difficult to realize I wouldn't have her to lean on or to talk to. First

Terri, then Gary, and now my whole family. It was difficult for me to sleep that night. I knew Tym would help, but I was about to go into a life where I'd truly be alone. I knew I wasn't prepared for it.

The next day, I packed up and drove into a little town high in the Appalachian Mountains. I found a pay phone and called my cousin Jimmy, who'd prepared the cabin for me. He said that he would meet me at the food market on the north edge of town. I found the market and waited. After about thirty minutes, Jimmy pulled into the parking lot. I hadn't seen him in five years, and I couldn't believe how much he'd aged. I wondered, with all I'd been through, if I looked like that to him.

The place was another twenty miles away, on a dirt road that spiraled to the left as it wound up and around the mountain. After completing two circles, we finally arrived. The unheated cabin was small but comfortable, having a living room, kitchen, bedroom, and bathroom. Jimmy helped me unload the heaviest items from the truck, then showed me how to operate the gas-powered generator. My water came from a spring-fed well. I watched Jimmy's car until it disappeared, and then I truly felt out of touch with the world.

I finished unloading the truck, then sat down on the porch to have a cigarette. The nearest neighbor was almost a mile away, and the view from the porch was breathtaking. As I sat back in my chair, a very strange feeling came over me. Thinking my diabetes was acting up, I checked my blood sugar, but it was normal. I returned to my chair and as I sat there enjoying the mountain air, I suddenly realized what the strange feeling was: I was actually relaxing!

I felt like standing on the porch and shouting this revelation to the world. I had survived two and a half years of almost unbearable stress from the ever-present fear that at any time I could take a bullet in the head. Relaxing had become as foreign to me as walking is to a baby. I don't know if it was the mountain air or my newfound peace, but I slept that night better than I had slept for a long, long time.

Tym Burkey

I hated to give up Dave as an informant. He'd been so valuable to us and had proven his integrity over and over. But snagging Kale Kelly before he could pull off a hit or worse was worth the loss. I wasn't yet certain that Dave would have to testify in federal court, but I did realize that his sudden absence would be interpreted, especially by someone as paranoid as Redfeairn, as a sign that he was an informant. We kept Redfeairn under surveillance, but it was difficult to know what he'd learned while Dave was on his way to his cousin's cabin.

I'd interviewed Kelly in Cincinnati myself over the past few days and he told me that if he hadn't been arrested that Tuesday morning, he'd have headed south early on Wednesday. He revealed that his plan had been to walk away from his apartment and catch a bus, and we'd caught him in the nick of time. I'd tried to learn what he'd intended to do, but he'd grown evasive, refusing to say anything more on the subject. That was his right, but it frustrated me. I was certain that Morris Dees, and possibly the Southern Poverty Law Center, had been his ultimate target. Dees himself apparently thought so, too, because a few days after Kelly's arrest, Dees sent a floral arrangement and a letter of gratitude to the Cincinnati Division. It was a simple act of recognition, and we appreciated it.

After Kelly appeared before a judge, we were legally required to give him the affidavit for the arrest warrant, so it was clear to him, although we never named Dave, who'd ratted him out. Later, he told me that he was not mad at Dave but was angry at Redfeairn, who'd brought Dave into the AN. By this time, suspicion of Redfeairn was high because he never seemed to get arrested, although everyone around him had been. Jason Swanson, too, was later arrested on gun charges.

Eventually Kelly threw us a bone. He admitted that he'd been planning to assassinate Dees. However, he refused to say anything about a bombing plot. Kelly was a hard enough con to know that just thinking about an act was not a crime, and the FBI would need an overt act before we could charge him with an assassination attempt. Still, we could get him on other charges and hold him for a long time.

I told all of this to Dave and then said, "You're a true American patriot."

He was silent for a moment, and I suspect that what we'd been through together had collected for him into an intense emotional moment. Dave then said, "If I've made a difference, then it was worth the sacrifice."

"You should be proud of yourself."

"I don't feel proud, Tym, but I do feel privileged to have had the opportunity to serve my country. Maybe our children will get to grow up in a more tolerant society and not one filled with hate."

"We sure made a dent, didn't we?"

"I guess we did."

Dave was scheduled to come back for a court appearance, getting his drunk-driving charge reduced to a charge of reckless operation of a vehicle. We kept the courthouse under surveillance to ensure his safety, and afterward he and I sat together in my car in a mall parking lot.

"Keep in touch," I told Dave. "If you need to talk, call me."

"Just let me know how it all turns out," he requested. "The payoff for me will be when Dees puts the Aryan Nations out of business." I smiled, thinking back to my initial thoughts about this tattooed biker whom I'd believed had little to offer. I was glad to say he'd proven me wrong.

As he got out of the car to go to his own, Dave turned and said, "Hail victory, Brother Tym."

I laughed. "Good luck, Dave."

26

AFTERMATH

Tym Burkey

Kelly was formally sentenced on July 30, 1999, on the charges of interstate transport of firearms and the possession of firearms by a convicted felon. He wouldn't admit that Redfeairn had any knowledge of his plan to assassinate Morris Dees. Kelly served several years in federal prison (where he claimed to have found God). After Kelly was released, he learned a trade and was gainfully employed. Kelly appears to have stayed out of trouble in that the FBI has had no further dealings with him.

On his second trip back from Tennessee, we learned that Kelly had stopped to see Steve Anderson, a white supremacist who had ties to the KKK and the Kentucky State Militia and who operated a pirate radio station called United Patriot Front. In 2001, Anderson made national news when he was in a shootout with Kentucky state troopers and went on the run for over a year. He was finally arrested in the mountains of North Carolina, and when the police searched his home, they found enough weapons to equip a small army. We thought it likely that Kelly had contacted Anderson about providing the weapon for Kelly to assassinate Dees.

Through another investigation, I finally learned that Kelly had in fact purchased a rifle for the assassination. He'd kept it at a friend's house in another state. I never had the rifle, so I couldn't charge Anderson in this plot.

Pastor Harold "Teflon Ray" Redfeairn, as we liked to call him, was not charged with anything, but he continued to be a thorn in the FBI's side as he strove to acquire more power in the Aryan Nations. Still, because he was the one who had brought Dave into the fold, he quickly lost much of his prominence. He'd sponsored Dave and allowed him to see the inner workings of the organization, as well as groomed him for a top-ranking role. No one trusted Redfeairn after that. During one of my interviews with him after he realized Dave's betrayal, he told me he wanted back the ring that he'd given to Dave, but he wanted it "with Dave's finger in it."

However, to our supreme satisfaction, the AN organization took a blow. Morris Dees sued Richard Butler and the Aryan Nations for the 1998 assault outside the Hayden Lake compound, and the jury returned a $6.3 million verdict against the group, essentially bankrupting Butler and breaking the AN's back. That, too, was Dave's contribution, since his work allowed Dees to survive.

After infighting among the remnants of the leadership, Ray split off and together with Morris Gulett formed the Church of the Sons of YHVH (the Hebrew spelling of Yahweh). He hoped to pick up where Butler had left off, to gather the combined forces of the various militant groups, but in October 2003, Ray Redfeairn died suddenly from a heart attack. The FBI sent agents to the morgue to verify that he was actually dead.

Mo returned to his hometown in Louisiana to start the southern branch of the church, promoting himself to senior pastor. In late 2003, Mo—the guy who'd been kicked out—posted Dave's picture on his website as a "known federal informant." But his ambitions were short-lived as well. In April 2005, Mo was caught on videotape plotting a bank robbery to finance his church and was arrested. He is currently serving time in a federal prison.

What Dave did for us during this investigation was unparalleled, but when we failed to arrest Redfeairn, I was disappointed. At that point, it seemed to me that losing Dave as an informant had been a high cost to pay for a single arrest and a yet-to-be-proven conspiracy. I lost my eyes and ears into the AN locally and nationally, and I had rewarded Dave by sending him into exile. Yet subsequent events showed that much larger things were astir.

As it turned out, the Kelly arrest had devastated the AN in Ohio and crippled them nationally. Because Dave had been so trusted, its members turned against one another with accusations of disloyalty. In addition, the fear of more arrests caused membership to drop even more than it already had, so Dave's work had wide-ranging repercussions. This was an important lesson regarding terrorism. The disruption factor should never be discounted; you never know what you might have prevented.

When working criminal cases, I had developed a personal creed of "If you do nothing, nothing will happen. But if you do something, even if it appears to have failed, something good will come from it." That seems to have been the case in this situation.

And lastly, what became of Dave?

Dave Hall

I've become something of a hermit. My only friends are the birds that frequent the feeders in my front yard and a dog, a beautiful boxer that's dumber than a box of rocks, but I love her just the same. Once or twice a year, I do arrange to meet with my mother for visits. Tym calls me from time to time to see how I'm doing, and in July 2002, I was honored to be invited to speak at the FBI National Conference on Domestic Terrorism in Indianapolis. Although the focus of my speech was the Aryan Nations, I also discussed my contacts with the KKK, the National Socialists, and other white supremacist groups while I was undercover. It was definitely one of the high points in my life.

I didn't emerge from this experience unscathed. I still experience panic attacks, and the constant bombardment of racial hatred that I had to endure during those years has subconsciously affected the way that I view Jews and people of color, lending credence to the old adage "When you dance with the devil, the devil doesn't change, the devil changes you." I can only hope that, with time, I'll heal.

Dave Hall and Tym Burkey

At the end of March in 2005, CNN reported that August Kreis, who took over the Aryan Nations leadership, was trying to become an ally of al-Qaeda. "You say they're terrorists," he was quoted as stating. "I say they're freedom fighters. And I want to instill the same jihadic feeling in our people's heart, in the Aryan race, that they have for their father, who they call Allah." He went on to identify their common enemies: Jews and the American government. At this time, Kreis refused to say how many followers he had in this effort. He had also decided to transform some of the old beliefs into what he views as a more viable stance for today's potential recruits. Nonwhites are no longer considered "mud people," says Kreis, because it's difficult to get people behind that type of racism, but it's not as hard to inspire them with white pride and antigovernment sentiment. That's where the idea of an Islamic terrorist alliance comes in, but the FBI stated in the same report that there was no evidence that he'd succeeded.

The Southern Poverty Law Center also keeps apprised of the continuing dangers of white supremacists, from neo-Nazi skinheads to the National Alliance to the Aryan Nations. In an article in 2006, they issued an intelligence report, accessible on their website, that documented a backlash of hate crimes from white supremacists in reaction to changing U.S. immigration policies.

On May 1, 2005, for example, a group of skinheads in California attacked a black man who'd brought a group of foster kids to a park. One skinhead jumped into a car and tried running down the victims, but by this time the police had arrived. They arrested the driver for attempted murder, while his two cohorts were brought in on aggravated assault charges. Since more minorities have moved into this area, white-power crimes have increased, including among high school students.

White supremacists dislike what they view as forced integration, and Tom Metzger, leader of the White Aryan Resistance, holds meetings in Riverside County, California, to thwart attempts to spread diversity and tolerance. Residing in this area are such groups as the High Desert Freak Boys and Angry Nazi Soldiers. They have stockpiled ammunition and weapons, large stashes of drugs (especially methamphetamine), and plenty of hate paraphernalia. One of the heavily armed arrestees was a high school football coach who was actively recruiting.

The motto of the Aryan Nations even today is "Violence solves everything." The home page of its website indicates that this was the sentiment of the late Pastor Ray Redfeairn. A statement posted on the same site urged sympathizers and members to do the following: "As we have been telling kinsman for years, what is needed is that we, those *racially aware,* must relocate to selected rural White towns and villages across this country and physically work to KEEP THEM WHITE! When a non-White, wetback scum or other, plans to or moves in, run them out and if that don't work BURN THEM OUT! This will send a STRONG resounding message to others that this particular town or village has NO TOLERANCE and is OFF LIMITS to non-whites! Now this is not a hypothetical solution, this is being practiced NOW in various locations across our country. White man, if you are not willing to do what needs to be done, if you are unwilling to FIGHT, then GET USED TO THE ALTERNATIVE for, if ignored, YOU LOOSE! [sic]"

Despite the AN's decline, there are still plenty of people with supremacist attitudes who are willing to resort to violence to protect what they believe are their rights and their welfare. The FBI continues to monitor these groups to prevent the kind of violence that Timothy McVeigh, *The Turner Diaries,* and Ray Redfeairn espoused.

GLOSSARY

Apocalypse: Taken from visions of St. John in the Book of Revelation in the Bible, this is the notion that the world as we know it will end in a great holy war. Many survivalists and white supremacists believed this might begin in the year 2000 with an international computer crash.

Aryan Nations: An extremist American antigovernment organization based on the anti-Semitic, racially biased notion of white supremacy. Founded by Richard G. Butler, the AN spread throughout prison gang networks and during the 1990s became one of the leading threats to national security. Between 1984 and 1991, at least four separate criminal entities emerged from the AN. These groups committed or conspired to commit acts of violence, including bombings, murders, attempted murders, and armed robberies in furtherance of their white supremacist goals.

Berg, Alan: A Denver-based Jewish talk show host who was gunned down by members of The Order, headed by Bob Mathews, as a way to hasten the inevitable race war against blacks and Jews.

Book of Revelation: The last book of the New Testament, in which John, a disciple of Jesus, recorded the visions of the end times that he experienced while in a penal colony. Many extremists groups view its message as a code and thus interpret the images to support antigovernment violence and their belief that the end times are upon us.

Britton, Neuman: National pastor of the Aryan Nations, he was selected in 1998 by Richard Butler to succeed him as the leader of the AN. Britton died in 2000.

Butler, Richard G.: Founded the Aryan Nations in honor of his hero, Adolf Hitler. He dreamed of an autonomous homeland based in his twenty-acre compound in Hayden Lake, Idaho (site of the annual Aryan Nations World Congress), with the idea of forcing five northwestern states away from the government to suit their own purposes. Also known as "the grandfather of hate," Butler died in September 2004.

Byrd, James, Jr.: A black man who was dragged to death in Jasper, Texas on June 7, 1998, an incident inspired by *The Turner Diaries* and the notion that a racial holy war could begin in 2000. John William King was convicted; he reportedly said that night, "We're going to start *The Turner Diaries* early."

Christian Identity movement: A philosophy that holds that Jews are satanic and anyone other than a white Caucasian is a member of subhuman, or "mud," races. Members of this movement are certain that the end times are approaching, along with the Second Coming of Christ, as stated in the Book of Revelation, during which the races will be "cleansed" through a violent struggle as a precursor to the establishment of Christ's Kingdom on Earth. The white race will triumph over the Jews and over all non-whites. This philosophy, in various renditions, unifies a group of loosely related churches and right-wing factions.

Church of Jesus Christ Christian: The religious movement that evolved in 1946 from Ku Klux Klan organizer Wesley Swift's anti-Semitic, antigovernment philosophy. Renamed in 1957 from the White Identity Church of Jesus Christ Christian, it became part of the Aryan Nations in 1978, when Richard Butler resumed ministry upon Swift's death. Among its doctrines are that only white people have souls.

Church of the Sons of YHVH: A splinter white supremacist Christian identity group formed by Ray Redfeairn and Morris Gulett, and controlled by Gulett after Redfeairn died in 2003.

Dees, Morris: Founder and chief trial attorney at the Southern Poverty Law Center; pledged to cripple hate groups via civil lawsuits that would drain their economic resources. Dees has been the target of several assassination attempts.

Furrow, Buford O., Jr.: A former security guard from the Aryan Nations Hayden Lake Compound, he married Bob Mathews' widow and went to California on August 10, 1999, where he shot into a Jewish community center, wounding five and murdering Filipino-American postal worker Joseph Ileto. He received a life sentence.

Gun control: Considered by militant groups to be the first step toward disarming Americans altogether, leaving them defenseless when foreign armies or the U.S. government take over their lives.

Harris, Larry Wayne: A microbiologist aligned with anti-Semitic, racist, and separatist movements. In 1995, he was arrested with three vials of a freeze-dried organism that causes bubonic plague. He received the samples for "research," but he did not have a lab license. Accepting a plea bargain in which he pled guilty to mail and wire fraud, he received eight months' probation. In February 1998, Harris was arrested again after supposedly carrying enough deadly anthrax germs to "wipe out" Las Vegas. However, when it was found to be nonlethal, the charges were dropped.

Hayden Lake, Idaho: Site of the 20-acre parcel of land owned by Richard G. Butler that became the headquarters for the AN and its annual World Congress; Butler hoped it would become the center of the whites-only homeland.

Hitler, Adolf: The Nazi leader responsible for creating the programs of annihilation that "purged" Germany of "undesirables"—Jews, homosexuals, Eastern Europeans, and so on—and supported the notion of a developing a pure race of Aryans of white Northern European stock. He is honored by white supremacists as a role model, and they celebrate his birthday annually.

Keenan, Victoria and Jason: After their car backfired near the Hayden Lake compound, they were chased and terrorized by several Aryan Nations guards. In September 2000, they won a lawsuit of $6.3 million, gaining Butler's property and ownership of the name of his church, which effectively crippled the organization.

Kehoe, Chevie: A white supremacist and associate of the Aryan Nations, convicted of three murders, conspiracy, and transportation of stolen property.

Ku Klux Klan: Founded in 1865 by veterans of the Confederate Army to resist Reconstruction, the KKK has dedicated itself to terrorizing and intimidating Jews, blacks, Catholics, and gay people, often with fatal violence. Destroyed by the Civil Rights Act of 1871, it resurfaced in 1915 as a white supremacist organization. Although its membership grew to the millions in the 1920s, it exists today in unrelated local chapters.

MacDonald, Andrew: *See* William Pierce.

Mathews, Robert Jay: An Odinist (*see* Odinism), founder of the neo-Nazi organization The Order in 1983. Mathews viewed the government as being under the control of a Jewish cabal, so he felt justified in committing robberies and bombings, as well as counterfeiting money. In 1984, during a shootout with police at Whidbey Island, Washington, Mathews burned to death when his cabin caught fire. White supremacists view him as a hero and martyr.

McVeigh, Timothy: A member of the Michigan Militia who on April 19, 1995, set off an ammonium nitrate and fuel oil bomb outside the Alfred P. Murrah federal building in Oklahoma City as a statement against the government and in honor of the standoff at Waco between the FBI/ATF and David Koresh that had taken eighty-eight lives. He was inspired by *The Turner Diaries.*

National Alliance: An American white Supremacist neo-Nazi faction founded by William L. Pierce, author of *The Turner Diaries.*

Northern Hammerskins: A racist faction of the skinheads, a group that originated in Britain in the 1960s as members of a working-class subculture. Their political views in subsequent decades and other countries have ranged from one extreme to the other. They often shave their heads to signal their membership. Some engage in the intimidation and bashing of racial groups they deplore.

Neo-Nazis: Groups in different countries that attempt to revive a racist form of fascism that raises white Caucasians above all other races and honors Adolf Hitler as their inspiration. They utilize the swastika and other Nazi-era insignias as symbols of their group identity.

The New Order: A splinter group from the Aryan Nations, founded by Dennis McGiffen and based on The Order. Its agenda was to perpetuate the same type of violence that Robert Mathews had advocated; they had planned assassinations and bombings before they were arrested in February 1998.

New world order conspiracy: The idea that when the crisis occurred in the year 2000, the United Nations planned to conquer the world.

Odinism: A pre-Christian religion based in Norse mythology, primarily the god Odin. Its current form allows members to believe in a god without having to accept the Christian values of tolerance and compassion. Violence is justified on behalf of their ideals.

The Order: An extremist group founded by Bob Mathews in response to the FBI shooting of Gordon Kahl after he'd run from a shoot-out in which two U.S. marshals were killed. The Order, founded in 1983, committed robberies of armored cars, counterfeited money, and was responsible for the murder of Alan Berg; the group crumbled when Mathews was killed late in 1984.

Phineas Priests: A splinter group that bases its ideology on chapter 25 of the Book of Numbers in the Bible; they view themselves as descendants of

Phineas, who was given everlasting priesthood, and justify violence against people who transgress the laws of God. They are strong adherents of racial purity.

Pierce, William L.: Founder of the National Alliance and the author of *The Turner Diaries* and *The Hunter,* under the pseudonym Andrew MacDonald.

Posse Comitatus: An antigovernment group that refuses to recognize government above the county level. In 1983, Gordon Kahl shot and killed two federal agents who arrived to arrest him, and was later killed in Arkansas during a shootout. Many members are also white supremacists and practice survivalism. During the 1990s, the Posse Comitatus was instrumental in helping citizens to form armed militias.

Southern Poverty Law Center: A nonprofit group located in Montgomery, Alabama, that is committed to crippling extremist violence by bringing civil lawsuits against members of hate groups. Morris Dees and Joe Levin founded it in 1971. They publish a quarterly intelligence report about extremist groups.

Swift, Wesley: An early figure in the extremist movement, Swift founded a church in the 1940s based on a mix of anti-Semitism, political militancy, and British Israelism that evolved in 1957 into the Church of Jesus Christ Christian.

The Turner Diaries: A piece of apocalyptic hate literature written by William L. Pierce under the pseudonym Andrew MacDonald as a result of his involvement with Nazi groups during the 1960s. *The Turner Diaries* was published as a serial in *Attack!,* a publication of the National Alliance; it was published as a book in 1978. Approximately eighty thousand words long, it tells the story of Earl Turner, a white man who joins an underground movement that in the early 1990s resists the so-called Jewish conspiracy that took over the American government and began confiscating everyone's guns. This book's sequel was *The Hunter.*

Waco, Texas: The site of the Branch Davidian compound run by cultist David Koresh, where a fatal clash occurred with the ATF, precipitating an

FBI standoff of fifty-one days, which terminated with more than eighty deaths inside the burning compound.

White separatism: The wish by some groups to obtain self-determination for whites and an existence entirely separate from people of other races. Many critics view this as a form of white supremacy.

White supremacy: The idea that the white race is superior to all others. Not all white supremacist groups adhere to Christian Identity doctrines.

Wickstrom, James: A Christian Identity minister and far-right racist talk show host based in Michigan. He preached the two-seed line racial identity covenant, wherein only whites are made in the image of God and are therefore the only race possessing a soul.

Y2K: The belief that in the year 2000, due to shortsightedness on the part of computer technology corporations, many computerized systems would shut down, leading to mass chaos. At that time, it was believed, groups would rise up and attempt to dominate, and the extremist groups feared that the United Nations would create a new world order by using foreign armies to subdue America. Many also believed that a racial holy war would be ignited, creating a new civilization based on white supremacy.

ZOG (Zionist Occupied Government): The belief of right-wing extremists that the federal government is controlled by Jews and is therefore a representative of Satan. The FBI is thus Satan's right arm.

INDEX

ABOUT THE AUTHORS

Dave Hall was born in the hills of southeastern Kentucky, the second of eleven children. Raised primarily by his grandparents, Hall, in his youth, secured a reputation as a hell-raising biker, then went to work for the FBI. Hall now lives in seclusion in an undisclosed location.

Tym Burkey has been a special agent with the FBI since 1991. He earned the first of his three FBI quality service incentive awards in 1999 for his work on the Aryan Nations investigation.

Katherine Ramsland is the author of thirty-one books, including *Inside the Mind of Serial Killers: Why They Kill*. She teaches forensic psychology at DeSales University in Pennsylvania and for the past six years has been a regular contributor to Court TV's *Crime Library*.